PHP

fast&easy
web development

2nd Edition

PHP

fast&easy.
web development
2nd Edition

Julie C. Meloni

Premier
P
Press

Publisher: Stacy L. Hiquet
Marketing Manager: Heather Buzzingham
Managing Editor: Sandy Doell
Acquisitions Editor: Todd Jensen
Project Editor: Kim V. Benbow
Editorial Assistant: Margaret Bauer
Marketing Coordinator: Kelly Poffenbarger
Technical Reviewer: Greg Perry
Copy Editor: Kim V. Benbow
Interior Layout: Scribe Tribe
Cover Design: Mike Tanamachi
Indexer: Johnna VanHoose Dinse

ISBN: 1-931841-87-X
Library of Congress Catalog Card Number: 2002104489
Printed in the United States of America
03 04 05 06 07 BH 10 9 8 7 6 5 4 3

Premier Press, a division of Course Technology
25 Thomson Place
Boston, MA 02210

Acknowledgments

Thanks as always to the PHP Group, Zend Technologies, the Apache Software Foundation, and MySQL AB for creating and maintaining such wonderful and accessible products for all users.

Thanks to every single PHP user and developer because without you, I wouldn't have anything to write about.

Great thanks to the all the editors who worked with me on both editions of this book!

Enormous thanks to everyone at i2i Interactive, for their never-ending support and encouragement.

About the Author

JULIE MELONI is the technical director for i2i Interactive, a multimedia company located in Campbell, CA (that's just down the street from San Jose). She's been developing Web-based applications since the Web first saw the light of day and remembers the excitement surrounding the first GUI Web browser. She is the author of several books and articles on Web-based programming languages and database topics, and you can find translations of her work in several languages, including Chinese, Italian, Portuguese, Polish, and even Serbian.

Contents at a Glance

Contents

Introduction

In the two years since the first edition of *PHP Fast & Easy Web Development* was published, I've received a significant amount of positive feedback regarding the teaching style of this book. I was originally skeptical when, about a month after the release of my first book, *PHP Essentials*, my editors decided that a Fast & Easy version was warranted. The Fast & Easy style is a step-by-step, learn-by-example path to learning a new programming language—with pictures included! Unlike the long, text-filled chapters upon chapters of most programming books, the Fast & Easy style did indeed appeal to users who are new to PHP, and especially to programming in general.

This second edition takes into account some of the feedback from the first edition, but holds true to the original structure and learning path. The first three chapters are dedicated to getting Apache, MySQL, and PHP up and running on your Windows or Linux machine. You may be surprised at how simple it is, and how quickly you'll be up and running.

A few additional chapters have been added to provide additional projects for practicing your new-found skills; and some appendices of additional database and programming information also round out this new edition. This book remains a solid introduction for the beginning user, who learns best by example. After completing this book, you will have a strong foundation in the basics before approaching advanced levels of application design.

Before jumping into all that, take a moment to familiarize yourself with PHP and its history.

What Is PHP?

Its official name is PHP: Hypertext Preprocessor, and it is a server-side scripting language. When your Web browser accesses a URL, it is making a request to a Web server. When you request a PHP page, something like http://www.yourcompany.com/home.php, the Web server wakes up the PHP parsing engine and says, "Hey! You've got to do something before I send a result back to this person's Web browser."

Then, the PHP parsing engine runs through the PHP code found in `home.php`, and returns the resulting output. This output is passed back to the Web server as part of the HTML code in the document, which in turn is passed on to your browser, which displays it to you.

A Brief History of PHP

In 1994, an incredibly forward-thinking man named Rasmus Lerdorf developed a set of tools that used a parsing engine to interpret a few macros here and there. They were not extravagant: a guest book, a counter, and some other "home page" elements that were cool when the Web was in its infancy. He eventually combined these tools with a form interpretation (FI) package he had written, added some database support, and released what was known as PHP/FI.

Then, in the spirit of Open Source software development, developers all over the world began contributing to PHP/FI. By 1997, more than 50,000 Web sites were using PHP/FI to accomplish different tasks—connecting to a database, displaying dynamic content, and so on.

At that point, the development process really started becoming a team effort. With primary assistance from developers Zeev Suraski and Andi Gutmans, the version 3.0 parser was created. The final release of PHP 3.0 occurred in June of 1998, when it was upgraded to include support for multiple platforms (it's not just for Linux anymore!) and Web servers, numerous databases, and SNMP (Simple Network Management Protocol) and IMAP (Internet Message Access Protocol).

Then, the birth of PHP 4.0 occurred. No small version change, PHP 4.0 marked a complete rethinking of the PHP core and a rewrite of the internals of the scripting language itself. The PHP development team and Zend Technologies produced a remarkable product with nearly a 50-fold performance improvement over version 3.0, with a long list of new and useful features.

So where are we now?

- Over 7 million Web servers worldwide run the 4.x version of PHP.

- PHP 4.x has been in use for over two years, with the current version being 4.2.1.

- PHP 4.x can work with just about any combination of Web server, operating system, and database you can think up.

- Companies such as Zend Technologies have released products to optimize and accelerate PHP, as well as "studio" environments for developing and testing PHP code.

- PHP usage has exploded as an enterprise application development solution—it's not just for home pages and small projects any more!

What Does PHP Do?

PHP does anything you want, except sit on its head and spin. Actually, with a little on-the-fly image manipulation and Dynamic HTML, it could probably do that, too.

According to the PHP manual, "The goal of the language is to allow Web developers to write dynamically generated pages quickly."

Here are some common uses of PHP:

- Perform system functions: create, open, read from, write to, and close files on your system; execute system commands; create directories; and modify permissions.

- Gather data from forms: save the data to a file, send data via e-mail, return manipulated data to the user.

- Access databases and generate content on-the-fly, or create a Web interface for adding, deleting, and modifying elements within your database.

- Set cookies and access cookie variables.

- Start sessions and use session variables and objects.

- Use PHP user authentication to restrict access to sections of your Web site.

- Create images on-the-fly.

- Encrypt data.

These are just everyday uses. PHP includes support for Java, Java Servlets, XML, and a myriad of other higher-level functions. The possibilities are endless.

Is PHP Right for Me?

Only you can decide if PHP should be your language of choice, whether you're developing sites for personal or commercial use on a small or large scale. I can only tell you that in the commercial realm, I've worked with all the popular server-side scripting languages—Active Server Pages (ASP), ColdFusion, Java Server Pages (JSP), Perl, and PHP—on numerous platforms and various Web servers, with varying degrees of success. PHP is the right choice for me: it's flexible, fast, and simple in its requirements, yet powerful in its output.

Before deciding whether to use PHP in a large-scale or commercial environment, consider your answers to these questions:

- Can you say with absolute certainty that you will always use the same Web server hardware and software? If not, look for something cross-platform that is available for all types of Web servers: PHP.

- Will you always have the exact same development team comprised entirely of ASP (or ColdFusion) developers? Or will you use whoever is available, thus necessitating a language that is easy to learn and syntactically similar to C and Perl? If you have reason to believe that your ASP or ColdFusion developers might drop off the face of the earth, don't use those tools—use PHP.

- Are memory and server load an issue? If so, don't use bloated third-party software that leaks precious memory—use PHP.

Here's the bottom line: PHP is simple, so just try it! If you like it, continue using it. It's Open Source, so help improve it. Join a mailing list, and help others. If you don't like it, you're only out about 25 bucks for this book, and the software can be uninstalled without rendering your machine completely inoperable.

More Stuff

This book has its own Web site. That figures, doesn't it? The URL is http://www.premierpressbooks.com/downloads.asp. At this site you can download all the code samples in this book. You can also use this site to alert me to bugs or other problems you might have with the examples. Although the code has been tested many times, one errant semicolon or quotation mark can cause the dreaded "Parse error."

P A R T I

Getting Started

1

Installing and Configuring MySQL

MySQL is the database of choice for a vast majority of Web developers who use PHP because of its efficiency and ease of use. Plus, MySQL is free, runs on multiple platforms, and its documentation is superb. When using MySQL with PHP, it's easiest to install MySQL first because, during the PHP installation and configuration process, you must tell the PHP configuration script where MySQL resides on your system in order to activate the MySQL–specific functions. In this chapter, you'll learn how to do the following:

- Install MySQL on Windows or Linux
- Create a sample database
- Create a sample table

Various MySQL Distributions

The most popular distribution of MySQL is the open source version from MySQL AB. However, there are also commercial versions of MySQL, as well as distributions of MySQL bundled with application server software. Some companies that offer these options are AbriaSoft (http://www.abriasoft.com/) and NuSphere (http://www.nusphere.com/). No matter which option you choose, a solution will be available for you on all platforms—any UNIX-like operating system, as well as on Windows 95/98/NT/2000/XP.

If you are using MySQL as part of a Web hosting package through an Internet service provider, you don't have to worry about downloading and installing the application in this chapter. Instead, you'll just need to work with your ISP to get your username and password. In almost all cases, your ISP will be running the MySQL distribution from MySQL AB. There's no harm in setting up MySQL on a development machine, if you have one available to you (your own workstation fits that bill), just to better understand the process. To that end, if you have a Linux workstation or server, MySQL was likely included on your OS distribution CDs as an installation option, and perhaps you even installed it already. In this case, you should check the MySQL Web site to compare the version numbers and download a newer version if one is available.

The installation instructions in this chapter are based on the MySQL version 4.0, distributed by MySQL AB. Earlier versions such as MySQL 3.23.x follow the same steps, should you run into problems while installing MySQL 4.0. You will be able to use all of the database-related examples in this book, whether using MySQL 3.23.x or MySQL 4.0.

Installing MySQL on Windows

The MySQL installation process on Windows 95/98/NT/2000/XP is based on an executable setup program provided by MySQL AB. Once you download the zip file, all you have to do is extract its contents into a temporary directory and run the `setup.exe` application. After the `setup.exe` application installs the MySQL server and client programs, you're ready to start the MySQL server.

1. Visit the MySQL 4.0 download page, at http://www.mysql.com/downloads/mysql-4.0.html and find the Windows section on the page. You want to download the "Installation files (zip)" rather than "Cygwin downloads (tar.bz2)."

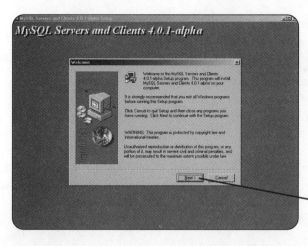

2. Clicking the Download link will take you to a page of mirror sites. Select the mirror site closest to you, and click on either the HTTP or FTP link to download the file. Using the HTTP method is usually quicker.

3. Once the Zip file is on your hard drive, extract its contents to a temporary directory.

4. From the temporary directory, find the setup.exe file and double-click it to start the installation. You will see the first screen of the installation wizard. Click Next to continue.

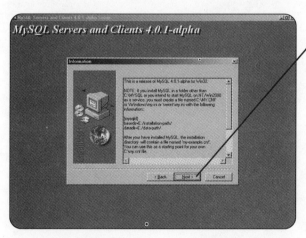

5. The second screen in the installation process contains valuable information regarding the installation location. The default installation location is C:\mysql, but if you plan to install MySQL in a different location, this screen shows you a few changes that you will have to make on your own. The information on this screen is also important for Windows NT users who wish to start MySQL as a service. Read the information and note anything relevant to your situation, then click Next to continue.

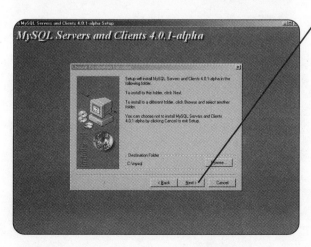

6. With the third screen in the installation process, you will select the installation location. If you want to install MySQL in the default location, click Next to continue. Otherwise, click Browse and navigate to the location of your choice, then click Next to continue.

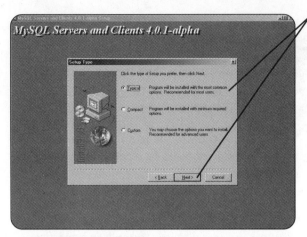

7. The fourth screen has you select the installation method, either Typical, Compact, or Custom. Select Typical, and click Next to continue.

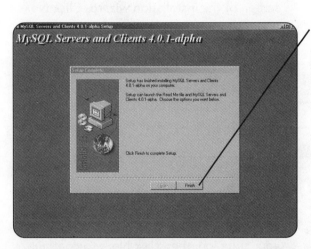

8. The installation process will now take over, and install files in their proper locations. When the process is finished, you will see a confirmation of completion. Click Finish to complete the setup process.

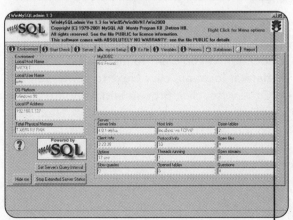

MySQL is now installed on your system. However, you won't find any shortcuts installed in your Windows Start menu after an installation of MySQL from MySQL AB, so now you must start the process yourself. If you navigate to the C:\mysql\bin directory, you will find numerous applications ready for action. One of these applications is called WinMySQLadmin, and is a great friend to Windows users who are just getting started with MySQL. If you double-click this file, it will start the MySQL server and place a Stoplight icon in your taskbar. If you right-click this icon, you can launch a graphical user interface to maintain and monitor your new server.

`WinMySQLadmin` will automatically interpret environment information, such as IP address, machine name, and so on. The tabs across the top allow you to view system information and also edit MySQL configuration options. To shut down the MySQL server and/or the `WinMySQLadmin` tool, right-click again on the Stoplight icon in your taskbar and select the appropriate choice. As long as the MySQL server is running, you can run additional applications through a console window, such as the MySQL monitor.

In the next section, you'll learn how to manually start MySQL and perform a few actions to familiarize yourself with the system.

Testing Your MySQL Installation

In this section, you will start and work with the MySQL utilities via the command line in a console window. When using MySQL with PHP, you'll issue the same types of commands, only within the context of the PHP code. Use the information in this section to familiarize yourself with the types of commands and responses you'll be working with later in the book.

Starting MySQL

To manually start MySQL, follow the steps below.

1. Open a DOS prompt or a console window (depending on your Windows version, it may be called one or the other).

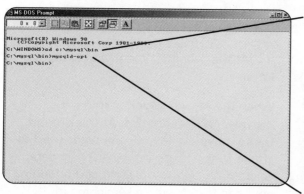

2. At the prompt, type **cd c:\mysql\bin** and press Enter.

NOTE

If you installed MySQL in a different directory, substitute that directory name in the command in step 2.

3. At the prompt, type **mysqld-opt** and press Enter.

The MySQL process will now be running in the background. You can now connect to MySQL and create databases and tables.

Creating a Test Database

Before going any further, you should know the following:

- A database is a collection of tables.

- A table contains a set of records, also referred to as rows.

- All records have the same number of fields.

- Each field categorizes a piece of a data.

In this section, you'll conquer the first element and create a database. The utility to use is the `mysqladmin` program, which allows you to administer MySQL from the command line.

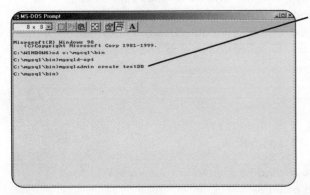

1. At the prompt, type **mysqladmin create testDB** and press Enter.

Next, you'll add a table to the `testDB` database.

Creating a Test Table

In this section, you'll create a table within the database you created in the preceding section. The utility to use is the `mysql` program, which allows you to work within the MySQL database system from the command line.

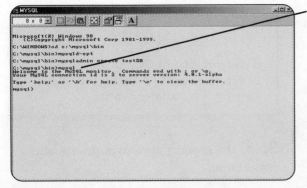

1. At the prompt, type **mysql** and press Enter.

When the MySQL Monitor starts, it provides its own prompt. At this prompt (`mysql>`) you will type commands used to create tables, explain tables, insert data, select data, and so on. Get used to ending your commands with a semicolon (;) because it's a common instruction terminator that is used in PHP as well.

Now that you've connected to the MySQL Monitor, you need to tell it which database to use.

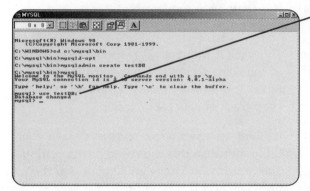

2. At the prompt, type **use testDB;** and press Enter.

The MySQL Monitor will respond with Database changed if the database exists and you have permission to access it.

It's time to create a test table. This table will have a column for an ID number and a column for some text.

NOTE

For more information about the specifics of creating tables, see Appendix D, "Basic MySQL Reference."

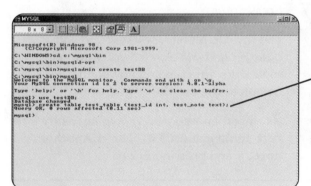

3. At the prompt, type **create table test_table (test_id int, test_note text);** and press Enter. This statement creates a table called test_table. Within the table, it creates a column called test_id of type int (integer). It also creates a column called test_note of type text.

The MySQL Monitor will respond with Query OK. It will also tell you how many rows were affected and how long it took to complete the task (in this case, 0.11 seconds).

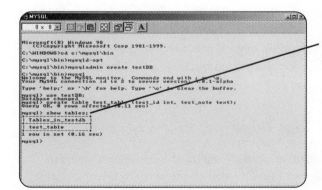

4. Verify the table creation by typing **show tables;** and pressing Enter.

The MySQL Monitor will respond with a list of all the tables in the current database.

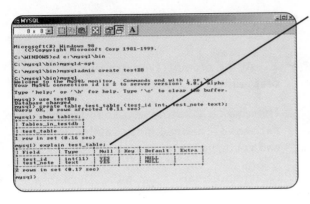

5. To verify the field names and types in a specific table, use the explain command. In this case, type **explain test_table;** and press Enter.

The MySQL Monitor will respond with a list of all the fields and their types in the selected table. This is a very handy command to use to keep track of your table design.

It's time to insert a few rows of data in your table, because this is getting pretty boring. The first row will have an ID of 1, and the note will be "This is a note."

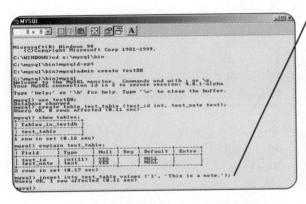

6. To insert this row, type **insert into test_table values('1', 'This is a note.');** and press Enter.

The MySQL Monitor will respond with Query OK. It will also tell you how many rows were affected and how long it took to complete the task.

7. Insert another row by typing **insert into test_table values('99', 'Look! Another note.');** and pressing Enter.

NOTE

For more information about the specifics of inserting data into tables, see Appendix D, "Basic MySQL Reference."

Now that you have some data in your table, even if it is only two rows, get familiar with selecting data. Keep the MySQL Monitor open because you'll be using it in the next section as well.

Selecting Data from Your Test Table

The SELECT command is very powerful and will likely be the command you use most often when working with PHP and MySQL. You can find more information about the SELECT command in Appendix D, "Basic MySQL Reference," but for now, let's do some simple data selections.

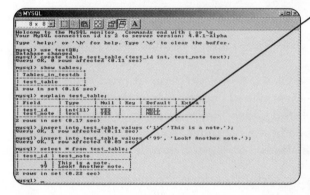

1. At the prompt, type **select * from test_table;** and press Enter.

This command simply selects all fields from all rows (that's what the * does) in the table called test_table and returns the data to the screen in a nicely formatted table. The MySQL Monitor tells you how many rows were returned and how long it took the query to run.

Add a little order to the results. Try to get the results ordered by ID number—largest number first.

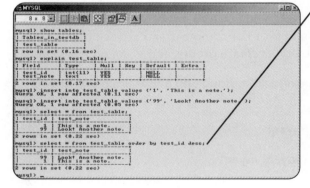

2. At the prompt, type **select * from test_table order by test_id desc;** and press Enter.

The result now shows the row with a test_id of 99 as the first row in the table. The desc in the command stands for descending. There is another option, asc, which stands for ascending. Ascending order is the default order.

The next section is for the installation of MySQL on Linux, so assuming you don't have two machines, skip ahead to Chapter 2, "Installing Apache," to install the Apache Web server.

Installing MySQL for Linux

This section will take you through the installation process of MySQL 4.0 on Linux, using the distribution from MySQL AB. If you're using another flavor of Linux, download the appropriate files and follow the instructions included with the distribution.

The recommended installation method for MySQL is with RPMs. There are several RPMs that make up a full distribution, but for a minimal installation you need

- `MySQL-VERSION.i386.rpm`—The MySQL server.

- `MySQL-client-VERSION.i386.rpm`—The standard MySQL client programs.

To download these files, visit the MySQL 4.0 download page, at http://www.mysql.com/downloads/mysql-4.0.html and find the "Linux downloads" section on the page. The RPMs are listed under "RedHat packages (rpm)." When you click on the Download link for one of the packages, you will be taken to a page of mirror sites. Select the mirror site closest to you, and download the files.

When the files are downloaded to your system, perform the minimal installation by typing the following at your prompt, replacing VERSION with the appropriate version number for your downloaded files:

```
#prompt> rpm -i MySQL-VERSION.i386.rpm MySQL-client-VERSION.i386.rpm
```

If the RPM method doesn't work for you, you can also install MySQL from a binary distribution, which requires gunzip and tar to uncompress and unpack the distribution and also requires the ability to create groups and users on the system.

In the first series of commands, you will add a group and a user, then unpack the distribution, as follows:

1. At the prompt, type **groupadd mysql**

2. At the prompt, type **useradd -g mysql mysql**

3. At the prompt, type **cd /usr/local**

NOTE

You can install MySQL in any directory. If you do not use `/usr/local/` as in the example above, be sure to modify subsequent commands appropriately.

---

4. At the prompt, type **gunzip < /path/to/mysql-VERSION-OS.tar.gz | tar xvf -**

5. To create a link with a shorter name, type **ln -s mysql-VERSION-OS mysql**

6. Change directories by typing **cd mysql**

Once the distribution is unpacked, the README and INSTALL files will walk you through the remainder of the installation process for the version of MySQL you've chosen. In general, the next series of commands will be used:

1. Type **scripts/mysql_install_db** to run the MySQL install script.

2. Type **chown -R root /usr/local/mysql** to change ownership of the mysql directory.

3. Type **chown -R mysql /usr/local/mysql/data** to change ownership of the mysql/data directory.

4. Type **chgrp -R mysql /usr/local/mysql** to change the group of the mysql directory.

5. Type **chown -R root /usr/local/mysql/bin** to change ownership of the mysql/bin directory.

If you have any problems during the installation of MySQL, the first place you should look is the "Problems and Common Errors" chapter of the MySQL manual, which is located at http://www.mysql.com/doc/P/r/Problems.html. Some common problems include

- Incorrect permissions do not allow you to start the MySQL daemon. If this is the case, be sure you have changed owners and groups to match those indicated in the installation instructions.

- If you see the message "Access denied" when connecting to MySQL, be sure you are using the correct username and password.

- If you see the message "Can't connect to server," make sure the MySQL daemon is running.

In the next section, you'll learn how to start MySQL and perform a few actions to familiarize yourself with the system.

Testing Your MySQL Installation

In this section, you will start and work with the MySQL utilities via the command line, in a console window. When using MySQL with PHP, you'll issue the same types of commands, only within the context of the PHP code. Use the information in this section to familiarize yourself with the types of commands and responses you'll be working with later in the book.

Starting MySQL

1. If you're not already there, enter the MySQL parent directory by typing **cd /usr/local/mysql** and pressing Enter.

2. Start the MySQL process by typing **./bin/safe_mysqld &** and pressing Enter.

The MySQL process will now be running in the background, and you can connect to MySQL and create databases and tables.

Creating a Test Database

Before going any further, you should know the following:

- A database is a collection of tables.

- A table contains a set of records, also referred to as rows.

- All records have the same number of fields.

- Each field categorizes a piece of a data.

In this section, you'll conquer the first element and create a database. The utility to use is the mysqladmin program, which allows you to administer MySQL from the command line.

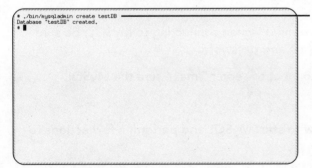

```
# ./bin/mysqladmin create testDB
Database "testDB" created.
#
```

1. At the prompt, type **./bin/mysqladmin create testDB** and press Enter.

As you can see by the system response, a database called testDB has been created. Next, you'll add a table to that database.

Creating a Test Table

In this section, you'll create a table within the database you created in the preceding section. The utility to use is the mysql program, which allows you to work within the MySQL database system from the command line.

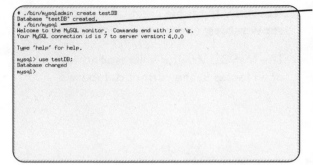

```
# ./bin/mysqladmin create testDB
Database "testDB" created.
# ./bin/mysql
Welcome to the MySQL monitor.  Commands end with ; or \g.
Your MySQL connection id is 7 to server version: 4.0.0

Type 'help' for help.

mysql> use testDB;
Database changed
mysql>
```

1. At the prompt, type **./bin/mysql** and press Enter.

The MySQL Monitor will start. The MySQL Monitor provides its own prompt. At this prompt (mysql>) you will type commands used to create tables, explain tables, insert data, select data, and so on. Get used to ending your commands with a semicolon (;) because it's a common instruction terminator that is used in PHP as well.

Now that you've connected to the MySQL monitor, you need to tell it which database to use.

2. At the prompt, type **use testDB;** and press Enter.

The MySQL Monitor will respond with Database changed if the database exists and you have permission to access it.

It's time to create a test table. This table will have a column for an ID number and a column for some text.

NOTE

For more information about the specifics of creating tables, see Appendix D, "Basic MySQL Reference."

```
# ./bin/mysqladmin create testDB
Database "testDB" created.
# ./bin/mysql
Welcome to the MySQL monitor.  Commands end with ; or \g.
Your MySQL connection id is 7 to server version: 4.0.0

Type 'help' for help.

mysql> use testDB;
Database changed
mysql> create table test_table (test_id int, test_note text);
Query OK, 0 rows affected (0.03 sec)

mysql>
```

3. At the prompt, type **create table test_table (test_id int, test_note text);** and press Enter. This statement creates a table called test_table. Within the table, it creates a column called test_id of type int (integer). It also creates a column called test_note of type text.

The MySQL Monitor will respond with Query OK. It will also tell you how many rows were affected and how long it took to complete the task (in this case, 0.03 seconds).

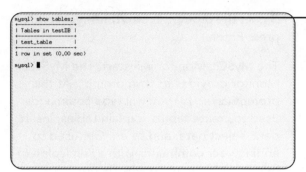

4. Verify the table creation by typing **show tables;** and pressing Enter.

The MySQL Monitor will respond with a list of all tables in the current database.

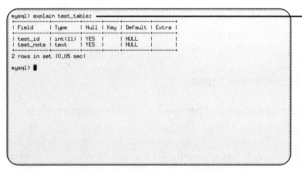

5. To verify the field names and types in a specific table, use the explain command. In this case, type **explain test_table;** and press Enter.

The MySQL Monitor will respond with a list of all the fields and their types in the selected table. This is a very handy command to use to keep track of your table design.

It's time to insert a few rows of data in your table because this is getting pretty boring. The first row will have an ID of 1, and the note will be "This is a note."

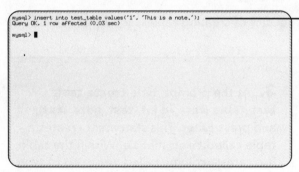

6. To insert this row, type **insert into test_table values('1', 'This is a note.');** and press Enter.

The MySQL Monitor will respond with Query OK. It will also tell you how many rows were affected and how long it took to complete the task.

7. Insert another row by typing **insert into test_table values('99', 'Look! Another note.');** and pressing Enter.

NOTE

For more information about the specifics of inserting data into tables, see Appendix D, "Basic MySQL Reference."

Now that you have some data in your table, even if it is only two rows, get familiar with selecting data. Keep the MySQL Monitor open because you'll be using it in the next section as well.

Selecting Data from Your Test Table

The SELECT command is very powerful and will likely be the command you use most often when working with PHP and MySQL. You can find more information about SELECT in Appendix D, "Basic MySQL Reference," but for now, we'll do some simple data selections.

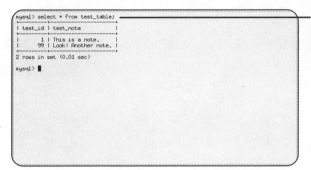

1. At the prompt, type **select * from test_table;** and press Enter.

This command simply selects all fields from all rows (that's what the * does) in the table called test_table and returns the data to the screen in a nicely formatted table. The MySQL Monitor tells you how many rows were returned and how long it took the query to run.

Add a little order to the results. Try to get the results ordered by ID number—largest number first.

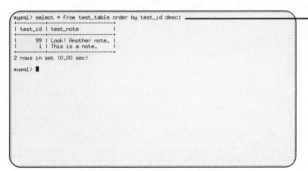

2. At the prompt, type **select * from test_table order by test_id desc;** and press Enter.

The result now shows the row with a test_id of 99 as the first row in the table. The desc in the command stands for descending. There is another option, asc, which stands for ascending. Ascending order is the default order.

In the next chapter, you'll install the Apache Web server and be one step closer to developing dynamic, database-driven Web sites!

2

Installing Apache

Since it's the most popular Web server in use, you might think that Apache is a complicated piece of software, but it's not difficult at all. In this chapter, you'll learn how to do the following:

- Install Apache on Windows or Linux
- Connect to your new Web server

Installing Apache for Windows

Installing Apache for Windows is a simple task, due in great part to the installation wizard distributed by the Apache Group. Whether you're using Windows 95, 98, ME, 2000, XP, or NT, the installation process of the precompiled binaries is definitely the way to go, and the same installation file is used for all versions of Windows.

Being able to use Apache on consumer-oriented operating systems such as Windows 95/98/ME/XP doesn't mean that you should, at least not in a production environment. Simply put, running any Web server on a Windows operating system is not as fast, stable, or secure as running a Web server on a Linux/UNIX machine. However, installing and configuring a development Web server on a Windows-based operating system is perfectly acceptable and how most users get their start.

NOTE

The Apache Group also distributes the source code for Apache on Windows, should you have a need to compile the code yourself. However, that process is well beyond the scope of this book!

To download the Apache distribution for Windows, start at the Apache Server Web site (http://httpd.apache.org/) and follow the link to "Download." Once in the download area, follow the links to "binaries" and then "win32." This will put you in the proper place for Windows distribution files and announcements. The direct URL to this download area is http://www.apache.org/dist/httpd/binaries/win32/.

Distribution files follow a naming convention, with "apache" followed by the version number, then `-win32-x86-no_src.exe`. As of this writing, the current version is 1.3.26, so the file used as an example throughout this section is `apache_1.3.26-win32-x86-no_src.exe`. Once you have downloaded the installation file to your hard drive, the following steps will take you through the installation wizard:

1. Double-click the file called `apache_1.3.26-win32-x86-no_src.exe`. The installer will start, and the installation wizard will begin. Click on Next to continue.

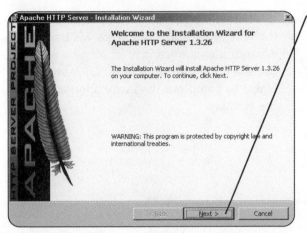

2. Read the licensing information on the screen, select the I Accept radio button, and then click on Next.

3. Read the general Apache information on the screen, and then click on Next.

4. The next screen requires you to fill in some details about your server: the network domain, server name, and the administrator's e-mail address.

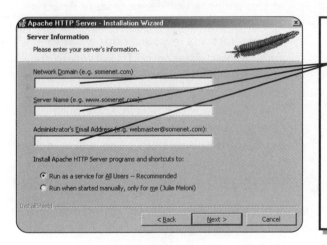

NOTE

If you do not know the network domain or server name at this point, enter some dummy information so that the installation moves forward. You will learn how to edit this information post-installation, so no matter what you enter in this step, you will soon be able to fix it. If you do know your domain and server name, go ahead and enter it.

5. Select the Run As Service For All Users radio button, and click Next.

6. Select the Complete set-up type, and click on Next.

7. Accept the default destination folder, then click on Next.

NOTE

If you elect to change the destination folder for the Apache installation files, please adjust the instructions and paths accordingly throughout this book.

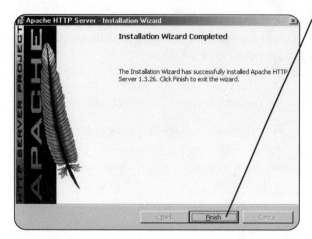

8. Select Install on the next screen, and the final installation sequence will begin. When the sequence is finished, you will see the confirmation screen. Click on Finish to complete the installation and close the installer.

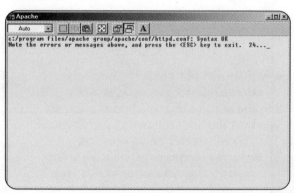

At this point, all of the necessary Apache files are installed, as well as a group of handy shortcuts in your Windows Start menu, called Apache HTTP Server. To run a basic test before moving forward into configuring your server, select Program Files, Apache HTTP Server, Configure Apache Server, Test Configuration from the Windows Start menu. This will launch a console window showing a successful installation.

If you have any errors at this point, rerun the installation program. In the next section, you'll make some minor changes to the Apache configuration file before you start Apache for the first time.

Configuring Apache on Windows

To run a basic installation of Apache, the only changes you need to make are to the server name, which you may already have done during the installation wizard. However, if you entered dummy information for the server name, or wish to modify any other part of the basic configuration, now is the time to do so.

The master configuration file for Apache is called `httpd.conf` and it lives in the `conf` directory, within the Apache installation directory. So if your installation directory is `C:\Program Files\Apache Group\Apache\`, the `httpd.conf` file will be in `C:\Program Files\Apache Group\Apache\conf\`.

Again with the handy shortcut, you can quickly access this file by selecting Program Files, Apache HTTP Server, Configure Apache Server, Edit The Apache `httpd.conf` Configuration File from the Windows Start menu. This shortcut is the same as opening a text editor and navigating to the file location. To modify the basic configuration, primarily the server name, look for a heading called "Section 2: 'Main' server configuration." You will find two important sections of text.

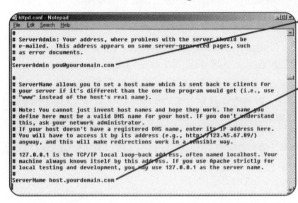

1. Change the value of `ServerAdmin` to your e-mail address, if it isn't already accurate.

2. Change the value of `ServerName` to something accurate, if it's isn't already.

3. Save the file.

The `ServerName` modification is the most important change you'll make to your Apache configuration file because if the `ServerName` isn't correct, you won't be able to connect to Apache. As it states in the configuration file itself, "You cannot just invent host names and hope they work." If you do not know your full machine name, you can use an IP number. If you have a static IP number (i.e., one that does not change), use it as your `ServerName`. If you have a dial-up connection that does not assign a static IP (i.e., your IP number changes each time you connect to your Internet service provider), then you will have to change the IP number in `httpd.conf` each time you dial up.

The `ServerName` changes described above are only relevant if you want people from the outside world to be able to connect to your new Web server. If you are the only person who will be accessing the server, then you can use the IP number 127.0.0.1, which is recognized by machines as the local loop-back address, also known as `localhost`. You can use either the word `localhost` or the IP number 127.0.0.1 as `ServerName` in `httpd.conf`. The IP number will probably work out better, as some Windows machines do not automatically know that `localhost` equals 127.0.0.1.

Once the appropriate modifications are made to the `httpd.conf` file, Apache is ready to run on your machine. In the next section, you'll start and connect to Apache.

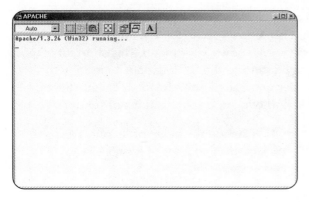

Starting and Connecting to Apache

To first start the Apache server, select Program Files, Apache HTTP Server, Start Apache In Console from the Windows Start menu. This will launch a console window.

Keep this window open, or your Apache process will end! You can minimize the window—just don't close it. Of course, you can close it if you want to shut down your server, but since the next step is to connect to the server via a Web browser, now would not be a good time to shut it down.

If the window is open and it states that Apache is running, you can connect to the server via your Web browser of choice. The URL will be whatever you used as ServerName—an actual name or IP, or localhost or IP.

NOTE

Remember, only you can connect to your Web server using 127.0.0.1 or the name localhost. This book assumes that you'll be using 127.0.0.1 as the ServerName, so if you are not, just substitute your machine name for 127.0.0.1 in the examples.

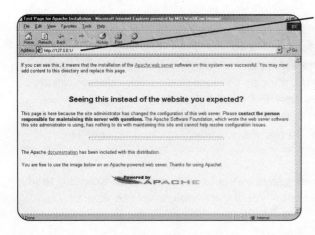

To finally test your installation, open your Web browser, type **http://127.0.0.1/** in the Address bar, and press Enter. You should see a default Web page.

This default start page comes from the htdocs directory within your Apache installation directory. You can go into that directory and delete all the default files if you want to, or you can leave them. They're not hurting anything, but you'll eventually be filling the htdocs directory with your own files and subdirectories, so you might want to delete them now for the sake of good housekeeping.

Move ahead to the next chapter, where you'll install PHP and make a few more minor changes to your Apache configuration files before you're ready for some action.

Installing Apache for Linux/UNIX

To download the Apache distribution for Linux, start at the Apache Server Web site (http://httpd.apache.org/) and follow the link to "Download." This is the proper place for Linux/UNIX distribution files and announcements.

Distribution files follow a naming convention, with "apache" followed by the version number, then the compression type (.tar.gz, .tar.Z and .zip). As of this writing, the current version is 1.3.26, and I prefer *.tar.gz files, so the file used as an example throughout this section is `apache_1.3.26.tar.gz`.

NOTE

The source code distribution should work for most flavors of UNIX, but if you have any concerns, read through the Apache documentation at the Apache Web site to find a better set of files for your specific operating system.

Once you have downloaded the file of choice to your hard drive, the following steps will build a basic version of Apache.

1. Type **cp apache_1.3.26.tar.gz /usr/local/** and press Enter to copy the Apache installation file to the `/usr/local/` directory.

NOTE

You can put Apache anywhere you want on your filesystem, such as `/usr/local/bin/` or `/opt/`. Just be sure to substitute your path for the path indicated in these directions.

---

2. Go to `/usr/local/` by typing **cd /usr/local/** and pressing Enter.

3. Unzip the Apache installation file by typing **gunzip apache_1.3.26.tar.gz** and pressing Enter.

4. Extract the files by typing **tar -xvf apache_1.3.26.tar** and pressing Enter. A directory structure will be created, and you'll be back at the prompt. The parent directory will be /usr/local/apache_1.3.26/.

5. Enter the parent directory by typing **cd apache_1.3.26** and pressing Enter.

6. Type the following and press Enter, to prepare to build Apache:

```
./configure --prefix=/usr/local/apache_1.3.26 --enable-module=so
```

NOTE

If the apache_1.3.26 directory resides elsewhere on your file system, such as /opt/ (as shown in the figures), use that path in the configuration directive in step 7.

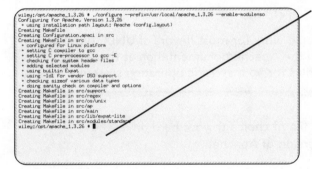

The configuration script will run through its process of checking your configuration and creating makefiles, and then will put you back at the prompt.

7. Type **make** and press Enter. This second step of the installation process will produce many lines of output on your screen. When it is finished, you will be back at the prompt.

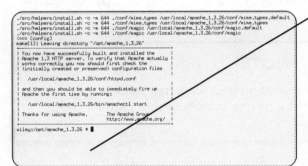

8. Type **make install** and press Enter. This final step of the installation process will again produce many lines of output on your screen. When it is finished, you will be back at the prompt.

If your installation process produces any errors up to this point, go through the process again or check the Apache Web site for any system-specific notes. In the next section, you'll make some minor changes to the Apache configuration file before you start Apache for the first time.

Configuring Apache on Linux/UNIX

To run a basic installation of Apache, the only changes you need to make are to the server name, which resides in the master configuration file called `httpd.conf`. This file lives in the `conf` directory, within the Apache installation directory. So if your installation directory is `/usr/local/apache_1.3.26/`, the configuration files will be in `/usr/local/apache_1.3.26/conf/`.

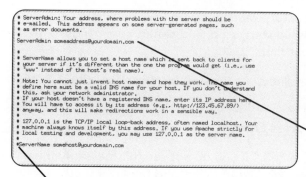

To modify the basic configuration, most importantly the server name, open the `httpd.conf` file with a text editor and look for a heading called "Section 2: 'Main' server configuration." You will find two important sections of text.

1. Change the value of `ServerAdmin` to your e-mail address.

2. Change the value of `ServerName` to something accurate, and remove the preceeding # so that the entry looks like this:

```
ServerName somehost.somedomain.com
```

You do not want it to look like this:

```
#ServerName somehost.somedomain.com
```

3. Save the file.

The `ServerName` modification is the most important change you'll make to your Apache configuration file because if the `ServerName` isn't accurate, you won't be able to connect to Apache on your machine. As it states in the configuration file itself, "You cannot just invent host names and hope they work." If you do not know your full machine name, you can use an IP number. If you have a static IP number (i.e., one that does not change), use it as your `ServerName`. If you have a dial-up connection that does not assign a static IP (i.e., your IP number changes each time you connect to your Internet service provider), then you will have to change the IP number in `httpd.conf` each time you dial up.

The `ServerName` changes described above are only relevant if you want people from the outside world to be able to connect to your new Web server. If you are the only person who will be accessing the server, then you can use the IP number 127.0.0.1, which is recognized by machines as the local loop-back address, also known as localhost. You can use either the word localhost or the IP number 127.0.0.1 as ServerName in httpd.conf. Once the appropriate modifications are made to the httpd.conf file, Apache is ready to run on your machine. In the next section, you'll start and connect to Apache.

Starting and Connecting to Apache

There's a handy utility in the bin directory within your Apache installation directory called apachectl. It allows you to issue start, stop, and restart commands. Use this utility to start Apache for the first time.

1. To get to the Apache installation directory, type **cd /usr/local/apache_1.3.26** and press Enter.

2. Type **./bin/apachectl start** and press Enter.

You should see a message: "httpd started." If you do not see this message, then you have an error somewhere in your configuration file, and the error message will tell you where to look.

To stop Apache, you can type **./bin/apachectl stop** and press Enter. For now, keep it running, as the next step is to connect to the server via a Web browser, and this would not be a good time to shut it down.

With Apache running, you can connect to the server via your Web browser of choice. The URL will be whatever you used as ServerName—an actual name or IP, or the localhost name or IP.

NOTE

Remember, only you can connect to your Web server using 127.0.0.1 or the name localhost. This book assumes that you'll be using 127.0.0.1 as the ServerName, so if you are not, just substitute your machine name for 127.0.0.1 in the examples.

To finally test your installation, open your Web browser, type **http://127.0.0.1/** in the location bar, and press Enter. You should see a default Web page.

This default start page comes from the `htdocs` directory within your Apache installation directory. You can go into that directory and delete all the default files if you want to, or you can leave them. They're not hurting anything, but you'll eventually be filling the `htdocs` directory with your own files and subdirectories, so you might want to delete them for the sake of good housekeeping.

Move ahead to the next chapter where you'll install PHP and make a few more minor changes to your Apache configuration files before you're ready for some action.

3

Installing PHP

This is it—the final piece of the puzzle that will get you started in the world of creating dynamic, database-driven Web sites. In this chapter, you'll learn how to do the following:

- Install PHP on Windows or Linux

- Make final modifications to Apache

- Use the `phpinfo()` function to retrieve system information

Installing PHP for Windows

Installing PHP for Windows doesn't occur through a wizard interface. Basically, you just unzip some files and move them around. No big deal. Just follow along very closely because this is the area where most people miss an instruction, and if you do that, it won't work.

NOTE

OK, so there is a Windows installer for PHP if you're going to use PHP with Microsoft IIS, Microsoft PWS, or the Xitami Web server. This book is based on a recommendation of using Apache as the Web server and to perform the manual installation of PHP. If you choose to install PHP with a different Web server or are using a different method, please read the installation instructions contained within the software you choose.

To download the PHP binary distribution for Windows, visit the Downloads page at the PHP Web site: http://www.php.net/downloads.php.

1. From the "Windows binaries" section, follow the link for "PHP 4.x.x zip package," where "x.x" refers to the version. Currently, the version for Windows is 4.2.1, and all subsequent installation instructions will be based on this version.

2. Once downloaded to your system, double-click on the file called `php-4.2.1-Win32.zip`. Your zipping program of choice, such as WinZip or PKZip, will open this file.

3. Extract the files to your hard drive, keeping the path names intact. This will create a directory called `C:\php-4.2.1-Win32`.

You now have all the basic PHP distribution files; you just need to move a few of them around.

NOTE

If you change the installation directory name, be sure to substitute your new directory name in the remaining instructions in this chapter.

---

1. Using Windows Explorer (or whatever method you prefer for moving through your file system), go to the `C:\php-4.2.1-Win32` directory.

2. Rename the `php.ini-dist` file to `php.ini` and move this file to `C:\WINDOWS\` or wherever you usually put your `*.ini` files.

3. Move `msvcrt.dll` and `php4ts.dll` to `C:\WINDOWS\SYSTEM\` or wherever you usually put your `*.dll` files.

NOTE

You might already have a copy of `msvcrt.dll` on your system. If you receive a warning when you try to move `msvcrt.dll`, you can ignore the warning and not copy the file. As long as this file is on your system, you don't necessarily need the one from the PHP distribution.

To get a basic version of PHP working with Apache, you'll need to make a few minor modifications to the Apache configuration file.

Configuring Apache to Use PHP

You can install PHP as a CGI binary or as an Apache module. The current recommendation by the PHP Group is to use the module version, as it offers greater performance and some additional functionality. However, you may encounter some conflicts with advanced functionality when using the module, depending on your particular operating system. Additionally, using the CGI version instead of the module version will allow you to create more secure virtual hosts, each with their own PHP CGI executable, therefore allowing PHP to run as a named user instead of the default Apache process owner.

In this section, you can choose which version you would like to use, or even go through both configuration processes just to better understand how these things work. You will be able to perform all of the exercises in the book regardless of the configuration you choose.

The CGI Version of PHP

To configure Apache to use the CGI version of PHP, you simply make a few modifications to the Apache configuration file, the `httpd.conf` file located in the `conf` directory within the Apache installation directory.

1. Open the `httpd.conf` file with a text editor such as Notepad.

2. Look for a section of text like the one shown in the figure.

3. Add a line like the following:

```
ScriptAlias /php/ "C:/php-4.2.1-win32/"
```

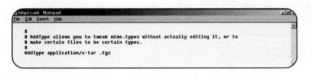

Next, you have to add a directive to the `httpd.conf` file to define the file extensions used by PHP files. Common extensions are .php and .phtml, but you can use whatever you'd like.

4. Look for a section of text like the one shown in the figure.

5. Add the following two lines:

```
AddType application/x-httpd-php .phtml .php
AddType application/x-httpd-php-source .phps
```

Make one more modification to the `httpd.conf` file, and you'll be done.

6. Look for a section of text like the one shown in the figure.

7. Add the following line:

```
Action application/x-httpd-php /php/php.exe
```

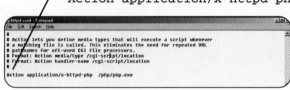

8. Save and close the `httpd.conf` file.

This final modification tells Apache that anytime a file with an extension of .php or .phtml is requested, Apache should first run that file through the PHP parser before sending any output to the Web browser.

The Apache Module Version of PHP

To configure Apache to use the module version, you have to move one piece of PHP and also make a few modifications to the Apache configuration file, the `httpd.conf` file located in the `conf` directory within the Apache installation directory.

1. In `C:\php-4.2.1-win32\` you should have a file called `php4ts.dll`. Move that file to `C:\Windows\system` (for Windows 98/Me) or to `C:\WINNT\system32` (for Windows NT/2000).

2. Open the `httpd.conf` file with a text editor such as Notepad.

3. Look for a section of text like the one shown in the figure.

4. Add a line like the following:

```
LoadModule php4_module c:/php-4.2.1-win32/sapi/php4apache.dll
```

```
httpd.conf - Notepad
File  Edit  Search  Help
#
# To be able to use the functionality of a module which was built as a DSO you
# have to place corresponding `LoadModule' lines at this location so the
# directives contained in it are actually available _before_ they are used.
# Please read the file README.DSO in the Apache 1.3 distribution for more
# details about the DSO mechanism and run `apache -l' for the list of already
# built-in (statically linked and thus always available) modules in your Apache
# binary.
#
# Note: The order in which modules are loaded is important.  Don't change
# the order below without expert advice.
#
# Example:
# LoadModule foo_module modules/mod_foo.so
#
#LoadModule vhost_alias_module modules/mod_vhost_alias.so
#LoadModule mime_magic_module modules/mod_mime_magic.so
#LoadModule status_module modules/mod_status.so
#LoadModule info_module modules/mod_info.so
#LoadModule speling_module modules/mod_speling.so
#LoadModule rewrite_module modules/mod_rewrite.so
#LoadModule anon_auth_module modules/mod_auth_anon.so
#LoadModule dbm_auth_module modules/mod_auth_dbm.so
#LoadModule digest_auth_module modules/mod_auth_digest.so
#LoadModule digest_module modules/mod_digest.so
#LoadModule proxy_module modules/mod_proxy.so
#LoadModule cern_meta_module modules/mod_cern_meta.so
#LoadModule expires_module modules/mod_expires.so
#LoadModule headers_module modules/mod_headers.so
#LoadModule usertrack_module modules/mod_usertrack.so
#LoadModule unique_id_module modules/mod_unique_id.so
LoadModule php4_module c:/php-4.2.1-win32/sapi/php4apache.dll
```

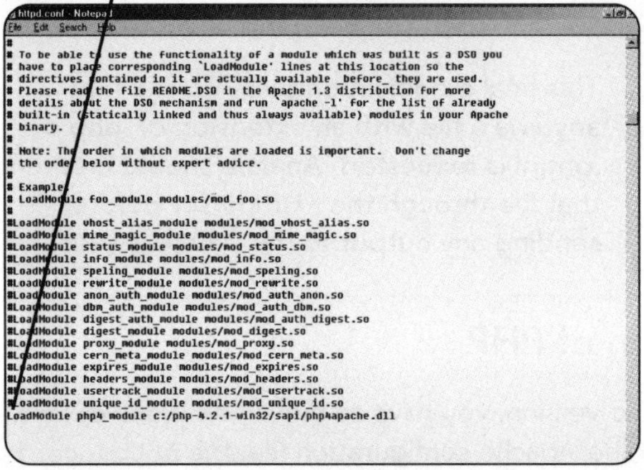

5. Directly beneath the text you just entered, look for a section of text like the one shown in the figure.

```
httpd.conf - Notepad
File  Edit  Search  Help
AddModule mod_imap.c
AddModule mod_actions.c
#AddModule mod_speling.c
AddModule mod_userdir.c
AddModule mod_alias.c
#AddModule mod_rewrite.c
AddModule mod_access.c
AddModule mod_auth.c
#AddModule mod_auth_anon.c
#AddModule mod_auth_dbm.c
#AddModule mod_auth_digest.c
#AddModule mod_digest.c
#AddModule mod_proxy.c
#AddModule mod_cern_meta.c
#AddModule mod_expires.c
#AddModule mod_headers.c
#AddModule mod_usertrack.c
#AddModule mod_unique_id.c
AddModule mod_so.c
AddModule mod_setenvif.c
```

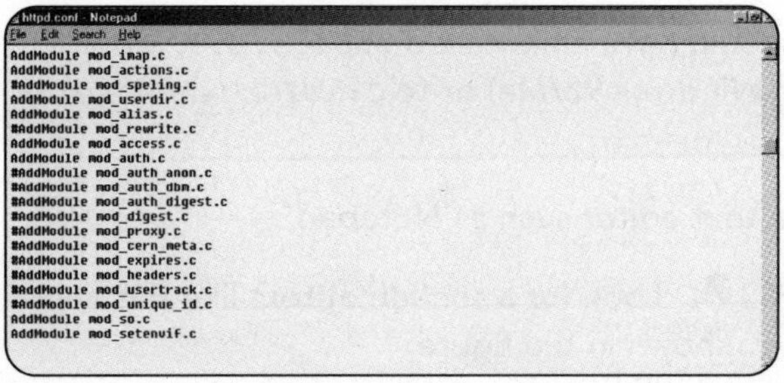

6. Add the following line:

```
AddModule mod_php4.c
```

```
httpd.conf - Notepad
File  Edit  Search  Help
AddModule mod_imap.c
AddModule mod_actions.c
#AddModule mod_speling.c
AddModule mod_userdir.c
AddModule mod_alias.c
#AddModule mod_rewrite.c
AddModule mod_access.c
AddModule mod_auth.c
#AddModule mod_auth_anon.c
#AddModule mod_auth_dbm.c
#AddModule mod_auth_digest.c
#AddModule mod_digest.c
#AddModule mod_proxy.c
#AddModule mod_cern_meta.c
#AddModule mod_expires.c
#AddModule mod_headers.c
#AddModule mod_usertrack.c
#AddModule mod_unique_id.c
AddModule mod_so.c
AddModule mod_setenvif.c
AddModule mod_php4.c
```

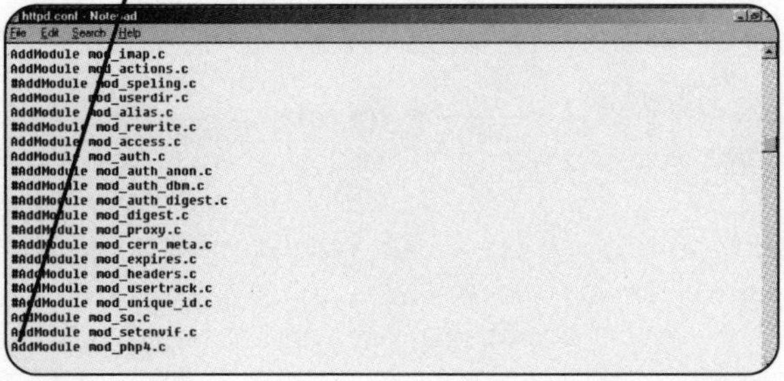

Next, you have to add a directive to the `httpd.conf` file to define the file extensions used by PHP files. Common extensions are .php and .phtml, but you can use whatever you'd like.

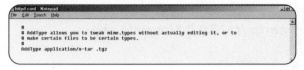

7. Look for a section of text like the one shown in the figure.

8. Add the following two lines:

```
AddType application/x-httpd-php .phtml .php
AddType application/x-httpd-php-source .phps
```

7. Save and close the `httpd.conf` file.

This final modification tells Apache that any time a file with an extension of .php or .phtml is requested, Apache should utilize the module version of the PHP parser before sending any output to the Web browser.

Testing the PHP Installation

Now that all of your modifications have been made to the `httpd.conf` file—no matter the configuration method—you can restart Apache using the method you learned in Chapter 2. To test that Apache and PHP are playing nice together, you'll next create a simple PHP script to test your installation. PHP scripts and other files (HTML, images, and so on) should be placed in the document root of your Web server. For Apache, the document root is the `htdocs` directory within your Apache installation directory.

1. Open a new file in your text editor and type the following:

```
<? phpinfo(); ?>
```

2. Save the file with the name `phpinfo.php` and place this file in the document root of your Web server

---

NOTE

Be absolutely sure your file extension is .php or .phtml (or another extension you configured for PHP). It is very common for Windows-based text editors to add a hidden file extension of .txt to the end of the file name. If that happens to you, then your script will not parse as PHP, only text. So keep an eye on your extension!

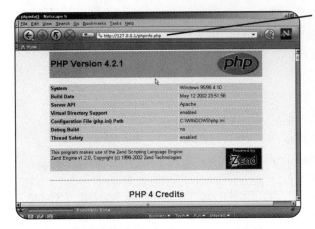

3. Open your Web browser and type **http://127.0.0.1/phpinfo.php**

The output of the `phpinfo.php` script should be a long page full of system and environment information. This information is very helpful when you're trying to figure out what's available to you. If you browse through the results, you'll see that the following extensions are preinstalled (along with many others):

- Regular expression support

- Dynamic library support

- Internal `sendmail` support

- Perl-compatible regular expression support

- ODBC support

- Session support

- XML support

- MySQL support

Having these items preinstalled means that no additional .dll files are necessary for these functions to be available to you. For more information on obtaining .dll files for additional PHP functionality, see Appendix A, "Additional Configuration Options."

You're now ready to move on to Part II, "The Absolute Basics of Coding in PHP," and learn the fundamentals of the PHP language.

Installing PHP for Linux

This section will show you how to install PHP on Linux as a dynamic module for Apache. By building a dynamic rather than a static module, you can upgrade or recompile PHP without having to recompile Apache as well. For example, all you'll be doing in this section is configuring PHP for MySQL support. If you decide you want additional options later in the game, such as image creation functions or additional encryption functions, you'll only have to change the configuration command for PHP, recompile the module, and restart Apache. No additional changes will be needed for the Apache installation, as just one PHP module file will be replacing another.

To download the PHP source distribution, visit the downloads page at the PHP Web site: http://www.php.net/downloads.php.

1. From the "Complete Source Code" section, follow the link for "PHP 4.x.x" where "x.x" refers to the version. The current source code version is 4.2.1, and that version number will be used in the steps below, although your version number (and therefore file name) may vary.

2. Once downloaded to your system, type **cp php-4.2.1.tar.gz /usr/local/** and press Enter to copy the PHP source distribution to the /usr/local/ directory.

NOTE

You can put PHP anywhere you want on your file system, such as /usr/local/bin/ or /opt/ or wherever you want to put the file. Just be sure to substitute your path for the path indicated in these directions.

---

3. Go to /usr/local/ by typing **cd /usr/local/** and pressing Enter.

4. Unzip the source file by typing **gunzip php-4.2.1.tar.gz** and pressing Enter.

5. Extract the files by typing **tar -xvf php-4.2.1.tar** and pressing Enter. This will create a directory structure, then put you back at the prompt. The parent directory will be /usr/local/php-4.2.1/.

6. Enter the parent directory by typing **cd php-4.2.1** and pressing Enter.

7. Type the following and press Enter to prepare to build PHP:

```
./configure --with-mysql=/usr/local/mysql/
--with-apxs=/usr/local/apache_1.3.26/bin/apxs
```

NOTE

In configuration directives, use your own paths to the MySQL and Apache directories, should they reside elsewhere on your file system.

The configuration script will run through its process of checking your configuration and creating makefiles, and then will put you back at the prompt.

8. Type **make** and press Enter. This second step of the installation process will produce many lines of output on your screen. When it is finished, you will be back at the prompt.

9. Type **make install** and press Enter. This final step of the installation process will produce many lines of output on your screen. When it is finished, you will be back at the prompt.

Now, to get a basic version of PHP working with Apache, all you need to do is to make a few modifications to the `httpd.conf` file.

Configuring Apache to Use PHP

The installation process will have placed a module in the proper place within the Apache directory structure. Now you must make some modifications to the `httpd.conf` file before starting up Apache with PHP enabled.

1. Open the `httpd.conf` file in your text editor of choice.

```
#
# AddType allows you to tweak mime.types without actually editing it, or to
# make certain files to be certain types.
#
# For example, the PHP 3.x module (not part of the Apache distribution - see
# http://www.php.net) will typically use:
#
#AddType application/x-httpd-php3 .php3
#AddType application/x-httpd-php3-source .phps
#
# And for PHP 4.x, use:
#
#AddType application/x-httpd-php .php
#AddType application/x-httpd-php-source .phps
```

2. Find a section of text that looks like the one shown in the figure.

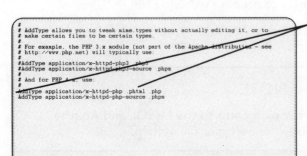

```
#
# AddType allows you to tweak mime.types without actually editing it, or to
# make certain files to be certain types.
#
# For example, the PHP 3.x module (not part of the Apache distribution - see
# http://www.php.net) will typically use:
#
#AddType application/x-httpd-php3 .php3
#AddType application/x-httpd-php3-source .phps
#
# And for PHP 4.x, use:
#
AddType application/x-httpd-php .phtml .php
AddType application/x-httpd-php-source .phps
```

3. Uncomment the last two lines by removing the #, and add `.phtml` as an option in the next-to-last line.

4. Save and close the `httpd.conf` file.

This modification tells Apache that anytime a file with an extension of `.php` or `.phtml` is requested, Apache should first run that file through the PHP parser before sending any output to the Web browser.

Additionally, during the process of building PHP, the appropriate Apache `LoadModule` directive should have been added. To verify this, look for a section of text in your `httpd.conf` file, like that in the figure. If the `LoadModule` line is present, then the installation was a success.

Once these changes have been made to `httpd.conf`, you're ready to start Apache and test your PHP installation.

Testing the PHP Installation

Now that all of your modifications have been made to the `httpd.conf` file, you can restart Apache using the method you learned in Chapter 2, "Installing Apache." To test that Apache and PHP are playing nice together, you'll next create a simple PHP script to test out your installation. PHP scripts and other files (HTML, images, and so on) should be located in the document root of your Web server. For Apache, the document root is the `htdocs` directory within your Apache installation directory.

1. Open a new file in your text editor and type the following:

```
<? phpinfo(); ?>
```

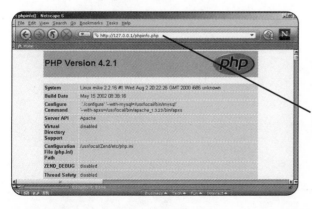

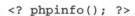

2. Save the file with the name `phpinfo.php`.

3. Place this file in the document root of your Web server.

4. Open your Web browser, type **http://127.0.0.1/phpinfo.php** and then hit Enter.

The output of the `phpinfo.php` script should be a long page full of system and environment information. This information is very helpful when you're trying to figure out what's available to you.

For more information on configuring and building additional functionality into your PHP installation, see Appendix A, "Additional Configuration Options."

You're now ready to move on to Part II, "The Absolute Basics of Coding in PHP," and learn the fundamentals of the PHP language.

PART II

The Absolute Basics of Coding in PHP

4

Mixing PHP and HTML

Now that you have a working development environment, with PHP, Apache, and MySQL happily running on your machine, it's time to delve into the PHP language. In this chapter, you'll learn how to do the following:

- Recognize and use the different kinds of PHP start and end tags
- Mingle PHP and HTML within your source code
- Escape special characters in your scripts to produce valid output

How PHP Is Parsed

So you have a file, and in that file you have some HTML and some PHP code. This is how it all works, assuming a PHP document with an extension of .php.

1. The Web browser requests a document with a .php extension.

2. The Web server says, "Hey! Someone wants a PHP file. Something else needs to deal with it," and sends the request on to the PHP parser.

3. The PHP parser finds the requested file and scans it for PHP code.

4. When the PHP parser finds PHP code, it executes that code and places the resulting output (if any) into the place in the file formerly occupied by the code.

5. This new output file is sent back to the Web server.

6. The Web server sends it along to the Web browser.

7. The Web browser displays the output.

Because the PHP code is parsed by the server, this method of code execution is called *server-side*. When code is executed by the browser, such as JavaScript, it is called *client-side*.

To combine PHP code with HTML, the PHP code must be set apart from the HTML. In the next section, you'll learn how this is done, using PHP start and end tags.

PHP Start and End Tags

The PHP parser recognizes a few different types of PHP start and end tags. It will attempt to execute anything between these tags, so it had better be valid code!

Study Table 4.1 to learn the three main sets of start and end tags recognized by the PHP parser.

Next, you'll use all three sets of tags in a script, which I promise will execute without errors.

1. Open a new file in your text editor.

Table 4.1 Basic PHP Start and End Tags

Opening Tag	Closing Tag
`<?php`	`?>`
`<?`	`?>`
`<script language="php">`	`</script>`

2. Type the following code, which uses the first tag type:

```
<?php
echo "<P>This is a test using the first tag type.</P>";
?>
```

3. Type the following code, which uses the second tag type:

```
<?
echo "<P>This is a test using the second tag type.</P>";
?>
```

4. Type the following code, which uses the third tag type:

```
<script language="php">
echo "<P>This is a test using the third tag type.</P>";
</script>
```

5. Save the file with the name `phptags.php`.

6. Place this file in the document root of your Web server.

7. Open your Web browser and type **http://127.0.0.1/phptags.php**

NOTE

While executing the examples in this book, if you are using PHP on an external Web server, substitute that server's domain name for 127.0.0.1 in the URL.

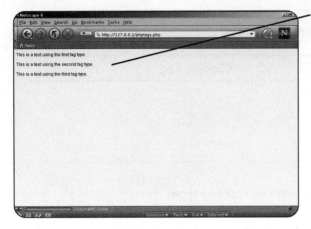

In your Web browser, you should see the results of your script.

In the next section, you'll learn that putting PHP blocks inside HTML is not a scary thing.

Code Cohabitation

In the previous section, your file consisted of three chunks of PHP code, each of which printed some HTML text. In this section, you'll create a script that has PHP code stuck in the middle of your HTML, and you'll learn how these two types of code can peacefully coexist.

1. Open a new file in your text editor.

2. Type the following HTML:

```
<HTML>
<HEAD>
<TITLE>My First PHP Script</TITLE>
</HEAD>
<BODY>
```

3. Type the following PHP code:

```
<?
echo "<P><em>Hello World! I'm using PHP!</em></P>";
?>
```

4. Add some more HTML so that the document is valid:

```
</BODY>
</HTML>
```

5. Save the file with the name firstscript.php.

6. Place this file in the document root of your Web server.

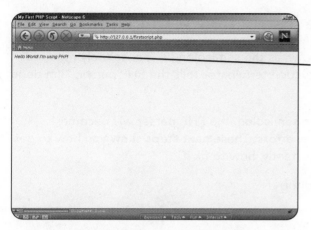

7. Open your Web browser and type **http://127.0.0.1/firstscript.php**

In your Web browser, you should see the results of your script.

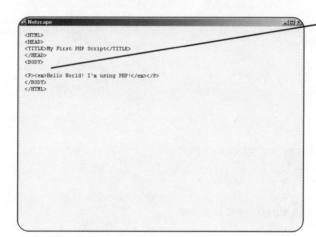

8. In your Web browser, view the source of this document.

Notice that the HTML source contains only HTML code. This block of PHP was executed:

```
<?
echo "<P><em>Hello World! I'm using PHP!</em></P>";
?>
```

This block contains three elements: the command (`echo`), the string (`<P><em>Hello World! I'm using PHP!</em></P>`), and the instruction terminator (`;`).

Familiarize yourself now with `echo`, because it will likely be your most often-used command. The `echo` statement is used to output information—in this case, to print this HTML output:

```
<P><em>Hello World! I'm using PHP!</em></P>
```

The next section discusses a common error, with the hope that you'll be able to avoid it.

The Importance of the Instruction Terminator

The instruction terminator, also known as the semicolon (;), is absolutely required at the end of commands. The instruction terminator tells the PHP parser, "I'm done with this thing, try the next one."

If you do not end commands with a semicolon, the PHP parser will become confused, and your code will display errors. These next steps show you how to get one of these errors and, more importantly, how to fix it.

1. Open a new file in your text editor.

2. Type the following HTML:

```
<HTML>
<HEAD>
<TITLE>Making an Error</TITLE>
</HEAD>
<BODY>
```

3. Type the following PHP code:

```
<?
echo "<P>I am trying to produce an error</P>"
echo "<P>Was I successful?</P>";
?>
```

4. Add some more HTML so that the document is valid:

```
</BODY>
</HTML>
```

5. Save the file with the name errorscript.php.

6. Place this file in the document root of your Web server.

7. Open your Web browser and type **http://127.0.0.1/errorscript.php**

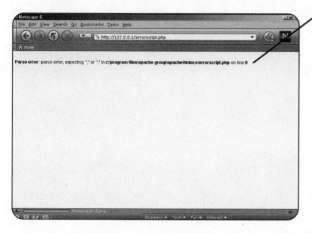

What a nasty error! The error message says that the error is on line 9. Take a look at lines 8 and 9 of the script:

```
echo "<P>I am trying to produce an
error</P>"
echo "<P>Was I successful?</P>";
```

Line 8 does not have an instruction terminator, and line 9 starts a new command. The PHP parser doesn't like this, and it tells you so by producing the parse error.

This error is easy enough to fix:

1. Open the errorscript.php file.

2. On line 8, add the instruction terminator (;) to the end of the line:

```
echo "<P>I am trying to produce an error</P>";
```

3. Save the file.

4. Place this file in the document root of your Web server.

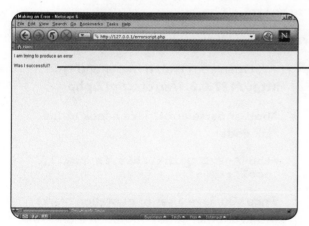

5. Open your Web browser and type **http://127.0.0.1//errorscript.php**

After you fix line 8, the PHP parser can deal with the file, and the rest of the output is successful. Avoid this and other errors by paying close attention to things such as semicolons and, as you'll learn in the next section, quotation marks!

Escaping Your Code

Right up there with remembering to end your commands with semicolons is remembering to escape things such as quotation marks. When you use quotation marks inside other quotation marks, the inner pairs must be delineated from the outside pair using the escape (\) character (also known as a backslash).

The following steps show you what happens when your code isn't escaped, and how to fix it.

1. Open a new file in your text editor.

2. Type the following HTML:

```
<HTML>
<HEAD>
<TITLE>Trying For Another Error</TITLE>
</HEAD>
<BODY>
```

3. Type the following PHP code:

```
<?
echo "<P>I think this is really "cool"!</P>";
?>
```

4. Add some more HTML so that the document is valid:

```
</BODY>
</HTML>
```

5. Save the file with the name `errorscript2.php`.

6. Place this file in the document root of your Web server.

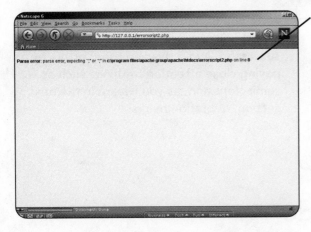

7. Open your Web browser and type **http://127.0.0.1/errorscript2.php**

Another parse error! Take a look at the PHP code:

```
echo "<P>I think this is really "cool"!</P>";
```

Since you have a set of quotation marks within another set of quotation marks, that inner set has to be escaped.

This error also has a simple fix:

1. Open the `errorscript2.php` file.

2. On line 8, escape the inner quotation marks by placing a backslash before each one:

```
echo "<P>I think this is really \"cool\"!</P>";
```

3. Save the file.

4. Place this file in the document root of your Web server.

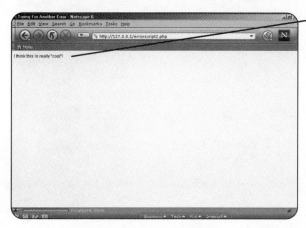

5. Open your Web browser and type **http://127.0.0.1/errorscript2.php**

Now that the inner quotation marks are escaped, the PHP parser will skip right over them, knowing that these characters should just be printed and have no other meaning. In the next section, you'll learn a good programming practice: commenting your code so people know what the heck is going on in it.

Commenting Your Code

Code commenting is a good habit to have. Entering comments in HTML documents helps you (and others who might have to edit your document later) keep track of areas of large documents. Commenting also allows you to write notes to yourself during the development process, or to comment out parts of code when you are testing your scripts.

HTML comments are ignored by the browser and are contained within `<!--` and `-->` tags. For example, the following comment reminds you that the code following it contains your logo graphic:

```
<!-- logo graphic goes here -->
```

PHP uses comments, too, which are ignored by the PHP parser. PHP comments are usually preceded by double slashes, like this:

```
// this is a comment in PHP code
```

But you can use other types of comments, such as

```
# This is shell-style style comment
```

and

```
/* This begins a C-style comment that runs
onto two lines */
```

Create a script full of comments so that you can see how they're ignored. Yes, I'm telling you to write a script that does absolutely nothing!

1. Open a new file in your text editor.

2. Type the following HTML:

```
<HTML>
<HEAD>
<TITLE>Code Comments</TITLE>
</HEAD>
<BODY>
<!-- This is an HTML comment. -->
```

3. Type the following PHP code:

```
<?
// This is a simple PHP comment.
/* This is a C-style, multiline comment. You can make this as
long as you'd like. */
# Used to shells? Use this kind of comment.
?>
```

4. Add some more HTML so that the document is valid:

```
</BODY>
</HTML>
```

5. Save the file with the name comments.php.

6. Place this file in the document root of your Web server.

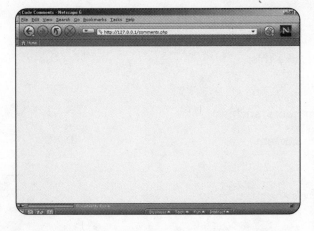

7. Open your Web browser and type **http://127.0.0.1/comments.php**

You should see absolutely nothing in your Web browser, because all you did was print an HTML comment (which is ignored). Since PHP comments are ignored by the PHP parser, the PHP block didn't contain any actual commands. If you view the source of this document in your Web browser, you will notice that only the HTML comment is visible. Although the PHP code was all comments, it was still parsed and is not visible to the end user.

HTML and PHP comments are used extensively throughout this book to explain blocks of code. Get used to reading comments, and try to pick up the habit of using them. Writing clean, bug-free code, with comments and white space, will make you popular among your developer peers because they won't have to work extra hard to figure out what your code is trying to do. In the next chapter, you'll learn all about variables, or, as I like to call them, "those things with the dollar signs."

5

Introducing Variables and Operators

In the last chapter, you were introduced to the process of parsing PHP code and how the code output is displayed in your Web browser. In the next few chapters, you'll learn a bit about the inner workings of the PHP language—all the bits and pieces that, when put together, actually produce a working program! In this chapter, you'll learn how to do the following:

- Recognize and use variables
- Recognize and use operators

What's a Variable?

A variable is a representation of a particular value, such as `blue` or `19349377`. By assigning a value to a variable, you can reference the variable in other places in your script, and that value will always remain the same (unless you change it, which you'll learn about later).

To create a variable, do the following:

1. Think of a good name! For instance, if I want to create a variable to hold a username, I name my variable:

```
username
```

2. Put a dollar sign ($) in front of that name:

```
$username
```

3. Use the equal sign after the name (=) to assign a literal value to that variable. Put the value in quotation marks:

```
$username = "joe"
```

4. Assigning a value to a variable is an instruction, and as such should be terminated with a semicolon:

```
$username = "joe";
```

There you have it—a variable called `username` with a value of `joe`. Later in this chapter, you'll do some exciting things (such as math) with your variables!

Naming Your Variables

As you've seen, variables begin with a dollar sign ($) and are followed by a meaningful name. The variable name cannot begin with a numeric character, but it can contain numbers and the underscore character (_). Additionally, variable names are case-sensitive, meaning that `$YOURVAR` and `$yourvar` are two different variables.

Creating meaningful variable names is another way to lessen headaches while coding. If your script deals with name and password values, don't create a variable called `$n` for the name and `$p` for the password—those are not meaningful names. If you pick up that script weeks later, you might think that `$n` is the variable for "number" rather than "name" and that `$p` stands for "page" rather than "password."

PHP Variable and Value Types

You will create two main types of variables in your PHP code: scalar and array. Scalar variables contain only one value at a time, and arrays contain a list of values, or even another array.

The example at the beginning of this chapter created a scalar variable, and the code in this book deals primarily with scalar variables. You can find information on arrays in Appendix B, "Basic PHP Language Reference."

When you assign a value to a variable, you usually assign a value of one of the following types:

- **Integers.** Whole numbers (numbers without decimals). Examples are 1,345 and 9922786. You can also use octal and hexadecimal notation: the octal 0123 is decimal 83 and the hexadecimal 0x12 is decimal 18.

- **Floating-point numbers ("floats" or "doubles").** Numbers with decimals. Examples are 1.5, 87.3446, and 0.88889992.

- **Strings.** Text and/or numeric information, specified within double quotes (" ") or single quotes (' ').

As you begin your PHP script, plan your variables and variable names carefully, and use comments in your code to remind yourself of the assignments you have made.

Create a simple script that assigns values to different variables and then simply prints the values to the screen.

1. Open a new file in your text editor and type the following HTML:

```
<HTML>
<HEAD>
<TITLE>Printing Variables</TITLE>
</HEAD>
<BODY>
```

2. Add a PHP block and create a variable that holds an integer:

```
<?
$intVar = "9554215464";
```

3. Create a variable that holds a floating-point number:

```
$floatVar = "1542.2232235";
```

4. Create a variable that holds a string:

```
$stringVar = "This is a string.";
```

5. Add an echo statement for each variable:

```
echo "<P>integer: $intVar</P>";
echo "<P>float: $floatVar</P>";
echo "<P>string: $stringVar</P>";
```

6. Close your PHP block and add some more HTML so that the document is valid:

```
?>
</BODY>
</HTML>
```

7. Save the file with the name `printvarscript.php` and place this file in the document root of your Web server.

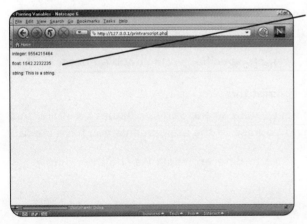

8. Open your Web browser and type **http://127.0.0.1/printvarscript.php**

You can see by this output that the values you assigned to the variables `$intVar`, `$floatVar`, and `$stringVar` were the values printed to the screen. In the next section, you'll learn how to use operators to change the values of your variables.

Local and Global Variables

Variables can be *local* or *global*, the difference having to do with their definition and use by the programmer, and where they appear in the context of the scripts you are creating. The variables described in the previous section, and for the majority of this book, are local variables.

When you write PHP scripts that use variables (and likely they always will), these variables can be used only by the script they live within. Scripts cannot magically reach inside other scripts and use the variables created and defined within them—unless you say they can and you purposefully link them together. When you do just that, such as when you create your own functions (blocks of reusable code that perform a particular task), you will define the shared variables as global. That is, able to be accessed by other scripts and functions which need them.

You can learn about creating your own functions, and using global as well as local variables, in Appendix C, "Writing Your Own Functions." For now, just understand that there are two different variable scopes—local and global—that will come into play as you write more advanced scripts.

Predefined Variables

In all PHP scripts, a set of predefined variables are in use. You may have seen some of these variables in the output of the `phpinfo()` function, if you scrolled and read through the entire results page. Some of these predefined variables are also called *superglobals*, essentially meaning that they are always present and available in your scripts.

Please study the following list of superglobals, as they will be used exclusively throughout this book. Each of these superglobals are actually arrays of other variables. Don't worry about fully understanding this concept now; it will be explained as you move along through the book.

- **$_GET** Any variables provided to a script through the GET method.

- **$_POST** Any variables provided to a script through the POST method.

- **$_COOKIE** Any variables provided to a script through a cookie.

- **$_FILES** Any variables provided to a script through file uploads.

- **$_ENV** Any variables provided to a script as part of the server environment.

- **$_SESSION** Any variables which are currently registered in a session.

NOTE

If you are using a version of PHP earlier than 4.1.x and cannot upgrade to a newer version of PHP as described in Chapter 3, "Installing PHP," you must adjust the names of these variables when following the scripts in this book. The old names are as follows: $HTTP_GET_VARS, $HTTP_POST_VARS, $HTTP_COOKIE_VARS, $HTTP_POST_FILES, $HTTP_ENV_VARS, and $HTTP_SESSION_VARS.

Using Constants

A *constant* is an identifier for a value that cannot change during the course of a script. Once it has a value, it remains through its execution lifetime. Constants can be user-defined, or you can use some of the predefined constants that PHP always has available. Unlike simple variables, constants do not have a dollar sign before their name, and they are usually uppercase to show their difference from a scalar variable. Next, you'll test out the user-defined type.

1. Open a new file in your text editor and open a PHP block:

```
<?
```

2. The function used to define a constant is called `define()` and it requires the name of the constant and the value you want to give it. Here you define a constant called `MYCONSTANT` with a value of `"This is a test of defining constants."`

```
define("MYCONSTANT", "This is a test of defining constants.");
```

3. Print the value of the constant, then close the PHP block:

```
echo MYCONSTANT;
```

4. Save the file with the name `constants.php` and place this file in the document root of your Web server.

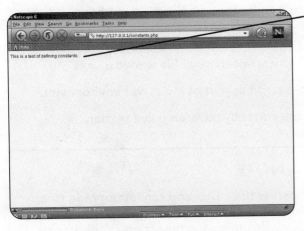

5. Open your Web browser and type **http://127.0.0.1/constants.php**

Some predefined constants include

- `__FILE__` The name of the script file being parsed

- `__LINE__` The number of the line in the script being parsed

- `PHP_VERSION` The version of PHP in use

- `PHP_OS` The operating system using PHP

Let's test them all out:

1. Open a new file in your text editor and open a PHP block:

```
<?
```

2. Use the echo statement to display an introductory string, and concatenate the __FILE__ constant to the end of it:

```
echo "<br>This file is ".__FILE__;
```

3. Use the echo statement to display an introductory string, and concatenate the __LINE__ constant to the end of it:

```
echo "<br>This is line number ".__LINE__;
```

4. Use the echo statement to display an introductory string, and concatenate the PHP_VERSION constant to the end of it:

```
echo "<br>I am using ".PHP_VERSION;
```

5. Use the echo statement to display an introductory string, and concatenate the PHP_OS constant to the end of it. Also close up the PHP block:

```
echo "<br>This test is being run on ".PHP_OS;
?>
```

6. Save the file with the name constants2.php and place this file in the document root of your Web server.

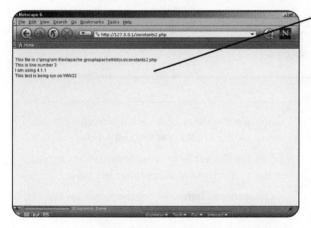

7. Open your Web browser and type **http://127.0.0.1/constants2.php**

You should see the strings you typed, plus the values of the constants. Your values will likely differ from those you see here.

What's an Operator?

In the previous section, you used an assignment operator (=) to assign values to your variables. There are other types of assignment operators, as well as other types of operators in general. The basic function of an operator is to do something with the value of a variable. That "something" can be to assign a value, change a value, or compare two or more values.

Here are the main types of PHP operators:

- **Assignment operators.** Assign a value to a variable. Can also add to or subtract from a variable's current value.

- **Arithmetic operators.** You know all of these operators! Addition, subtraction, division, and multiplication occur when these operators are used.

- **Comparison operators.** Compare two values and return either true or false. You can then perform actions based on the returned value.

- **Logical operators.** Determine the status of conditions.

The rest of this chapter is devoted to discussing some of the main operators used in PHP. You'll be writing scripts for each, so hang on to your hat!

Assignment Operators

You've already seen an assignment operator at work: the equal sign is the basic assignment operator. Burn this into your brain: = does *not* mean "equal to"! Instead, == (two equal signs) means "equal to," and the single = means "is assigned to." In fact, you've also seen the concatenation operator in this chapter, as it is used to put strings together.

Take a look at the assignment operators in Table 5.1 and prepare to write a new script.

Table 5.1 Assignment Operators

Operator	Example	Action
+=	$a += 3;	Changes the value of a variable to the current value plus the value on the right side.
-=	$a -= 3;	Changes the value of a variable to the current value minus the value on the right side.
.=	$a .= "string";	Concatenates (adds on to) the value on the right side with the current value.

Create a simple script to show how all of these assignment operators work. This script will assign an original value to one variable and then change that value as the script executes, all the while printing the result to the screen.

1. Open a new file in your text editor and type the following HTML:

```
<HTML>
<HEAD>
```

```
<TITLE>Using Assignment Operators</TITLE>
</HEAD>
<BODY>
```

2. Start a PHP block. Create a variable with a value of 100 and then print it:

```
<?
$origVar = 100;
echo "<P>Original value is $origVar</P>";
```

3. Add to that value and then print it:

```
$origVar += 25;
echo "<P>Added a value, now it's $origVar</P>";
```

4. Subtract from that value and then print it:

```
$origVar -= 12;
echo "<P>Subtracted a value, now it's $origVar</P>";
```

5. Concatenate a string and then print it:

```
$origVar .= " chickens";
echo "<P>Final answer: $origVar</P>";
```

6. Close your PHP block and add some more HTML so that the document is valid:

```
?>
</BODY>
</HTML>
```

7. Save the file with the name `assignscript.php` and place this file in the document root of your Web server.

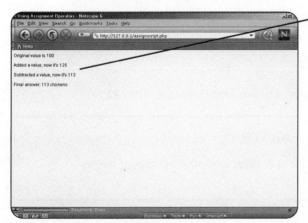

8. Open your Web browser and type **http://127.0.0.1/assignscript.php**

The results of your calculations will be printed to the screen. Next we move to arithmetic operators, none of which should be strange to you as long as you made it through your first few years of school.

Arithmetic Operators

Arithmetic operators are just basic math! Take a look at Table 5.2, be sure you remember your basic math, and start creating the test script for this section.

Table 5.2 Arithmetic Operators

Operator	Example	Action
+	$b = $a + 3;	Adds values
–	$b = $a – 3;	Subtracts values
*	$b = $a * 3;	Multiplies values
/	$b = $a / 3;	Divides values
%	$b = $a % 3;	Returns the modulus, or remainder

Create a simple script to show how all of these arithmetic operators work. This script will assign original values to two variables, perform mathematical operations, and print the results to the screen.

1. Open a new file in your text editor and type the following HTML:

```
<HTML>
<HEAD>
<TITLE>Using Arithmetic Operators</TITLE>
</HEAD>
<BODY>
```

2. Start a PHP block, create two variables with values, and print the values:

```
<?
$a = 85;
$b = 24;
echo "<P>Original value of \$a is $a and \$b is $b</P>";
```

NOTE

If you escape the dollar sign (\$), it will print literally instead of being interpreted as a variable.

3. Add the two values and print the result:

```
$c = $a + $b;
echo "<P>Added \$a and \$b and got $c</P>";
```

4. Subtract the two values and print the result:

```
$c = $a - $b;
echo "<P>Subtracted \$b from \$a and got $c</P>";
```

5. Multiply the two values and print the result:

```
$c = $a * $b;
echo "<P>Multiplied \$a and \$b and got $c</P>";
```

6. Divide the two values and print the result:

```
$c = $a / $b;
echo "<P>Divided \$a by \$b and got $c</P>";
```

7. Check the modulus of the two values and print the result:

```
$c = $a % $b;
echo "<P>The modulus of \$a and \$b is $c</P>";
```

8. Close your PHP block and add some more HTML so that the document is valid:

```
?>
</BODY>
</HTML>
```

9. Save the file with the name `arithmeticscript.php` and place this file in the document root of your Web server.

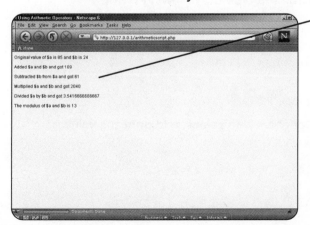

10. Open your Web browser and type **http://127.0.0.1/arithmeticscript.php**

Your original values, as well as the results of the various calculations, will be printed to the screen.

Next we move to comparison operators, which are quite necessary, but not nearly as much fun as arithmetic operators.

Comparison Operators

It should come as no surprise that comparison operators compare two values. As with the arithmetic operators, you already know most of the comparison operators but might not know what they are called. Take a look at Table 5.3 and then start creating the test script for this section.

Table 5.3 Comparison Operators

Operator	Definition
==	Equal to
!=	Not equal to
>	Greater than
<	Less than
>=	Greater than or equal to
<=	Less than or equal to

The result of any of these comparisons is either true or false. This isn't much fun, but you can act on the result using control statements such as `if…else` and `while` to perform a specific task.

Create a simple script to show the result of some comparisons, using the `if…else` control statements to print a result to the screen.

1. Open a new file in your text editor and type the following HTML:

```
<HTML>
<HEAD>
<TITLE>Using Comparison Operators</TITLE>
</HEAD>
<BODY>
```

2. Start a PHP block, create two variables with values, and print the values:

```
<?
$a = 21;
$b = 15;
echo "<P>Original value of \$a is $a and \$b is $b</P>";
```

3. Within an if...else statement, test whether $a is equal to $b. Depending on the answer (true or false), one of the echo statements will print:

```
if ($a == $b) {
echo "<P>TEST 1: \$a equals \$b</P>";
} else {
echo "<P>TEST 1: \$a is not equal to \$b</P>";
}
```

NOTE

Conditional expressions are enclosed in parentheses.

4. Within an if...else statement, test whether $a is not equal to $b. Depending on the answer (true or false), one of the echo statements will print:

```
if ($a != $b) {
echo "<P>TEST 2: \$a is not equal to \$b</P>";
} else {
echo "<P>TEST 2: \$a is equal to \$b</P>";
}
```

NOTE

The curly braces { } separate the blocks of statements within a control structure.

5. Within an if...else statement, test whether $a is greater than $b. Depending on the answer (true or false), one of the echo statements will print:

```
if ($a > $b) {
echo "<P>TEST 3: \$a is greater than \$b</P>";
} else {
echo "<P>TEST 3: \$a is not greater than \$b</P>";
}
```

6. Within an `if…else` statement, test whether $a is less than $b. Depending on the answer (true or false), one of the `echo` statements will print:

```
if ($a < $b) {
echo "<P>TEST 4: \$a is less than \$b</P>";
} else {
echo "<P>TEST 4: \$a is not less than \$b</P>";
}
```

7. Within an `if…else` statement, test whether $a is greater than or equal to $b. Depending on the answer (true or false), one of the `echo` statements will print:

```
if ($a >= $b) {
echo "<P>TEST 5: \$a is greater than or equal to \$b</P>";
} else {
echo "<P>TEST 5: \$a is not greater than or equal to \$b</P>";
}
```

8. Within an `if…else` statement, test whether $a is less than or equal to $b. Depending on the answer (true or false), one of the `echo` statements will print:

```
if ($a <= $b) {
echo "<P>TEST 6: \$a is less than or equal to \$b</P>";
} else {
echo "<P>TEST 6: \$a is not less than or equal to \$b</P>";
}
```

9. Close your PHP block and add some more HTML so that the document is valid:

```
?>
</BODY>
</HTML>
```

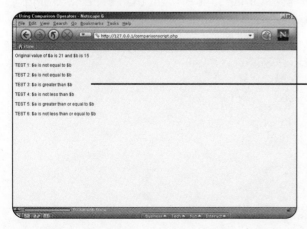

10. Save the file with the name `comparisonscript.php` and place this file in the document root of your Web server.

11. Open your Web browser and type **http://127.0.0.1/comparisonscript.php**

The original values, as well as the results of the various comparisons, will be printed to the screen. The last type of operators you'll tackle are logical operators, which are also used frequently inside blocks of code.

Logical Operators

Logical operators allow your script to determine the status of conditions (such as the comparisons in the preceding section). In the context of your if...else or while statements, logical operators execute certain code based on which conditions are true and which are false.

For now, focus on the && (and) and || (or) operators to determine the validity of a few comparisons.

1. Open a new file in your text editor and type the following HTML:

```
<HTML>
<HEAD>
<TITLE>Using Logical Operators</TITLE>
</HEAD>
<BODY>
```

2. Start a PHP block and create two variables with values. The comparisons in this script will be based on these two variables:

```
<?
$degrees = "95";
$hot = "yes";
```

3. Within an if...else statement, test whether $degrees is greater than 100 or if the value of $hot is yes. Depending on the result of the two comparisons, one of the echo statements will print:

```
if (($degrees > 100) || ($hot == "yes")) {
echo "<P>TEST 1: It's <strong>really</strong> hot!</P>";
} else {
echo "<P>TEST 1:It's bearable.</P>";
}
```

NOTE

Since your conditional expression is actually made up of two smaller conditional expressions, an extra set of parentheses surrounds it.

---

4. Within an if...else statement, test whether $degrees is greater than 80 and whether the value of $hot is yes. Depending on the result of the two comparisons, one of the echo statements will print:

```
if (($degrees > 80) && ($hot == "yes")) {
echo "<P>TEST 2: It's <strong>really</strong> hot!</P>";
} else {
echo "<P> TEST 2: It's bearable.</P>";
}
```

5. Close your PHP block and add some more HTML so that the document is valid:

```
?>
</BODY>
</HTML>
```

6. Save the file with the name logicalscript.php and place this file in the document root of your Web server.

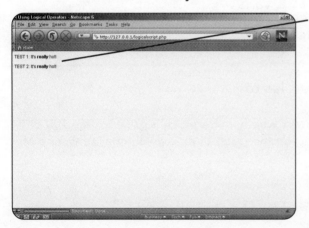

7. Open your Web browser and type **http://127.0.0.1/logicalscript.php**

The text message associated with the comparison result will be printed to the screen. Both expressions in this example are true. In the first test, only one expression has to be true, and that is satisfied by $hot having a value of yes. In the second test, both expressions have to be true, and they are; $degrees has a value of 95, which is greater than 80, and $hot has a value of yes.

Numerous other types of operators are used in PHP. They will be explained as they appear throughout the book. The operators listed in this chapter give you a pretty good head start. In the next chapter, you'll use your newly acquired knowledge of variables and operators to build scripts that perform more intriguing actions than those explained so far.

6

Using Variables

Now that you know a little bit about variables in general, it's time to take that knowledge one step further and do more interesting things with variables. In this chapter, you'll learn how to do the following:

- Use HTML forms to send variables to your scripts
- Use environment variables

Getting Variables from Forms

HTML forms should contain the following elements:

- A method
- An action
- A submit button

In your HTML code, the first line of a form will look something like this:

```
<FORM METHOD="POST" ACTION="yourscript.php">
```

When you click on a submit button in an HTML form, variables are sent to the script specified by the ACTION via the specified METHOD. The method can be either POST or GET. Variables passed from a form to a PHP script are placed in the global associative array (or superglobal) called $_POST or $_GET, depending on the form method. In the next section, you'll see how this works by creating an HTML form and accompanying PHP script that performs calculations depending on the form input.

Creating a Calculation Form

In this section, you'll create the front end to a calculation script. This form will contain two input fields and a radio button to select the calculation type.

1. Open a new file in your text editor.

2. Type the following HTML:

```
<HTML>
<HEAD>
<TITLE>Calculation Form</TITLE>
</HEAD>
<BODY>
```

3. Begin your form. Assume that the method is POST and the action is a script called calculate.php:

```
<FORM METHOD="POST" ACTION="calculate.php">
```

4. Create an input field for the first value, with a text label:

```
<P>Value 1: <INPUT TYPE="text" NAME="val1" SIZE=10></P>
```

5. Create an input field for the second value, with a text label:

`<P>Value 2: <INPUT TYPE="text" NAME="val2" SIZE=10></P>`

6. Add a submit button:

`<P><INPUT TYPE="submit" NAME="submit" VALUE="Calculate"></P>`

7. Close your form and add more HTML so that the document is valid:

```
</FORM>
</BODY>
</HTML>
```

8. Save the file with the name `calculate_form.html` and place this file in the document root of your Web server.

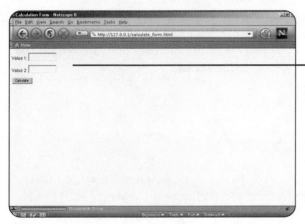

9. Open your Web browser and type **http://127.0.0.1/calculate_form.html**

You will see a form containing the Value 1 and Value 2 fields, along with a Calculate button. Take a moment to examine the HTML form, to understand just how variables will get their names.

When submitted, this form will send two variables to your script, `$_POST[val1]` and `$_POST[val2]`, because those are the NAMEs used in each text field. The values for those variables will be the values typed in the form fields by the user.

There's one more item to add: a series of radio buttons to determine the type of calculation to perform on the two values.

1. Open `calculate_form.html` in your text editor.

2. Add the following block before the submit button:

```
<P>Calculation:<br>
<INPUT TYPE="radio" NAME="calc" VALUE="add"> add<br>
<INPUT TYPE="radio" NAME="calc" VALUE="subtract"> subtract<br>
<INPUT TYPE="radio" NAME="calc" VALUE="multiply"> multiply<br>
<INPUT TYPE="radio" NAME="calc" VALUE="divide"> divide</P>
```

3. Save the file and place it in the document root of your Web server.

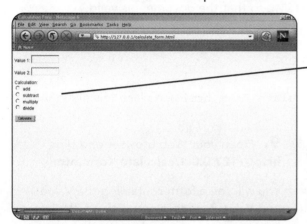

4. Open your Web browser and type **http://127.0.0.1/calculate_form.html**

Your form will now contain the Value 1 and Value 2 fields, a set of radio buttons, and a Calculate button. Now, in addition to the two values ($_POST[val1] and $_POST[val2]), a variable called $_POST[calc] will be sent to your script. Move on to the next section and create the calculation script.

Creating the Calculation Script

According to the form action in calculate_form.html, you need a script called calculate.php. The goal of this script is to accept the two values ($_POST[val1] and $_POST[val2]) and perform a calculation depending on the value of $_POST[calc].

1. Open a new file in your text editor.

2. Start a PHP block and prepare an if statement that checks for the presence of the three values:

```
<?
if (($_POST[val1] == "") || ($_POST[val2] == "") || ($_POST[calc]
=="")) {
    // more code goes here
}
```

This statement says "If any of these three variables do not have a value, do something else."

3. Replace the "more code goes here" with the following two lines:

```
header("Location: http://127.0.0.1/calculate_form.html");
exit;
```

The first of these two lines outputs a `header` statement—in this case, printing a new location: the URL of the form. The second line exits the script. So, if any of the three variables do not have a value, the user will be redirected to the original form.

NOTE

Be sure that there are no line breaks, spaces, or any other text before your PHP block starts. You cannot use the `header()` function if output has already been sent to the browser.

---

4. Begin an `if…else` statement to perform the correct calculation, based on the value of `$_POST[calc]`, starting with a value of `add`:

```
if ($_POST[calc] == "add") {
    $result = $_POST[val1] + $_POST[val2];
```

5. Continue the statement for the remaining three calculation types and then close your PHP block:

```
} else if ($_POST[calc] == "subtract") {
    $result = $_POST[val1] - $_POST[val2];
} else if ($_POST[calc] == "multiply") {
    $result = $_POST[val1] * $_POST[val2];
} else if ($_POST[calc] == "divide") {
    $result = $_POST[val1] / $_POST[val2];
}
?>
```

6. Start the HTML output:

```
<HTML>
<HEAD>
<TITLE>Calculation Result</TITLE>
</HEAD>
<BODY>
```

7. Using HTML mingled with PHP code, display the value of `$result`:

```
<P>The result of the calculation is: <? echo "$result"; ?></P>
```

8. Add some more HTML so that the document is valid:

```
</BODY>
</HTML>
```

```
<?
if (($_POST[val1] == "") || ($_POST[val2] == "") || ($_POST[calc] =="")) {
        header("Location  http://127.0.0.1/calculate_form.html");
}

if ($_POST[calc] == "add") {
        $result = $_POST[val1] + $_POST[val2];
} else if ($_POST[calc] == "subtract") {
        $result = $_POST[val1] - $_POST[val2];
} else if ($_POST[calc] == "multiply") {
        $result = $_POST[val1] * $_POST[val2];
} else if ($_POST[calc] == "divide") {
        $result = $_POST[val1] / $_POST[val2];
}
?>
<HTML>
<HEAD>
<TITLE>Calculation Result</TITLE>
</HEAD>
<BODY>
<P>The result of the calculation is: <? echo "$result"; ?></P>
</BODY>
</HTML>
```

9. Save the file with the name `calculate.php`, and place this file in the document root of your Web server.

Your code should look something like this.

In the next section, you'll submit the form and even try to break it, which is just a bit of good, healthy debugging.

Submitting Your Form and Getting Results

Now that you've created both the front end (form) and the back end (script), it's time to hold your breath and test it.

1. To access the calculation form, open your Web browser and type **http://127.0.0.1/calculate_form.html**

2. Click on the Calculate button without typing anything in the form fields. Your Web browser will reload the page because you didn't enter any values for the three required fields.

3. Enter a value for Value 1, but not for Value 2, and do not select a calculation option. After you click on Calculate, the page should reload.

4. Enter a value for Value 2, but not for Value 1, and do not select a calculation option. After you click on Calculate, the page should reload.

5. Enter a value for Value 1 and for Value 2, but do not select a calculation option. After you click on Calculate, the page should reload.

6. Select a calculation option, but do not enter any values for Value 1 or Value 2. After you click on Calculate, the page should reload.

Now that you've debugged the script by attempting to bypass your validation routine, try some calculations:

1. Enter 9732 for Value 1 and 27 for Value 2.

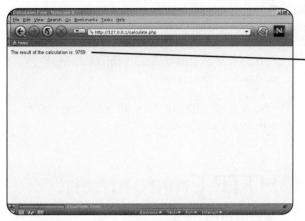

2. Select Add, and click on the Calculate button.

The result of the addition calculation is printed to the screen.

3. Use the Back button to return to the form, then enter 432 for Value 1 and 947 for Value 2.

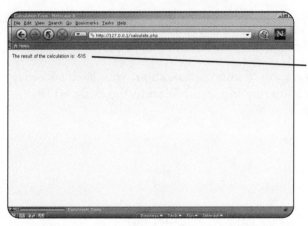

4. Select Subtract, and click on the Calculate button.

The result of the subtraction calculation is printed to the screen.

5. Use the Back button to return to the form, then enter 8562 for Value 1 and 81 for Value 2.

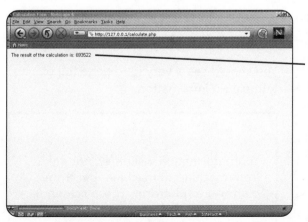

6. Select Multiply, and click on the Calculate button.

The result of the multiplication calculation is printed to the screen.

7. Use the Back button to return to the form, then enter 4893 for Value 1 and 7143 for Value 2.

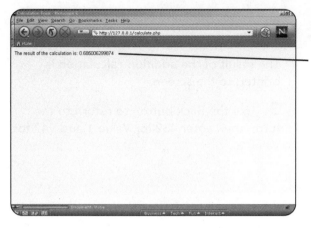

8. Select Divide, and click on the Calculate button.

The result of the division calculation is printed to the screen.

Knock yourself out by trying all sorts of number calculations!

HTTP Environment Variables

When a Web browser makes a request of a Web server, it sends along with the request a list of extra variables. These are called *environment variables*, and they can be very useful for displaying dynamic content or authorizing users.

The `phpinfo()` function displays a wealth of information about your Web server software and the version of PHP you are running, in addition to the basic HTTP environment. Let's see what you have.

1. Open a new file in your text editor.

2. Type the following line of PHP code:

```
<? phpinfo(); ?>
```

3. Save the file with the name `phpinfo.php` and place this file in the document root of your Web server.

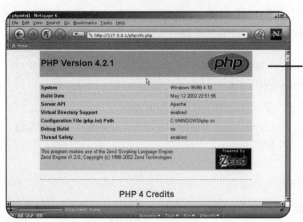

4. Open your Web browser and type **http://127.0.0.1/phpinfo.php**

You should see a very long page full of interesting information.

NOTE

Your information will differ, not only from machine to machine, but from platform to platform. These screen shots were taken on a Windows development machine.

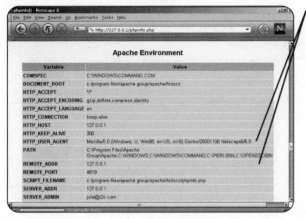

As you scroll down, look for a section titled Apache Environment. In the next sections, you'll learn how to use two environment variables: REMOTE_ADDR and HTTP_USER_AGENT. For an explanation of some of the HTTP environment variables shown in the phpinfo() output, visit http://hoohoo.ncsa.uiuc.edu/cgi/env.html.

Retrieving and Using REMOTE_ADDR

By default, environment variables are available to PHP scripts as $VAR_NAME. For example, the REMOTE_ADDR environment variable is already contained as $REMOTE_ADDR. However, to be absolutely sure that you're reading the correct value, use the getenv() function to assign a value to a variable of your choice.

The REMOTE_ADDR environment variable contains the IP address of the machine making the request. Let's get the value of your REMOTE_ADDR.

1. Open a new file in your text editor.

2. Open a PHP block, then use getenv() to place the value of REMOTE_ADDR in a variable called $address:

```
<?
$address = getenv("REMOTE_ADDR");
```

3. Print the value of $address to the screen, and close your PHP block:

```
echo "Your IP address is $address.";
?>
```

4. Save the file with the name remoteaddress.php, then place this file in the document root of your Web server.

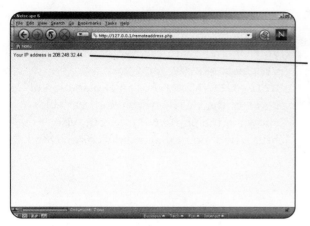

5. Open your Web browser and type **http://127.0.0.1/remoteaddress.php**

Your current IP address will be printed to the screen.

> ### NOTE
> Your IP address will differ from that shown above.

In the next section, you'll get the value of another handy environment variable, `HTTP_USER_AGENT` (Web browser).

Retrieving and Using HTTP_USER_AGENT

The `HTTP_USER_AGENT` variable contains the browser type, browser version, language encoding, and platform. For example, the following value string refers to the Netscape (Mozilla) browser, version 4.61, in English, on the Windows 98 platform:

```
Mozilla/4.61 - (Win98; I)
```

Here are some other `HTTP_USER_AGENT` values, for my own browser library:

```
Mozilla/4.0 (compatible; MSIE 5.5; Windows 98)
```

This value refers to Microsoft Internet Explorer (MSIE) version 5.0 on Windows 98. Sometimes you will see MSIE return an `HTTP_USER_AGENT` value that looks like a Netscape value, until you notice that the value says it's "compatible" and is actually "MSIE 5.0."

I am one of those die-hard Lynx users. Don't count out the text-only browsers! A Lynx `HTTP_USER_AGENT` value looks like this:

```
Lynx/2.8rel.3 libwww-FM/2.14
```

Let's find your HTTP_USER_AGENT.

1. Open a new file in your text editor.

2. Open a PHP block, then use getenv() to place the value of HTTP_USER_AGENT in a variable called $agent:

```
<?
$agent = getenv("HTTP_USER_AGENT");
```

3. Print the value of $agent to the screen, then close your PHP block:

```
echo " You are using $agent.";
?>
```

4. Save the file with the name useragent.php, then place this file in the document root of your Web server.

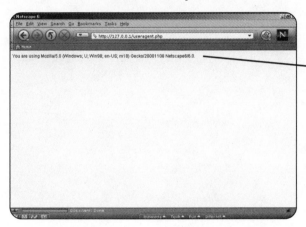

5. Open your Web browser and type **http://127.0.0.1/useragent.php**

Your current HTTP_USER_AGENT value will be printed to the screen.

NOTE

Your user agent string might be different than the one shown.

In the next chapter, you'll learn many of the basic tasks for Web developers, including displaying dynamic content, sending e-mail, and working with your file system.

PART III

Start with Simple Stuff

7

Displaying Dynamic Content

The Web is a dynamic environment, so why not use your programming skills to display dynamic content? Dynamic content can be as simple or as complex as you want it to be. In this chapter, you'll learn how to do the following:

● Display browser-specific HTML

● Display platform-specific HTML

● Use PHP string functions on HTML form input

● Create a redirection menu using an HTML form and the header() function

Displaying Browser-Specific HTML

In the previous chapter, you learned to retrieve and print the HTTP_USER_AGENT environment variable to the screen. In this chapter, you'll do something a bit more interesting with the value of HTTP_USER_AGENT, and that's to print browser-specific HTML.

However, having seen some of the possible values of HTTP_USER_AGENT in the last chapter, you can imagine that there are hundreds of slightly different values. So it's time to learn some basic pattern matching.

You'll use the preg_match() function to perform this task. This function needs two arguments: what you're looking for, and where you're looking:

```
preg_match("/[what you're looking for]/", "[where you're
looking]");
```

This function will return a value of true or false, which you can use in an if...else block to do whatever you want. The goal of the first script is to determine if a Web browser is Microsoft Internet Explorer, Netscape, or something else. This can be a little tricky, but not because of PHP.

Within the value of HTTP_USER_AGENT, Netscape always uses the string Mozilla to identify itself. Unfortunately, the value of HTTP_USER_AGENT for Microsoft Internet Explorer also uses Mozilla to show that it's compatible. Luckily, it also uses the string MSIE, so you can search for that. If the value of HTTP_USER_AGENT doesn't contain either Mozilla or MSIE, chances are very good that it's not one of those Web browsers.

1. Open a new file in your text editor and start a PHP block, then use getenv() to place the value of HTTP_USER_AGENT in a variable called $agent:

```
<?
$agent = getenv("HTTP_USER_AGENT");
```

2. Start an if...else statement to find which of the preg_match() functions is true, starting with the search for MSIE:

```
if (preg_match("/MSIE/i", "$agent")) {
    $result = "You are using Microsoft Internet Explorer.";
}
```

3. Continue the statement, testing for `Mozilla`:

```
else if (preg_match("/Mozilla/i", "$agent")) {
    $result = "You are using Netscape.";
}
```

4. Finish the statement by defining a default:

```
else {
    $result = "You are using $agent";
}
```

NOTE

The `i` in the `preg_match()` function performs a case-insensitive search.

---

5. Close your PHP block and add some HTML to begin the display:

```
?>
<HTML>
<HEAD>
<TITLE>Browser Match Results</TITLE>
</HEAD>
<BODY>
```

6. Type the following PHP code to print the result of the `if...else` statement:

```
<? echo "<P>$result</P>"; ?>
```

7. Add some more HTML so that the document is valid:

```
</BODY>
</HTML>
```

8. Save the file with the name `browsermatch.php` and place this file in the document root of your Web server.

9. Open your Web browser and type **http://127.0.0.1/browsermatch.php**

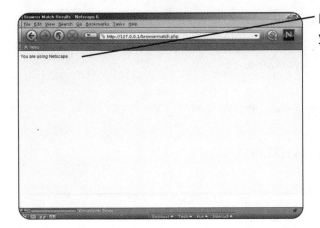

Depending on the Web browser you use, you might see a result such as this

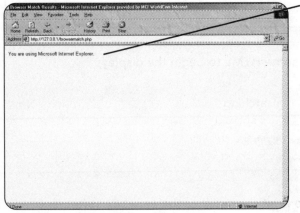

or this.

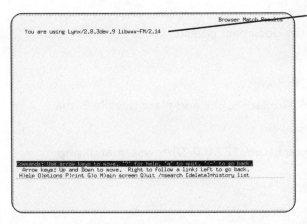

If you're using neither Netscape nor Microsoft Internet Explorer, the actual value of HTTP_USER_AGENT will be printed.

The Browser War rages on: no one Web browser is used by a vast majority of Web surfers. Various versions of Microsoft Internet Explorer (MSIE) account for approximately 78 percent of Web browsers in use, while versions of Netscape (NS) take up about 15 percent. Throw in the die-hard Lynx, Opera, Konquerer, and other users to reach 100 percent.

Although an 80/20 split might seem like a majority, if 500 million people have access to the Internet, 100 million non-Microsoft users is a huge number of users to consider when developing a good Web site. HotWired maintains a browser reference at http://hotwired.lycos.com/webmonkey/reference/browser_chart/. This chart shows you some of the differences between the major browsers. In the next section, you'll take into consideration how not all platforms are created equal, and in fact do not display HTML the same either.

Displaying Platform-Specific HTML

There are differences not only between browsers, but also between platforms. This difference is most clear with regard to fonts and font sizes. In the Windows world, you have fonts such as Times New Roman and Courier New. Slight variations of these fonts appear on the Macintosh and Linux/UNIX platforms; they are called Times and Courier. It doesn't end there—the font sizes all display differently. A 10-point font on Macintosh or Linux is sometimes barely legible, but if you bump it up to 11 or 12 point, you're in business. If that same 12-point font is viewed on Windows, however, it might look like your text is trying to take over the world.

So what to do? Use your new pattern-matching skills to extract the platform from the HTTP_USER_AGENT string, and then display platform-specific HTML. As with matching on a keyword—which you did in the previous section—to nail down the platform you need to know what you're looking for. In the next script, you'll check for the keywords "Win" and "Linux" and print an appropriate style sheet block in your HTML result page.

1. Open a new file in your text editor, start a PHP block, and use getenv() to place the value of HTTP_USER_AGENT in a variable called $agent:

```
<?
$agent = getenv("HTTP_USER_AGENT");
```

2. Start an if...else statement to find which of the preg_match() functions is true, starting with the search for "Win":

```
if (preg_match("/Win/i", "$agent")) {
    $style = "win";
}
```

3. Continue the statement, testing for "Linux":

```
else if (preg_match("/Linux/i", "$agent")) {
    $style = "linux";
}
```

4. Create a basic style sheet block for Windows users:

```
$win_style = "
<style type=\"text/css\">\n
p, ul, ol, li{font-family:Arial;font-size:10pt;font-
weight:normal;}\n
h1 {font-family:Arial;font-size:16pt;font-weight:bold;}\n
h2 {font-family:Arial;font-size:14pt;font-weight:bold;}\n
strong{font-family:Arial;font-size:10pt;font-weight:bold;}\n
em {font-family:Arial;font-size:10pt;font-style:italic;}\n
</style>
";
```

NOTE

When you use quotation marks inside other quotation marks, the inner pair must be delineated from the outside pair using the escape (\) character (also known as a backslash).

---

5. Create a basic style sheet block for Linux users:

```
$linux_style = "
<style type=\"text/css\">\n
p, ul, ol, li{font-family:Times;font-size:12pt;font-
weight:normal;}\n
h1 {font-family:Times;font-size:18pt;font-weight:bold;}\n
h2 {font-family:Times;font-size:16pt;font-weight:bold;}\n
strong{font-family:Times;font-size:12pt;font-weight:bold;}\n
em {font-family:Times;font-size:12pt;font-style:italic;}\n
</style>
";
```

NOTE

The use of the new line (\n) character ensures that your code will print on multiple lines. This is helpful when you are viewing your HTML source.

---

6. Close your PHP block and add the following HTML:

```
?>
<HTML>
<HEAD>
<TITLE>Platform Matching</TITLE>
```

7. Type the following PHP code, creating an `if...else` statement used to print the correct style sheet block:

```
<?
if ($style == "win") {
    echo "$win_style";
} else if ($style == "linux") {
    echo "$linux_style";
}
?>
```

8. Close the top section of your HTML and start the body:

```
</HEAD>
<BODY>
```

9. Type the following HTML to show the use of your style sheet:

```
<h1 align=center>This is a level 1 heading</h1>
<h2 align=center>Look! A level 2 heading</h2>
<P align=center>This is a simple paragraph with some
<strong>bold</strong> and <em>emphasized</em> text.</P>
```

10. Add some more HTML so that the document is valid:

```
</BODY>
</HTML>
```

11. Save the file with the name `platformmatch.php` and place it in the document root of your Web server.

12. Open your Web browser and type **http://127.0.0.1/platformmatch.php**

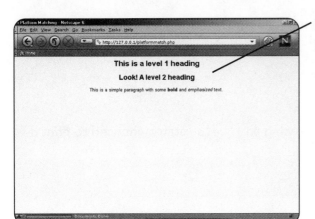

Depending on the Web browser you use, you might see a result such as this

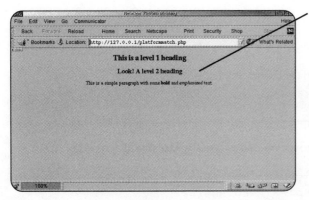

or this.

You can see that the proper style sheet block was printed, based on the result of the platform match. In the next section, you'll move away from pattern matching and work with some of the string functions in PHP to modify form input before displaying it back to the browser.

Working with String Functions

Numerous string functions are built into PHP, all of which are designed to make your life easier. Suppose you have to normalize strings for news headlines or product ID numbers, or calculate the length of a string before trying to stuff it into a database field. Those are just a few of the string functions you'll learn about in the next section. For more string functions, take a look at the PHP manual at http://www.php.net/manual/. The function list seems to grow daily as more people contribute to the language.

Creating an Input Form

In this section, you'll create the front end to a string modification script. This form will contain one text area and several radio buttons. The radio buttons will determine the string function to use.

1. Open a new file in your text editor and type the following HTML:

```
<HTML>
<HEAD>
<TITLE>Generic Input Form</TITLE>
</HEAD>
<BODY>
```

2. Begin your form. Assume that the method is POST and the action is a script called display_input.php:

```
<FORM METHOD="POST" ACTION="display_input.php">
```

3. Create a text area with a text label:

```
<P><strong>Text Field:</strong><br>
<TEXTAREA NAME="text1" COLS=45 ROWS=5 WRAP=virtual></TEXTAREA></P>
```

4. Add this block of radio buttons:

```
<P><strong>String Function:</strong><br>
<INPUT TYPE="radio" NAME="func" VALUE="md5" checked> get md5<br>
<INPUT TYPE="radio" NAME="func" VALUE="strlen"> get length of
string<br>
<INPUT TYPE="radio" NAME="func" VALUE="strrev"> reverse the
string<br>
<INPUT TYPE="radio" NAME="func" VALUE="strtoupper"> make string
uppercase<br>
<INPUT TYPE="radio" NAME="func" VALUE="strtolower"> make string
lowercase<br>
<INPUT TYPE="radio" NAME="func" VALUE="ucwords"> make first letter
of all words uppercase</P>
```

NOTE

The value for each option button is its exact PHP function name. This will make the back-end script very simple to create, as you'll see in the next section.

---

5. Add a submit button:

```
<P><INPUT TYPE="submit" NAME="submit" VALUE="Do Something With the
String"></P>
```

6. Close your form and add some more HTML so that the document is valid:

```
</FORM>
</BODY>
</HTML>
```

7. Save the file with the name `generic_form.html` and place this file in the document root of your Web server.

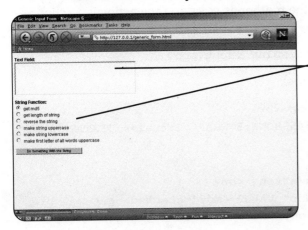

8. Open your Web browser and type **http://127.0.0.1/generic_form.html**

You'll see a form with a text area and several radio buttons, along with a Do Something With The String form submission button. In the next section, you'll create the back-end script. That script will expect two variables: `$_POST[text1]` and `$_POST[func]`.

Creating a Script to Display Form Values

According to the form action in `generic_form.html`, you need a script called `display_input.php`. The goal of this script is to accept the text in `$_POST[text1]` and use a particular string function (the value of `$_POST[func]`) to get a new result (`$result`).

1. Open a new file in your text editor and type the following PHP:

```
<? $result = $_POST[func]($_POST[text1]); ?>
```

2. Start the HTML output:

```
<HTML>
<HEAD>
<TITLE>Generic Input Results</TITLE>
</HEAD>
<BODY>
```

3. Display the value of `$result`:

```
<? echo "$result"; ?>
```

4. Add a link back to the form:

```
<P><a href="generic_form.html">Go again!</a></P>
```

5. Add some more HTML so that the document is valid:

```
</BODY>
</HTML>
```

6. Save the file with the name `display_input.php` and place this file in the document root of your Web server.

```
<? $result = $_POST[func]($_POST[text1]); ?>
<HTML>
<HEAD>
<TITLE>Generic Input Results</TITLE>
</HEAD>
<BODY>
<? echo "$result"; ?>
<P><a href="generic_form.html">Go again!</a></P>
</BODY>
</HTML>
```

Your code should look something like this.

In the next section, you'll submit the form and see all these different types of string functions at work.

Submitting Your Form and Getting Results

Now that you've created both a front-end form and a back-end script, it's time to try them out.

1. Open your Web browser and type **http://127.0.0.1/generic_form.html**

2. Type the following text in the text area:

I think PHP is just the coolest server-side scripting language around! Who knew it would be this simple?

NOTE

You might want to copy that chunk of text to the Clipboard because it will be used in all of the following examples.

---

3. Select the get md5 radio button, and click on the Do Something With The String button.

NOTE

The md5() function gets a *hash* of the string. A hash is like a digital summary of the string. It can be used to compare versions of strings (or files) to see if the versions differ.

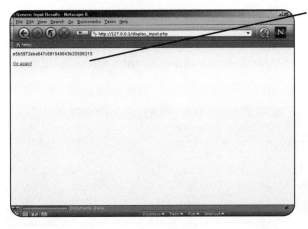

You should see a hash of the string, along with a link back to the form. Next, use the strlen() function to find the length of the string, including white space and all characters.

1. Click on the Go again! link.

2. Enter the same text in the text area:

I think PHP is just the coolest server-side scripting language around! Who knew it would be this simple?

3. Select the get length of string radio button.

4. Click on the Do Something With The String button.

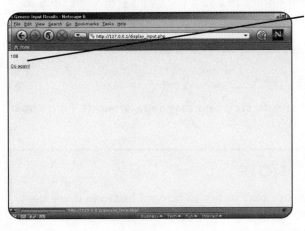

You should see a number representing the character length of the string along with a link back to the form. Next, use the strrev() function to return the original string, completely reversed.

1. Click on the Go again! link.

2. Enter the same text in the text area:

I think PHP is just the coolest server-side scripting language around! Who knew it would be this simple?

3. Select the reverse the string radio button.

4. Click on the Do Something With The String button.

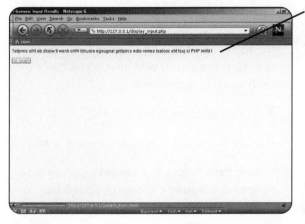

You should see the reverse of the original string, along with a link back to the form. Next, use the `strtoupper()` function to return the string with all letters in uppercase.

1. Click on the Go again! link.

2. Enter the same text in the text area:

I think PHP is just the coolest server-side scripting language around! Who knew it would be this simple?

3. Select the make string uppercase radio button.

4. Click on the Do Something With The String button.

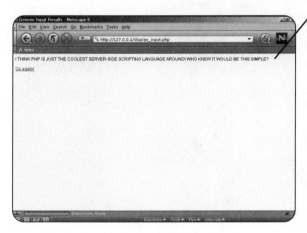

You should see the string completely in uppercase letters, along with a link back to the form. Next, use the `strtolower()` function to return the string with all letters in lowercase.

1. Click on the Go again! link.

2. Enter the same text in the text area:

I think PHP is just the coolest server-side scripting language around! Who knew it would be this simple?

3. Select the make string lowercase radio button.

4. Click on the Do Something With The String button.

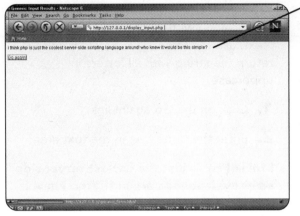

You should see the string completely in lowercase letters, along with a link back to the form. Next, use the `ucwords()` function to return the string with the first letter of each word in uppercase.

1. Click on the Go again! link.

2. Enter the same text in the text area:

I think PHP is just the coolest server-side scripting language around! Who knew it would be this simple?

3. Select the make first letter of all words uppercase radio button.

4. Click on the Do Something With The String button.

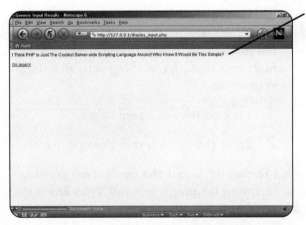

You should see the string, with the first letter of each word capitalized, along with a link back to the form.

To add some error checking to your script, check for the value of `$_POST[func]` as well as the value of `$_POST[text1]` before any other action occurs. Replace your first block of PHP code with this:

```
<?
if (($_POST[func] == "") || ($_POST[text1] == "")){
    header("Location: http://127.0.0.1/generic_form.html");
    exit;
}
$result = $_POST[func]($_POST[text1]);
?>
```

Now if some rogue user directly accesses the script without using the form, he'll be redirected back to the form, and no errors will occur.

Redirecting to a New Location

Redirecting a user to a new location means that your script has sent an HTTP header to the browser, indicating a new location. HTTP headers of any kind (authentication, redirection, cookies, and so on) must be sent to the browser before anything else, including white space, line breaks, and any characters.

In the next section, you'll create a redirection menu and a redirection form. The goal is to have the user select a new location from the menu and then have the script automatically send him there.

Creating a Redirection Form

In this section, you'll create the front end to a redirection script. This form will contain a drop-down list of the names of various Web sites. The value for each option is the Web site's URL.

1. Open a new file in your text editor and type the following HTML:

```
<HTML>
<HEAD>
<TITLE> Redirection Menu</TITLE>
</HEAD>
<BODY>
```

2. Begin your form. Assume that the method is POST and the action is a script called do_redirect.php:

```
<FORM METHOD="POST" ACTION="do_redirect.php">
```

3. Add this drop-down list:

```
<P>Send me to:
<SELECT name="location">
    <OPTION value="http://www.premierpressbooks.com/">Premier
Press</OPTION>
    <OPTION value="http://www.thickbook.com/">thickbook.com
</OPTION>
    <OPTION value="http://www.i2ii.com/">i2i Interactive</OPTION>
```

```
<OPTION value="http://www.php.net/">PHP.net</OPTION>
<OPTION value="http://www.zend.com/">Zend Technologies</OPTION>
</SELECT>
```

4. Add a submit button:

```
<P><INPUT TYPE="submit" NAME="submit" VALUE="Go!"></P>
```

5. Close your form, and add some more HTML so that the document is valid:

```
</FORM>
</BODY>
</HTML>
```

6. Save the file with the name `redirect_form.html` and place this file in the document root of your Web server.

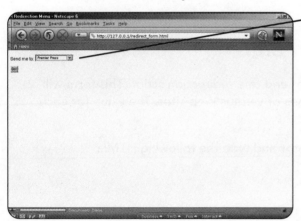

7. Open your Web browser and type **http://127.0.0.1/redirect_form.html**

In the next section, you'll create the back-end script. That script will expect one variable: `$_POST[location]`.

Creating the Redirection Script and Testing It

According to the form action in `redirect_form.html`, you need a script called `do_redirect.php`. The goal of this script is to accept the value of `$_POST[location]` and print that value within the `header()` function so that the user is redirected to the chosen location.

1. Open a new file in your text editor and type the following PHP to create the proper redirection header:

```
<?
header( "Location: $_POST[location]");
exit;
?>
```

2. Save the file with the name do_redirect.php and place this file in the document root of your Web server.

3. Open your Web browser and type **http://127.0.0.1/redirect_form.html**

4. Select Premier Press from the drop-down list, and click on the Go! button.

Users will now be redirected to the Premier Press Web site.

To add some error checking to your script, check for the value of $_POST[location] before trying to do the redirection. Replace your PHP code with this:

```
<?
if ($_POST[location] == "") {
    header("Location: http://127.0.0.1/redirect_form.html");
    exit;
} else {
    header("Location: $_POST[location]");
    exit;
}
?>
```

Now if a user directly accesses the script, he'll be redirected back to the form, and no errors will occur.

8

Sending E-Mail

Using PHP to send the contents of a form to a specified e-mail address is so easy that you'll wonder why more people don't do it every day. In this chapter, you'll learn how to do the following:

- Modify the PHP configuration file so you can send mail
- Create and send a simple feedback form
- Use the $_SERVER[PHP_SELF] variable to create a feedback form with custom error messages

Using an SMTP Server

An SMTP (Simple Mail Transfer Protocol) server is a machine that transports mail, just like a Web server is a machine that displays Web pages when requested. An SMTP server is sometimes referred to as an outgoing mail server, which brings me to the point—you need one in order to complete the exercises in this chapter. On Linux/UNIX, Sendmail and Qmail are popular packages. On Windows, the SMTP service in the Windows NT Service Pack, or the service built into the Windows 2000 operating system, is typically used.

If you have installed Apache, PHP, and MySQL as part of a development environment on your personal machine, you probably do not have SMTP running locally. If that's the case, you can access an outgoing mail server that may already be available to you.

NOTE

If you skipped the first three chapters of this book and are using PHP as part of an Internet service provider's virtual hosting package, the SMTP server should already be installed on that machine and PHP should be properly configured to access it.

If your machine is connected to the Internet via a dial-up connection, DSL, cable, or other type of access, you can use your Internet service provider's outgoing mail server. For example, if your development machine is a Windows 98 box with a 56Kbps modem connected to the Internet via EarthLink, then you can use `mail.earthlink.net` as your SMTP server. Whatever you have configured within your e-mail client (Eudora, Outlook, Netscape Mail, and so on) as your outgoing mail server will also function within your PHP code as your SMTP server. The trick is making PHP aware of this little fact, which you'll learn about next.

SMTP-Related Changes in php.ini

In the `php.ini` master configuration file, there are a few directives that need to be set up so that the `mail()` function works properly. Open `php.ini` with a text editor and look for these lines:

```
[mail function]
; For Win32 only.
SMTP = localhost
```

```
; For Win32 only.
sendmail_from = me@localhost.com
; For Unix only.  You may supply arguments as well (default:
'sendmail -t -i').
;sendmail_path =
```

If you are using Windows, you'll need to modify the first two directives, SMTP and sendmail_from. If you plan to use the outgoing mail server of your ISP (in this example, EarthLink), the entry in php.ini would look like this:

```
SMTP = mail.earthlink.net
```

The second configuration directive is sendmail_from, and this is the e-mail address used in the From header of the outgoing e-mail. It can be overwritten in the mail script itself but normally operates as the default value. For example

```
sendmail_from = youraddress@yourdomain.com
```

Of course, replace youraddress@yourdomain.com with your own address.

If you're on Linux or a Unix variant, sendmail_path is all you need to worry about, and it should look something like this:

```
sendmail_path = /usr/sbin/sendmail
```

Or, if you're using Qmail

```
sendmail_path = /var/qmail/bin/sendmail
```

In the sendmail_path directive, you can also set configuration flags to specify queuing options or to explicitly set the Return_Path header, such as

```
sendmail_path = /usr/sbin/sendmail -t -fyou@yourdomain.com
```

After making changes to the php.ini file, restart the Web server and use the phpinfo() function to verify that the changes have been made. When that's done, you're ready to send some e-mail using PHP.

A Simple Feedback Form

A simple feedback form contains fields for the user's name and e-mail address, and a text area for some sort of message. In this section, you'll create two files: one for the feedback form, and one for the PHP script to process the form, send the mail, and return a response to the browser.

Creating the Feedback Form

1. Open a new file in your text editor.

2. Type the following HTML:

```
<HTML>
<HEAD>
<TITLE>Simple Feedback Form</TITLE>
</HEAD>
<BODY>
```

3. Begin your form. Assume that the method is POST and the action is a script called send_simpleform.php:

```
<FORM METHOD="POST" ACTION="send_simpleform.php">
```

4. Create an input field for the user's name with a text label:

```
<P><strong>Your Name:</strong><br>
<INPUT type="text" NAME="sender_name" SIZE=30></P>
```

5. Create an input field for the user's e-mail address with a text label:

```
<P><strong>Your E-Mail Address:</strong><br>
<INPUT type="text" NAME="sender_email" SIZE=30></P>
```

6. Create a text area to hold the message with a text label:

```
<P><strong>Message:</strong><br>
<TEXTAREA NAME="message" COLS=30 ROWS=5 WRAP=virtual></TEXTAREA></P>
```

7. Add a submit button:

```
<P><INPUT TYPE="submit" NAME="submit" VALUE="Send This Form"></P>
```

8. Close your form and add some more HTML so that the document is valid:

```
</FORM>
</BODY>
</HTML>
```

9. Save the file with the name simple_form.html, and place this file in the document root of your Web server.

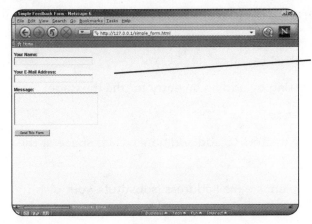

10. Open your Web browser and type **http://127.0.0.1/simple_form.html**

You will see a form containing a text field for the person's name, a text field for the person's e-mail address, a text area for the message, and a button that says Send This Form.

In the next section, you'll create the back-end script. That script will expect three variables: $_POST[sender_name], $_POST[sender_email], and $_POST[message].

Creating a Script to Mail Your Form

According to the form action in simple_form.html, you need a script called send_simpleform.php. The goal of this script is to accept the text in $_POST[sender_name], $_POST[sender_email], and $_POST[message] format, send an e-mail, and display a confirmation to the Web browser.

1. Open a new file in your text editor.

2. Begin a PHP block, then start building a message string:

```
<?
$msg = "E-MAIL SENT FROM WWW SITE\n";
```

4. Continue building the message string by adding an entry for the sender's name:

```
$msg .= "Sender's Name:\t$_POST[sender_name]\n";
```

NOTE

The next few steps will continue building the message string by concatenating smaller strings to form one long message string. *Concatenating* is a fancy word for "smashing together." The concatenation operator (.=) is used.

5. Continue building the message string by adding an entry for the sender's e-mail address:

```
$msg .= "Sender's E-Mail:\t$_POST[sender_email]\n";
```

6. Continue building the message string by adding an entry for the message:

```
$msg .= "Message:\t$_POST[message]\n\n";
```

The final line contains two new line characters to add additional white space at the end of the string.

7. Create a variable to hold the recipient's e-mail address (substitute your own):

```
$to = "you@youremail.com";
```

8. Create a variable to hold the subject of the e-mail:

```
$subject = "Web Site Feedback";
```

9. Create a variable to hold additional mailheaders:

```
$mailheaders = "From: My Web Site <> \n";
```

10. Add to the `$mailheaders` variable:

```
$mailheaders .= "Reply-To: $_POST[sender_email]\n\n";
```

11. Add the `mail()` function:

```
mail($to, $subject, $msg, $mailheaders);
```

12. Close your PHP block:

```
?>
```

```
<?
$msg = "E-MAIL SENT FROM WWW SITE\n";
$msg .= "Sender's Name:\t$_POST[sender_name]\n";
$msg .= "Sender's E-Mail:\t$_POST[sender_email]\n";
$msg .= "Message:\t$_POST[message]\n\n";

$to = "you@youremail.com";
$subject = "Web Site Feedback";

$mailheaders = "From: My Web Site <> \n";
$mailheaders .= "Reply-To: $_POST[sender_email]\n\n";

mail($to, $subject, $msg, $mailheaders);

?>
```

You're not done yet, but your code should look something like this.

Although this code will send the mail, you should return something to the user's screen so that he knows the form has been sent. Otherwise, he might sit there and continually click the Send This Form button.

1. Start the HTML output:

```
<HTML>
<HEAD>
<TITLE>Simple Feedback Form Sent</TITLE>
</HEAD>
<BODY>
```

2. Add some information to tell the user what has happened:

```
<H1>The following e-mail has been sent:</H1>
```

3. Add the text label for the Your Name field and display the user's input:

```
<P><strong>Your Name:</strong><br>
<? echo "$_POST[sender_name]"; ?>
```

4. Add the text label for the Your E-Mail Address field and display the user's input:

```
<P><strong>Your E-Mail Address:</strong><br>
<? echo "$_POST[sender_email]"; ?>
```

5. Add the text label for the Message field and display the user's input:

```
<P><strong>Message:</strong><br>
<? echo "$_POST[message]"; ?>
```

6. Add some more HTML so that the document is valid:

```
</BODY>
</HTML>
```

```
<?
$msg = "E-MAIL SENT FROM WWW SITE\n";
$msg .= "Sender's Name :\t$_POST[sender_name]\n";
$msg .= "Sender's E-Mail :\t$_POST[sender_email]\n";
$msg .= "Message:\t$_POST[message]\n\n";

$to = "you@youremail.com";
$subject = "Web Site Feedback";

$mailheaders = "From: My Web Site <> \n";
$mailheaders .= "Reply-To: $_POST[sender_email]\n\n";

mail($to, $subject, $msg, $mailheaders);
?>
<HTML>
<HEAD>
<TITLE>Simple Feedback Form Sent</TITLE>
</HEAD>
<BODY>

<H1>The following e-mail has been sent:</H1>

<P><strong>Your Name:</strong><br>
<? echo "$_POST[sender_name]"; ?>

<P><strong>Your E-Mail Address:</strong><br>
<? echo "$_POST[sender_email]"; ?>

<P><strong>Message:</strong><br>
<? echo "$_POST[message]"; ?>

</BODY>
</HTML>
```

7. Save the file with the name
send_simpleform.php and place this file
in the document root of your Web server.
Your code should look something like this.

In the next section, you'll submit the form
and see all these different types of string
functions at work.

Submitting Your Form and Getting Results

Now that you've created both a front-end form and a back-end script, it's time to try them out.

1. Open your Web browser and type **http://127.0.0.1/simple_form.html**

2. Type your name in the Your Name field.

3. Type your e-mail address in the Your E-Mail Address field.

4. Type the following message in the Message field:

PHP is so cool!

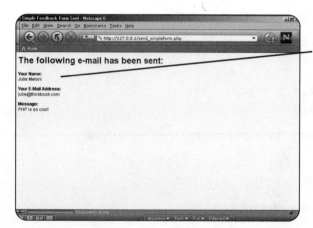

5. Click on the Send This Form button.

The information you entered, along with a confirmation that your e-mail has been sent, will appear.

Now check your e-mail, and see if a message is waiting for you.

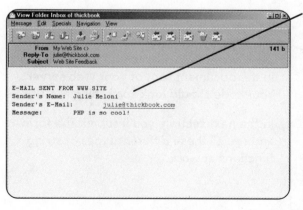

An e-mail sent through this form will look something like this. If it drives you crazy that the tabbed text doesn't line up properly, you can insert as much white space as you'd like in the message string.

1. Open send_simpleform.php in your text editor.

2. Modify the string containing Sender's Name by replacing the tab character (\t) with two spaces:

```
$msg .= "Sender's Name:  $_POST[sender_name}\n";
```

3. Modify the string containing Sender's E-Mail by replacing the tab character (\t) with four spaces:

```
$msg .= "Sender's E-Mail:     $_POST[sender_email]\n";
```

4. Modify the string containing Message by replacing the tab character (\t) with 10 spaces:

```
$msg .= "Message:               $_POST[message]\n\n";
```

5. Save the file.

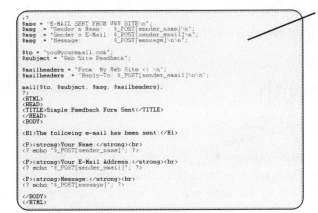

This new section of code should look like this.

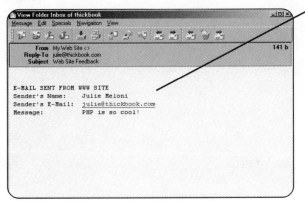

Submit the form again. When you receive the e-mail, this time it should all line up.

Just like previous scripts in this book, you should add some error checking to
`send_simpleform.php`. Check that `$_POST[sender_name]`,
`$_POST[sender_email]`, and `$_POST[message]` all have values before you
perform any other actions. Add this after the first open PHP tag:

```
if (($_POST[sender_name] == "") || ($_POST[sender_email] == "") ||
($_POST[message] == "")) {
    header("Location: http://127.0.0.1/simple_form.html");
    exit;
}
```

In the next section, you'll create custom error messages for when fields are blank,
and you'll streamline the two-step process of sending mail into one cohesive script.

A Feedback Form with Custom Error Messages

In the previous section, you created two separate files. One file contained the front
end (form), and the other contained the back end (script). In this section, you'll
learn how to use the `$_SERVER[PHP_SELF]` variable in a form action to create a
single file that holds both form and script, and how to create custom error
messages when required fields are not completed.

Creating the Initial Script

1. Open a new file in your text editor.

2. Type the following HTML:

```
<HTML>
<HEAD>
<TITLE>All-In-One Feedback Form</TITLE>
</HEAD>
<BODY>
```

3. Start a PHP block, then create a variable called `$form_block`, which will hold
the entire form. Start with the form action, and assume that the method is `POST`
and the action is `$_SERVER[PHP_SELF]`:

```
<?
$form_block = "
<FORM METHOD=\"POST\" ACTION=\"$_SERVER[PHP_SELF]\">
```

TIP

Since you're putting a long string inside a variable, chances are good that you'll have a quotation mark or two. Remember to escape all your quotation marks with a backslash!

---

4. Create an input field for the user's name with a text label:

```
<P><strong>Your Name:</strong><br>
<INPUT type=\"text\" NAME=\"sender_name\" SIZE=30></P>
```

5. Create an input field for the user's e-mail address with a text label:

```
<P><strong>Your E-Mail Address:</strong><br>
<INPUT type=\"text\" NAME=\"sender_email\" SIZE=30></P>
```

6. Create a text area to hold the message with a text label:

```
<P><strong>Message:</strong><br>
<TEXTAREA NAME=\"message\" COLS=30 ROWS=5 WRAP=virtual>
</TEXTAREA></P>
```

7. Add a submit button:

```
<P><INPUT TYPE=\"submit\" NAME=\"submit\" VALUE=\"Send This
Form\"></P>
```

8. Close the form, and then add the ending quotation marks and instruction terminator (semicolon):

```
</FORM>";
```

9. Close the PHP block, then add some more HTML so that the document is valid:

```
?>
</BODY>
</HTML>
```

10. Save the file with the name `allinone_form.php`.

```
<HTML>
<HEAD>
<TITLE>All-In-One Feedback Form</TITLE>
</HEAD>
<BODY>

<?
$form_block = "
<FORM METHOD=\"POST\" ACTION=\"$_SERVER[PHP_SELF]\">

<P><strong>Your Name:</strong><br>
<INPUT type=\"text\" NAME=\"sender_name\" SIZE=30></P>

<P><strong>Your E-Mail Address:</strong><br>
<INPUT type=\"text\" NAME=\"sender_email\" SIZE=30></P>

<P><strong>Message:</strong><br>
<TEXTAREA NAME=\"message\" COLS=30 ROWS=5 WRAP=virtual></TEXTAREA></P>

<P><INPUT TYPE=\"submit\" NAME=\"submit\" VALUE=\"Send This Form\"></p>
</FORM>";

?>
```

You're not done yet, but your code should look something like this.

If you looked at this code in your Web browser, you'd only see a title in the title bar. The burning question should be, "Why do we need all that HTML in a variable called $form_block?" In the next section, you'll add to the script so that it displays particular chunks of code based on certain actions. The string in $form_block is one of those chunks.

Adding Error Checking to the Script

The plan is to use the global variable $_SERVER[PHP_SELF], which has a value of the script's current name. So really, $_SERVER[PHP_SELF] will have a value of allinone_form.php in this instance. When you use $_SERVER[PHP_SELF] as a form action, you're saying, "When the submit button is clicked, reload this script and do something," instead of "When the submit button is clicked, go find another script and do something."

Now that you have a shell of a script, think about what this all-in-one script must do:

- Display the form
- Submit the form
- Check for errors
- Print error messages without sending the form
- Send the form if no errors are found

Make a few modifications to the script to help it determine which actions it should take. Inside the $form_block variable, before the HTML code for the submit button, add this line:

```
<INPUT type=\"hidden\" name=\"op\" value=\"ds\">
```

This line creates a hidden variable called $_POST[op], which has a value of ds. The "op" stands for "operation," and "ds" stands for "do something." I made these names up; they have nothing to do with any programming language. You can call them whatever you want, as long as you understand what they do (which you'll soon see).

The $_POST[op] variable will be present only if the form has been submitted. So if the value of $_POST[op] is not ds, the user hasn't seen the form. If the user hasn't seen the form, we need to show it, so add the following if...else statement before the end of the PHP block:

```
if ($_POST[op] != "ds") {
// they need to see the form
echo "$form_block";
}
```

```
<HTML>
<HEAD>
<TITLE>All-In-One Feedback Form</TITLE>
</HEAD>
<BODY>

<?
$form_block = "
<FORM METHOD=\"POST\" ACTION=\"$_SERVER[PHP_SELF]\">

<P><strong>Your Name:</strong><br>
<INPUT type=\"text\" NAME=\"sender_name\" SIZE=30></P>

<P><strong>Your E-Mail Address:</strong><br>
<INPUT type=\"text\" NAME=\"sender_email\" SIZE=30></P>

<P><strong>Message:</strong><br>
<TEXTAREA NAME=\"message\" COLS=30 ROWS=5 WRAP=virtual></TEXTAREA></P>
<INPUT type=\"hidden\" name=\"op\" value=\"ds\">

<P><INPUT TYPE=\"submit\" NAME=\"submit\" VALUE=\"Send This Form\"></p>
</FORM>";

if ($_POST[op]!= "ds") {
    // they need to see the form
    echo "$form_block";

}
?>
```

You're not done yet, but your code should now look something like this.

You'll make a few more modifications in the next step to add your error messages. If the form is submitted, the value of $_POST[op] will be ds, and now you must account for that. Assume that all the form fields are required; after checking for the value of $_POST[op], you'll check for a value in all the fields.

1. Continue the if...else statement:

```
else if ($_POST[op] == "ds") {
```

2. Add an if statement within the parent statement to check for values. Start with $_POST[sender_name]:

```
if ($_POST[sender_name] == "") {
```

3. Create an error message for $_POST[sender_name] called $name_err:

```
$name_err = "<font color=red>Please enter your name!</font><br>";
```

4. Set the value of $send to no:

```
$send = "no";
```

5. Create a similar if statement for $_POST[sender_email]:

```
if ($_POST[sender_email] == "") {
$email_err = "<font color=red>Please enter your e-mail address!
</font><br>";
$send = "no";
}
```

6. Create a similar `if` statement for `$_POST[message]`:

```
if ($_POST[message] == "") {
$message_err = "<font color=red>Please enter a message!
</font><br>";
$send = "no";
}
```

7. Start an `if...else` statement to handle the value of `$send`:

```
if ($send != "no") {
    // it's ok to send!
```

8. Create a variable to hold the recipient's e-mail address (substitute your own):

```
$to = "you@youremail.com";
```

9. Create a variable to hold the subject of the e-mail:

```
$subject = "All-in-One Web Site Feedback";
```

10. Create a variable to hold additional mail headers:

```
$mailheaders = "From: My Web Site <> \n";
```

11. Add to the `$mailheaders` variable:

```
$mailheaders .= "Reply-To: $_POST[sender_email]\n\n";
```

12. Build the message string:

```
$msg = "E-MAIL SENT FROM WWW SITE\n";
$msg .= "Sender's Name:    $_POST[sender_name]\n";
$msg .= "Sender's E-Mail:  $_POST[sender_email]\n";
$msg .= "Message:          $_POST[message]\n\n";
```

13. Add the `mail()` function:

```
mail($to, $subject, $msg, $mailheaders);
```

14. Add a simple statement to let the user know the mail has been sent, and close the `if` statement:

```
echo "<P>Mail has been sent!</p>";
}
```

15. Continue the `if...else` statement to deal with a value of `no` for `$send`:

```
else if ($send == "no") {
```

16. Print the error messages:

```
echo "$name_err";
echo "$email_err";
echo "$message_err";
```

17. Print the form again:

```
echo "$form_block";
```

18. Close the current if…else block:

```
}
```

19. Close the parent if…else block:

```
}
```

20. Save the file.

The entire code should look something like this:

```
<HTML>
<HEAD>
<TITLE>All-In-One Feedback Form</TITLE>
</HEAD>
<BODY>
<?
$form_block = "
<FORM METHOD=\"POST\" ACTION=\"$_SERVER[PHP_SELF]\">
<P><strong>Your Name:</strong><br>
<INPUT type=\"text\" NAME=\"sender_name\"  SIZE=30></P>
<P><strong>Your E-Mail Address:</strong><br>
<INPUT type=\"text\" NAME=\"sender_email\"  SIZE=30></P>
<P><strong>Message:</strong><br>
<TEXTAREA NAME=\"message\" COLS=30 ROWS=5 WRAP=virtual>
</TEXTAREA></P>
<INPUT type=\"hidden\" name=\"op\" value=\"ds\">
<P><INPUT TYPE=\"submit\" NAME=\"submit\" VALUE=\"Send This
Form\"></p>
</FORM>";

if ($_POST[op] != "ds") {
    // they need to see the form
    echo "$form_block";
} else if ($_POST[op] == "ds") {
```

```
    // check value of $_POST[sender_name]
    if ($_POST[sender_name] == "") {
    $name_err = "<font color=red>Please enter your name!
</font><br>";
    $send = "no";
    }
    // check value of $_POST[sender_email]
    if ($_POST[sender_email] == "") {
    $email_err = "<font color=red>Please enter your e-mail
address!</font><br>";
    $send = "no";
    }
    // check value of $_POST[message]
    if ($_POST[message]== "") {
    $message_err = "<font color=red>Please enter a message!
</font><br>";
    $send = "no";
    }
    if ($send != "no") {
    // it's ok to send, so build the mail
    $msg = "E-MAIL SENT FROM WWW SITE\n";
    $msg .= "Sender's Name:     $_POST[sender_name]\n";
    $msg .= "Sender's E-Mail:   $_POST[sender_email]\n";
    $msg .= "Message:           $_POST[message]\n\n";

    $to = "you@yourdomain.com";
    $subject = "All-in-One Web Site Feedback";
    $mailheaders = "From: My Web Site <> \n";
    $mailheaders .= "Reply-To: $_POST[sender_email]\n\n";
    //send the mail
    mail($to, $subject, $msg, $mailheaders);
    //display confirmation to user
    echo "<P>Mail has been sent!</p>";
    } else if ($send == "no") {
    //print error messages
    echo "$name_err";
    echo "$email_err";
    echo "$message_err";
    echo "$form_block";
    }
}
?>
```

Submitting Your Form and Getting Results

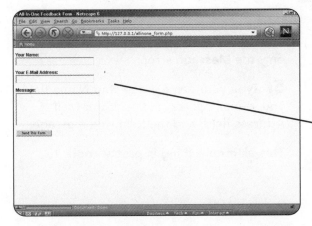

Now that you've created both a front-end form and a back-end script, it's time to try them out.

1. Open your Web browser and type **http://127.0.0.1/allinone_form.php**

You will see a form containing a text field for the person's name, a text field for the person's e-mail address, a text area for the message, and a button that says Send This Form.

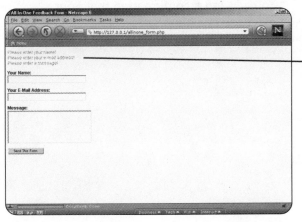

2. Submit the form without typing anything in any of the fields.

The form, with all three error messages at the top, will appear in your browser window.

3. Type your name in the Your Name field and then submit the form.

The form will reappear, without the Name error message.

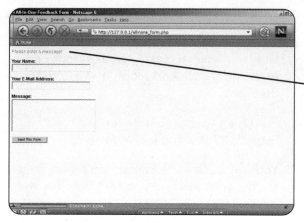

4. Type your name in the Your Name field and your e-mail address in the Your E-Mail Address field, then submit the form.

The form will reappear again, this time with only the Message error.

5. Type your name in the Your Name field, your e-mail address in the Your E-Mail Address field, and the following message:

This all-in-one thing is pretty cool!

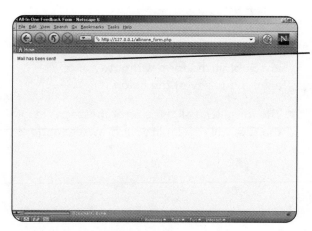

6. Submit the form.

You will see a confirmation that your message has been sent.

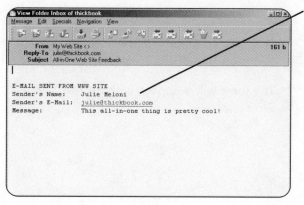

Check your e-mail, and see if a message is waiting for you.

Saving the Values If You Make an Error

One thing you probably noticed in the original script is that if you made an error, the form was reset and you lost the values you had entered. A simple modification to the original `$form_block` will take care of that problem. Just add a VALUE attribute to the form field to hold any previous value for the given variable.

1. Open `allinone_form.php` in your text editor.

2. Inside the `$form_block` variable, modify the input field for Your Name:

```
<INPUT type=\"text\" NAME=\"sender_name\"
VALUE=\"$_POST[sender_name]\" SIZE=30></P>
```

3. Modify the input field for Your E-Mail Address:

```
<INPUT type=\"text\" NAME=\"sender_email\"
VALUE=\"$_POST[sender_email]\" SIZE=30></P>
```

4. Modify the text area for Message:

```
<TEXTAREA NAME=\"message\" COLS=30 ROWS=5
WRAP=virtual>$_POST[message]</TEXTAREA></P>
```

NOTE

There's no VALUE attribute for TEXTAREA. Instead, the value goes between the start and end tags.

---

5. Save the file, then open your Web browser and type **http://127.0.0.1/ allinone_form.php**

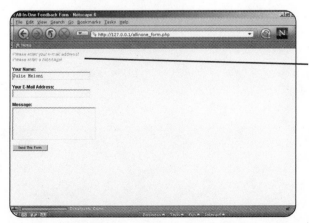

6. Type your name in the Your Name field, then submit the form.

The form, complete with error messages, will appear. This time, though, your name has been saved!

Repeat the process for the other fields in the form to verify that the values were saved.

9

Using Your File System

Using simple PHP scripts, you can do anything with your file system—it's yours, after all! In this chapter, you'll learn how to do the following:

- Display the contents of a directory
- Create a new file
- Open an existing file and append data to it
- Copy, rename, and delete files

File Paths and Permissions

The scripts used in these chapters can be executed on both Windows and Linux/ UNIX operating systems. If you are using Windows, you can use both the forward slash (/) and the backslash (\) in file paths, whereas other operating systems use only the forward slash. The scripts in this chapter use the forward slash method in all instances. This method works even if you don't specify a drive letter. For example:

```
$path = "/Program Files/Apache Group/Apache/htdocs";
```

This path, on Windows, is assumed to be on the current drive (in my case, C:/). If you need to specific a drive letter, go for it:

```
$path = "K:/Program Files/Apache Group/Apache/htdocs/";
```

You'll have to modify file paths to fit your own directory structure, but you shouldn't have to do anything more than that.

For each directory specified in this chapter, you must have the proper permissions to create, modify, and delete files within it. This is an especially important note for non-Windows users, whose operating system is multi-user by nature. If you are unsure how to assign or modify permissions on your system, please contact your system administrator.

Displaying Directory Contents

Believe it or not, this script will be the most complicated in this chapter, and it has only 32 lines! The goal is to open a directory, find the names of all the files in the directory, and print the results in a bullet list.

1. Open a new file in your text editor and start a PHP block:

```
<?
```

2. Create a variable to hold the full path name of a directory:

```
$dir_name = "/My Documents/misc/";
```

NOTE

This directory is one that exists on my own machine. Substitute your own directory name so that this works for you!

---

3. Create a handle and use the `opendir()` function to open the directory specified in step 2.

```
$dir = opendir($dir_name);
```

> ## NOTE
>
> The term *handle* will be used to refer to the open directory in subsequent directory-related functions.

4. You'll eventually place the results in a bullet list inside a string called `$file_list`. Start that bullet list now:

```
$file_list = "<ul>";
```

5. Start a `while` loop that uses the `readdir()` function to determine when to stop and start the loop. The `readdir()` function returns the name of the next file in the directory, and in this case assigns the value to a variable called `$file_name`:

```
while ($file_name = readdir($dir)) {
```

6. Get rid of those "." and ".." file names using an `if` statement:

```
if (($file_name != ".") && ($file_name != "..")) {
```

7. If `$file_name` is neither of the "dot" file names, add it to `$file_list` using the concatenation assignment operator:

```
$file_list .= "<li>$file_name";
```

8. Close the `if` statement and the `while` loop:

```
}
}
```

9. Add the closing tag to the bullet list:

```
$file_list .= "</ul>";
```

10. Close the open directory:

```
closedir($dir);
```

11. Close your PHP block and then add some HTML to begin the display:

```
?>
<HTML>
```

```
<HEAD>
<TITLE>Directory Listing</TITLE>
</HEAD>
<BODY>
```

12. Mingle some HTML and PHP to print the name of the directory you just read:

```
<P>Files in: <? echo "$dir_name"; ?></P>
```

13. Print the file list, then close your HTML tags so the document is valid:

```
<? echo "$file_list"; ?>
</BODY>
</HTML>
```

14. Save the file with the name `listfiles.php`.

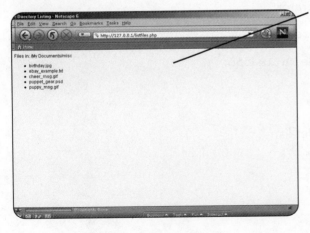

Your code should look something like this.

To test it out, place the file in the document root of your Web server, then open your Web browser and type **http://127.0.0.1/ listfiles.php**.

Assuming that this worked, try it for other directories on your system. If a directory doesn't exist, the script won't return an error—it just won't have any results.

In the next section, you'll work with the `fopen()` and `fclose()` functions to open and close specific files.

Working with fopen() and fclose()

Before you jump headfirst into working with files, you need to learn a bit about the fopen() function, which is used to open files. This function requires a file name and mode, and it returns a file pointer. A file pointer provides information about the file and is used as a reference.

The file name is the full path to the file you want to create or open, and the mode can be any of the modes listed in Table 9.1.

Table 9.1 Modes Used with fopen()

Mode	Usage
r	Opens an existing file and reads data from it. The file pointer is placed at the beginning of the file.
r+	Opens an existing file for reading or writing. The file pointer is placed at the beginning of the file.
w	Opens a file for writing. If a file with that name does not exist, the function creates a new file. If the file exists, the function deletes all existing contents and places the file pointer at the beginning of the file.
w+	Opens a file for reading and writing. If a file with that name does not exist, the function creates a new file. If the file exists, the function deletes all existing content and places the file pointer at the beginning of the file.
a	Opens a file for writing. If a file with that name does not exist, the function creates a new file. If the file exists, the function places the file pointer at the end of the file.
a+	Opens a file for reading and writing. If a file with that name does not exist, the function attempts to create a new file. If the file exists, the function places the file pointer at the end of the file.

Creating a New File

Compared to the first section of this chapter, this next task will be a piece of cake. The goal is simply to create a new, empty file in a specified location.

1. Open a new file in your text editor and start a PHP block:

```
<?
```

2. Create a variable to hold the full path name to a file:

```
$filename = "/My Documents/mydata.txt";
```

> ### NOTE
>
> This directory is one that exists on my own machine. Substitute your own directory name so that this works for you!

3. Create a file pointer and use the `fopen()` function to open the file specified in step 3 for reading and writing. The `die()` function will cause the script to end and a message to display if the file doesn't open properly.

```
$newfile = fopen($filename, "w+") or die("Couldn't create file.");
```

> ### NOTE
>
> The term *file pointer* will be used to refer to the open file in subsequent file-related functions.

4. Close the file pointer:

```
fclose($newfile);
```

5. Create a message to print upon success, then close your PHP block:

```
$msg = "<P>File created!</P>";
?>
```

6. Add this HTML:

```
<HTML>
<HEAD>
<TITLE>Creating a New File</TITLE>
</HEAD>
<BODY>
```

7. Print the message:

```
<? echo "$msg"; ?>
```

8. Add some more HTML so that the document is valid:

```
</BODY>
</HTML>
```

9. Save the file with the name `newfile.php` and place this file in the document root of your Web server.

10. Open your Web browser and type **http://127.0.0.1/newfile.php**

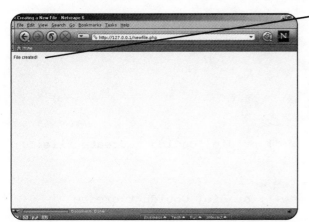

If the file creation was successful, you should see the success message.

However, if your file creation failed, you will see a nasty parse error. You can force an error by using an invalid value for `$filename`, such as this:

```
$filename = "/bozo/mydata.txt";
```

When you run your script, you'll see something like this.

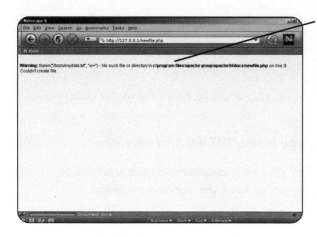

Although the `die()` function did its job by printing the specified message, you can prevent this nastiness by suppressing errors and warnings using the @ sign in front of functions.

Change this line

```
$newfile = fopen($filename, "w+") or die("Couldn't create file.");
```

to this:

```
$newfile = @fopen($filename, "w+") or die("Couldn't create
file.");
```

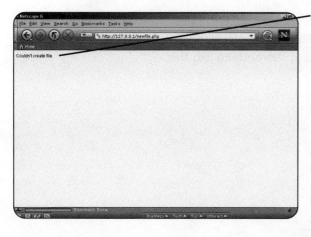

Save the file and access the script via your Web browser. You'll now see just the message from the `die()` function, and no other warnings.

Checking If a File Already Exists

To avoid any possible housekeeping errors when running around your file system, you can use the `file_exists()` function to check if a file already exists before you create it. This next script will do just that and will print a message one way or the other.

1. Open a new file in your text editor and start a PHP block:

```
<?
```

2. Create a variable to hold the full path name to a file (use your own file path):

```
$filename = "/My Documents/mydata.txt";
```

> **NOTE**
>
> Yes, this is the same file you probably created in the previous section. That's fine because it can trip the error checking!

3. Start an `if...else` statement that checks for a true/false result to the `file_exists()` function:

```
if (file_exists($filename)) {
```

4. Create a variable to hold a message regarding the file's existence:

```
$msg = "<P>File already exists.</P>";
```

5. Continue the `else` statement to do something if the file doesn't exist:

```
} else {
```

6. Create a file pointer and use the `fopen()` function to open the file specified in step 2 for reading and writing. The `die()` function will cause the script to end and a message to display if the file doesn't open properly.

```
$newfile = @fopen($filename, "w+") or die("Couldn't create
file.");
```

7. Create a variable to hold a success message:

```
$msg = "<P>File created!</P>";
```

8. Close the file pointer, the `if...else` statement, and your PHP block:

```
fclose($newfile);
}
?>
```

9. Add this HTML:

```
<HTML>
<HEAD>
<TITLE>Creating a New File</TITLE>
</HEAD>
<BODY>
```

10. Print the message:

```
<? echo "$msg"; ?>
```

11. Add some more HTML so that the document is valid:

```
</BODY>
</HTML>
```

12. Save the file with the name `newfile_checkfirst.php` and place this file in the document root of your Web server.

13. Open your Web browser and type **http://127.0.0.1/newfile_checkfirst.php**

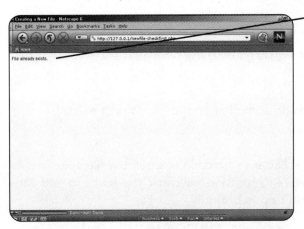

Assuming that you used the filename of a previously created file, you should see the failure message.

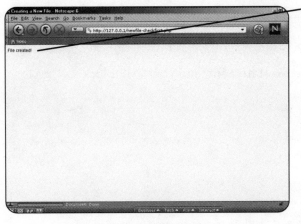

If you change the value of `$filename` to a file that doesn't exist and then access the script again, you'll see the success message.

Since just creating a file is boring, in the next section you'll learn to write data to the file.

Appending Data to a File

The goal of the next script is to append data to a file. If the file exists, the script will just write data into it. If the file doesn't exist, it will be created before data is written to it.

1. Open a new file in your text editor and start a PHP block:

```
<?
```

2. Create a variable to hold the full path name to a file (use your own file path):

```
$filename = "/My Documents/textfile.txt";
```

3. Create a variable called `$newstring` to hold the string you want to write to the file. Populate that string with this very exciting message:

```
$newstring = "
Check it out!\n

I've created a new file and stuck all this text into it!";
```

NOTE

The use of the new line character causes a line break to occur at that point in the text.

---

4. Create a file pointer and use the `fopen()` function to open the file specified in step 2 for reading and writing. The `die()` function will cause the script to end and a message to display if the file doesn't open properly.

```
$myfile = @fopen($filename, "w+") or die("Couldn't open file.");
```

5. Use the `fwrite()` function to place the text (`$newstring`) inside the file (`$myfile`). The `die()` function will cause the script to end and a message to display if the `fwrite()` function fails.

```
@fwrite($myfile, $newstring) or die("Couldn't write to file.");
```

6. Create a variable to hold a success message:

```
$msg = "<P>File has data in it now...</p>";
```

7. Close the file pointer and the PHP block:

```
fclose($myfile);
?>
```

8. Add this HTML:

```
<HTML>
<HEAD>
<TITLE>Adding Data to a File</TITLE>
</HEAD>
<BODY>
```

9. Print the message:

```
<? echo "$msg"; ?>
```

10. Add some more HTML so that the document is valid:

```
</BODY>
</HTML>
```

11. Save the file with the name `writedata.php` and place this file in the document root of your Web server.

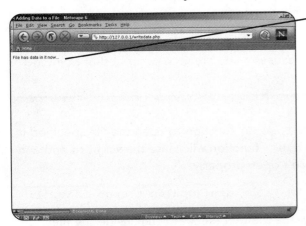

12. Open your Web browser and type **http://127.0.0.1/writedata.php**

In the next section, you'll read the data from the text file created by this script.

Reading Data from a File

You'll now create a script to read the data from the file you created in the previous section. You could just open that file in a text editor, but where's the fun in that? PHP has a handy function called `fread()` that does the job for you.

1. Open a new file in your text editor and start a PHP block:

```
<?
```

2. Create a variable to hold the full path name to the file you created in the previous section (use your own path):

```
$filename = "/My Documents/textfile.txt";
```

3. Create a file pointer and use the `fopen()` function to open the file specified in step 2 for reading only. The `die()` function will cause the script to end and a message to display if the file doesn't open properly.

```
$whattoread = @fopen($filename, "r") or die("Couldn't open file");
```

4. Create a variable called `$file_contents`, and use the `fread()` function to read all the lines from the open file pointer (`$whattoread`) for as long as there are lines in the file:

```
$file_contents = fread($whattoread, filesize($filename));
```

> **NOTE**
>
> Using the `filesize()` function on an existing file lets PHP do the work for you. The second argument of the `fread()` function is for the length of the file. If you don't know the length, but you know you want all of it, you can use `filesize($filename)` to get that length.

5. Create a variable to print a message, including the contents of the file:

```
$msg = "The file contains:<br>$file_contents";
```

6. Close the file pointer and your PHP block:

```
fclose($whattoread);
?>
```

7. Add this HTML:

```
<HTML>
<HEAD>
<TITLE>Reading Data From a File</TITLE>
</HEAD>
<BODY>
```

8. Print the message:

```
<? echo "$msg"; ?>
```

9. Add some more HTML so that the document is valid:

```
</BODY>
</HTML>
```

10. Save the file with the name `readdata.php` and place this file in the document root of your Web server.

11. Open your Web browser and type **http://127.0.0.1/readdata.php**

That's definitely the string written to the file, but what happened to that line break? The new line character means nothing to a Web browser, which renders only HTML. Luckily, the PHP development team had great forethought and created the nl2br() function (new-line-to-break; get it?). Make some slight adjustments to the readdata.php script:

1. Add this line after the line containing the fread() function:

```
$new_file_contents = nl2br($file_contents);
```

2. Modify the $msg string so that it looks like this:

```
$msg = "The file contains:<br>$new_file_contents";
```

3. Save the file.

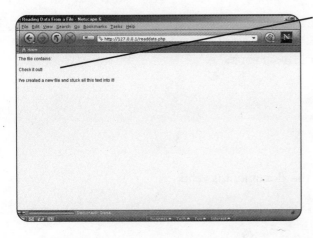

Now open this file in your Web browser, and notice the line break.

In the next section, you'll read the same message, but instead of printing it on the screen, you'll send it via e-mail.

Sending File Contents via E-Mail

If you're saving the results of HTML forms to a plain text file, which you want to read only at specific times, you can write a little script that mails the contents of the file to you on demand.

1. Open a new file in your text editor and start a PHP block:

```
<?
```

2. Create a variable to hold the full path name to the file containing the data (use your own path):

```
$filename = "/My Documents/textfile.txt";
```

3. Create a file pointer and use the `fopen()` function to open the file specified in step 2 for reading only. The `die()` function will cause the script to end and a message to display if the file doesn't open properly.

```
$whattoread = @fopen($filename, "r") or die("Couldn't open file");
```

4. Create a variable called `$file_contents`, and use the `fread()` function to read all the lines from the open file pointer (`$whattoread`) for as long as there are lines in the file:

```
$file_contents = fread($whattoread, filesize($filename));
```

5. Create a variable to hold your e-mail address:

```
$to = "you@yourdomain.com";
```

6. Create a variable for the subject of the e-mail:

```
$subject = "File Contents";
```

7. Create a variable for additional mail headers:

```
$mailheaders = "From: My Web Site <> \n";
```

8. Populate the `mail()` function using the `$file_contents` string as the third argument (the message):

```
mail($to, $subject, $file_contents, $mailheaders);
```

9. Create a variable to print a message to the screen:

```
$msg = "<P>Check your mail!</P>";
```

10. Close the file pointer and your PHP block:

```
fclose($whattoread);
?>
```

11. Add this HTML:

```
<HTML>
<HEAD>
```

```
<TITLE>Mailing Data From a File</TITLE>
</HEAD>
<BODY>
```

12. Print the message:

```
<? echo "$msg"; ?>
```

13. Add some more HTML so that the document is valid:

```
</BODY>
</HTML>
```

14. Save the file with the name `mailcontents.php` and place this file in the document root of your Web server.

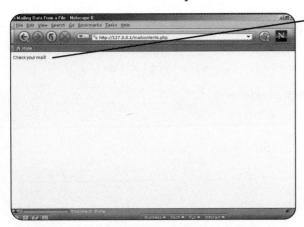

15. Open your Web browser and type **http://127.0.0.1/mailcontents.php**

Like the message says, go check your mail.

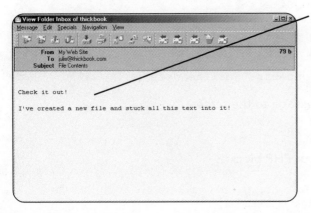

Unlike with the previous script, you didn't need to use the `nl2br()` function, since you weren't displaying text in a Web browser window. The plain-text e-mail will keep the original line break.

File System Housekeeping

The next series of scripts will help you perform very basic file system tasks, such as copying, renaming, and deleting files. Remember that you can perform file system functions only if the proper permissions are in place for the PHP user.

Copying Files

The `copy()` function is very simple: it needs to know the original file name and a new file name, and that's all there is to it.

1. Open a new file in your text editor and start a PHP block:

```
<?
```

2. Create a variable to hold the full path name to the original file (use your own path):

```
$orig_filename = "/My Documents/textfile.txt";
```

3. Create a variable to hold the full path name to the new file (use your own path):

```
$new_filename = "/My Documents/textfile.bak";
```

4. Create a variable to hold the true/false result of the function. Suppress warnings by using the @ in front of the function, and use `die()` to print a message if the function fails:

```
$success = @copy($orig_filename, $new_filename) or die("Couldn't copy file.");
```

5. Start an `if...else` statement to print the proper message based on the outcome of the function:

```
if ($success) {
```

6. The message string, if successful, should print a confirmation of the copy:

```
$msg = "Copied $orig_filename to $new_filename";
```

7. Continue the statement for a failure, then close the PHP block:

```
} else {
    $msg = "Could not copy file.";
}
?>
```

NOTE

Using the `else` statement in this case is actually unnecessary, but it's good practice for providing a default result. If the `copy()` function fails, the `die()` function will exit the script and print the error before even getting to the `if...else` part of the script.

---

8. Add this HTML:

```
<HTML>
<HEAD>
<TITLE>Copy a File</TITLE>
</HEAD>
<BODY>
```

9. Print the message:

```
<? echo "$msg"; ?>
```

10. Add some more HTML so that the document is valid:

```
</BODY>
</HTML>
```

11. Save the file with the name `copyfile.php` and place this file in the document root of your Web server.

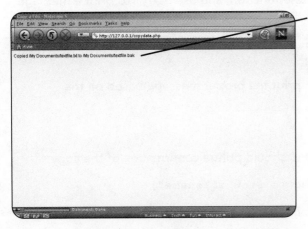

12. Open your Web browser and type **http://127.0.0.1/copyfile.php**

See if your error handling works by changing the value of `$new_filename` to something that doesn't exist:

```
$new_filename = "/bozo/textfile.bak";
```

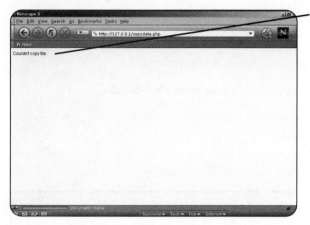

Access the script via your Web browser, and you should see something like this.

Next, move on to renaming files. The script is remarkably similar!

Renaming Files

Like the `copy()` function, the `rename()` function just needs to know the original file name and a new file name. In this case, you're just renaming the original, not copying it.

1. Open a new file in your text editor and start a PHP block:

```
<?
```

2. Create a variable to hold the full path name to the original file (use your own path):

```
$orig_filename = "/My Documents/textfile.bak";
```

3. Create a variable to hold the full path name to the new file (use your own path):

```
$new_filename = "/My Documents/textfile.old";
```

4. Create a variable to hold the true/false result of the function. Suppress warnings by using the @ in front of the function, and use `die()` to print a message if the function fails:

```
$success = @rename($orig_filename, $new_filename) or die("Couldn't
rename file.");
```

5. Start an if...else statement to print the proper message based on the outcome of the function:

```
if ($success) {
```

6. The message string, if successful, should print a confirmation of the renaming function:

```
$msg = "Renamed $orig_filename to $new_filename";
```

7. Continue the statement for a failure, then close your PHP block:

```
} else {
    $msg = "Could not rename file.";
}
?>
```

> ## NOTE
>
> Using the `else` statement in this case is actually unnecessary, but it's good practice for providing a default result. If the `rename()` function fails, the `die()` function will exit the script and print the error before even getting to the `if…else` part of the script.

8. Add this HTML:

```
<HTML>
<HEAD>
<TITLE>Rename a File</TITLE>
</HEAD>
<BODY>
```

9. Print the message:

```
<? echo "$msg"; ?>
```

10. Add some more HTML so that the document is valid:

```
</BODY>
</HTML>
```

11. Save the file with the name `renamefile.php` and place this file in the document root of your Web server.

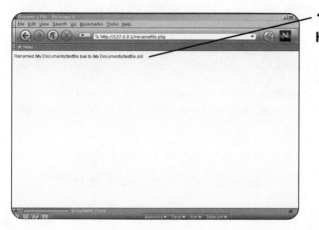

12. Open your Web browser and type **http://127.0.0.1/renamefile.php**

See if your error handling works by changing the value of $new_filename to something that doesn't exist:

```
$new_filename = "/bozo/textfile.bak";
```

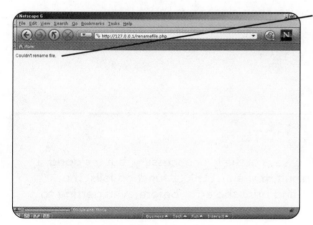

Access the script via your Web browser, and you should see this.

There's one more housekeeping function in the next section: deleting a file.

Deleting Files

Be very careful when using the `unlink()` function because once you've deleted a file, it's gone for good.

1. Open a new file in your text editor and start a PHP block:

```
<?
```

2. Create a variable to hold the full path name to the file you want to delete (use your own path):

```
$filename = "/My Documents/textfile.old";
```

3. Create a variable to hold the true/false result of the function. Suppress warnings by using the @ in front of the function, and use die() to print a message if the function fails:

```
$success = @unlink($filename) or die("Couldn't delete file.");
```

4. Start an if...else statement to print the proper message based on the outcome of the function:

```
if ($success) {
```

5. The message string, if successful, should print a confirmation of the deletion:

```
$msg = "Deleted $filename";
```

6. Continue the statement for a failure, then close your PHP block:

```
} else {
    $msg = "Could not delete file.";
}
?>
```

NOTE

Using the else statement in this case is actually unnecessary, but it's good practice for providing a default result. If the unlink() function fails, the die() function will exit the script and print the error before even getting to the if...else part of the script.

---

7. Add this HTML:

```
<HTML>
<HEAD>
<TITLE>Delete a File</TITLE>
</HEAD>
<BODY>
```

8. Print the message:

```
<? echo "$msg"; ?>
```

9. Add some more HTML so that the document is valid:

```
</BODY>
</HTML>
```

10. Save the file with the name `deletefile.php` and place this file in the document root of your Web server.

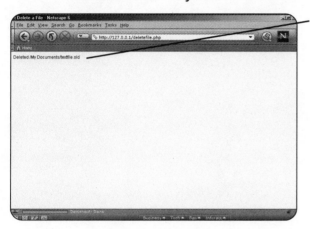

11. Open your Web browser and type **http://127.0.0.1/deletefile.php**

See if your error handling works by changing the value of `$filename` to something that doesn't exist:

```
$filename = "/bozo/textfile.old";
```

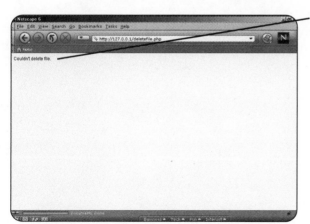

Access the script via your Web browser, and you should see this.

In the next chapter, you'll create a two-step process (front-end form and back-end script) to initiate file uploads from a Web browser to your file system.

10

Uploading Files to Your Web Site

If you need a quick interface for uploading files to your Web site from a remote location, you can create a two-step form and script interface with PHP. In this chapter, you'll learn how to do the following:

● Create an HTML form for file uploads

● Create a PHP script to handle file uploads

Check Your php.ini File

Before you start uploading files, check a few values in your `php.ini` file. Look for this section of text:

```
;;;;;;;;;;;;;;;;;
; File Uploads ;
;;;;;;;;;;;;;;;;;
; Whether to allow HTTP file uploads.
file_uploads = On

; Temporary directory for HTTP uploaded files (will use system
default if not
; specified).
;upload_tmp_dir =

; Maximum allowed size for uploaded files.
upload_max_filesize = 2M
```

To ensure the file upload process will work smoothly, make the following modifications:

1. Uncomment the `upload_tmp_dir` line by deleting the initial semicolon.

2. Enter a directory name after the = for `upload_tmp_dir`.

3. If you want to allow larger uploads, change the number of bytes for `upload_max_filesize`.

For example, on a Windows system, this section of the `php.ini` file may look like

```
;;;;;;;;;;;;;;;;;
; File Uploads ;
;;;;;;;;;;;;;;;;;

; Whether to allow HTTP file uploads.
file_uploads = On

; Temporary directory for HTTP uploaded files (will use system
default if not
; specified).
upload_tmp_dir = /Windows/temp

; Maximum allowed size for uploaded files.
upload_max_filesize = 2M
```

If you are not using Windows, you won't have to modify the value for `upload_tmp_dir`, as long as you want files to be placed in `/tmp` (the default).

Understanding the Process

The process of uploading a file to a Web server through an HTML form interface puzzles a lot of people. Take a moment to understand the process you'll create in the following sections.

To start and finish this process, you need the following:

- An HTML form
- A file to upload
- A place to put the file
- A script to put it there

The process itself goes something like this:

1. The user accesses the HTML form and sees a text field and the Browse button in his Web browser.

2. The user browses his hard drive for the file he wants to upload and then selects a file.

3. The full file path and file name appear in the text field.

4. The user clicks on the Submit button.

5. The selected file goes out, lands at the Web server, and sits around in a temporary directory.

6. The PHP script used in the form action checks that a file was sent and executes a copy command on the temporary file to move it to a real directory on the Web server.

7. The PHP script confirms the action for the user.

> **NOTE**
>
> The PHP user (the user under which PHP runs, such as "nobody" or "www" or "joe") must have write permissions in the temporary directory as well as the target directory for the file.

Start with simply creating the HTML form interface in the next section.

Creating the Form

Start out by creating a one-field form. You can create a form to upload as many files as you like after you get this sequence to work with one file.

1. Open a new file in your text editor and type the following HTML:

```
<HTML>
<HEAD>
<TITLE>Upload a File</TITLE>
</HEAD>
<BODY>
<H1>Upload a File</H1>
```

2. Begin your form. Assume that the method is POST and the action is a script called do_upload.php. Because you'll be sending more than just text, use the ENCTYPE attribute.

```
<FORM METHOD="POST" ACTION=" do_upload.php" ENCTYPE="multipart/
form-data">
```

3. Create an input field for the file with a text label. Assume that you'll be uploading an image file, and name the input field img1:

```
<p><strong>File to Upload:</strong><br>
<INPUT TYPE="file" NAME="img1" SIZE="30"></P>
```

> **NOTE**
>
> The TYPE="file" attribute in the form field will display an input field with a Browse button. The Browse button launches a file manager through which you select the file to upload.

4. Add a submit button, then close your form and add some more HTML so that the document is valid:

```
<P><INPUT TYPE="submit" NAME="submit" VALUE="Upload File"></P>
</FORM>
</BODY>
</HTML>
```

5. Save the file with the name `upload_form.html` and place this file in the document root of your Web server.

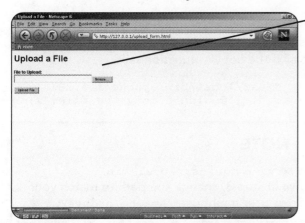

6. Open your Web browser and type **http://127.0.0.1/upload_form.html**

In the next section, you'll create the script that handles the file upload.

Creating the Upload Script

Take a moment to commit the following list to memory—it contains the variables that are automatically placed in the $_FILES superglobal after a successful file upload. The base of img1 comes from the name of the input field in the original form.

- **$_FILES[$img1][tmp_name]**. The value refers to the temporary file on the Web server.

- **$_FILES[img1][name]**. The value is the actual name of the file that was uploaded. For example, if the name of the file was me.jpg, the value of $_FILES[img1][name] is me.jpg.

- **$_FILES[img1][size]**. The size of the uploaded file in bytes

- **$_FILES[img1][type]**. The mime type of the uploaded file, such as image/jpg

The goal of this script is to take the uploaded file and copy it to the document root of the Web server and return a confirmation to the user containing values for all the variables in the preceding list.

1. Open a new file in your text editor and start a PHP block:

```
<?
```

2. Create an `if...else` statement that checks for a value in `$_FILES[img1]`.

```
if ($_FILES[img1] != "") {
```

3. If `$_FILES[img1]` is not empty, execute the copy function. Use `@` before the function name to suppress warnings, and use the `die()` function to cause the script to end and a message to display if the `copy()` function fails.

```
@copy($_FILES[img1][tmp_name], "/usr/local/bin/apache_1.3.26/
htdocs/".$_FILES[img1][name]) or die("Couldn't copy the file.");
```

NOTE

If the document root of your Web server is not `/usr/local/bin/apache_1.3.26/htdocs/` as shown in step 3, change the path to match your own system. For example, a Windows user might use `/Apache/htdocs/`.

---

4. Continue the `else` statement to handle the lack of a file for upload:

```
} else {
    die("No input file specified");
```

5. Close the `if...else` statement, then close your PHP block:

```
}
?>
```

6. Add this HTML:

```
<HTML>
<HEAD>
<TITLE>Successful File Upload</TITLE>
</HEAD>
<BODY>
<H1>Success!</H1>
```

7. Mingle HTML and PHP, printing a line that displays values for the various elements of the uploaded file (name, size, type):

```
<P>You sent: <? echo $_FILES[img1][name]; ?>, a <? echo
$_FILES[img1][size]; ?> byte file with a mime type of <? echo
$_FILES[img1][type]; ?>.</P>
```

8. Add some more HTML so that the document is valid:

```
</BODY>
</HTML>
```

9. Save the file with the name do_upload.php.

```
<?
if ($_FILES[img1] != "") {
        @copy($_FILES[img1][tmp_name],
        "/usr/local/bin/apache_1.3.24/htdocs/".$_FILES[img1][name])
        or die("Couldn't copy the file ");
} else {
        die("No input file specified");
}
?>
<HTML>
<HEAD>
<TITLE>Successful File Upload</TITLE>
</HEAD>
<BODY>
<H1>Success!</H1>
<P>You sent: <? echo $_FILES[img1][name]; ?>, a <? echo $_FILES[img1][size]; ?>
byte file with a mime type of <? echo $_FILES[img1][type]; ?>.</P>
</BODY>
</HTML>
```

The code should look something like this.

In the next section, you'll finally get to upload a file!

Uploading a File Using Your Form and Script

This is the moment of truth, where you hold your breath and test the script.

1. Open your Web browser and type **http://127.0.0.1/upload_form.html**

2. Use the Browse button to locate a file you want to upload.

NOTE

This example uses a file on my own machine, so the figures won't look quite the same as your results.

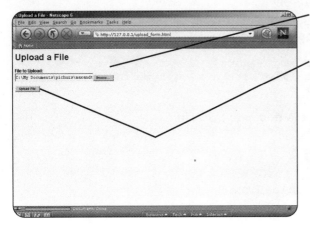

The full path to the file should appear in the form field.

3. Click on the Upload File button.

The results screen should appear, providing information about the file you just uploaded.

> ## NOTE
>
> Only allow your file upload script to be used by yourself or other trusted sources, unless you limit the types of files you wish to upload by checking the file type before copying to the system.

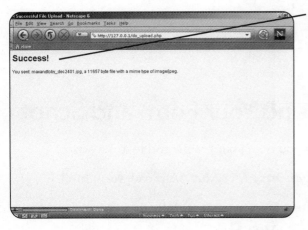

There's nothing to it! You're now a file system wizard. In the next section, you'll become a database wizard as well.

PART IV

Getting to Know Your Database

11

Establishing a Connection

During the process of installing and testing MySQL in Chapter 1, you should have created a sample database as well as a sample table, and even inserted and selected some data. The next several chapters focus on making the same types of connections and queries and using PHP scripts for the front end. In this chapter, you'll learn how to do the following:

- Connect to MySQL
- List all databases on localhost
- List all tables in a database
- Create a database
- Drop (delete) a database

Working with User Privileges in MySQL

When you installed the MySQL database in Chapter 1, you were working as the anonymous or root user. Before you begin working regularly with databases, you should create a real user with a real password. To do this, you need to understand a bit about the MySQL privilege system.

NOTE

If you are accessing MySQL through an Internet service provider, you probably have only one user and one database available to you. By default, that one user has access to all tables in the database and is allowed to perform all commands. If this is the case, you can skip the information in this section and proceed to the script creation sections. In all instances where a username and password are used, use the one given to you by your ISP.

Creating a New User

If you have proper permissions for adding a user, the simplest method for performing this task is the GRANT command. The basic syntax of the GRANT command follows, where [privilege list] is a placeholder for the privileges you want to give to the new user.

```
GRANT [privilege list] ON databasename.tablename TO username@host
IDENTIFIED BY "password";
```

You can grant many types of privileges, and for more information, please visit the MySQL manual topic at http://www.mysql.com/doc/G/R/GRANT.html. For now, you will just grant all privileges to your new user, on all tables in the database.

NOTE

The following commands are exactly the same for MySQL on Windows and Linux/UNIX platforms.

---

1. Start the MySQL Monitor.

2. Select the database called `mysql` by typing the following at the `mysql>` prompt:

```
use mysql;
```

3. Type the following SQL statement, substituting your own username and password if you want. The wildcard (*) grants permissions on all databases and tables:

```
GRANT ALL ON *.* TO spike@localhost IDENTIFIED BY "9sj7En4";
```

4. Exit the MySQL Monitor by typing the following at the `mysql>` prompt:

```
exit
```

5. Issue the command to reload the grant tables using the `mysqladmin` program:

```
mysqladmin reload
```

The new user (`spike`) will now have access to all databases and tables when using the password `9sj7En4`. This user will be the sample user in all database connectivity scripts from this point forward. Please substitute your own username and password where appropriate.

Connecting to MySQL

The goal of this script is simply to connect to MySQL, running on your machine (`localhost`).

1. Open a new file in your text editor and start a PHP block:

```
<?
```

2. Create a variable to hold the result of the `mysql_connect()` function:

```
$connection = mysql_connect("localhost", "spike", "9sj7En4")
```

NOTE

The `mysql_connect()` function requires a host name, username, and password (in that order).

3. Add a `die()` function to the `mysql_connect()` line to cause the script to end and a message to display if the connection fails. Within the `die()` function, use the `mysql_error()` function. The message that will be printed upon error is the exact error as sent by MySQL. The new line should read as follows:

```
$connection = mysql_connect("localhost", "spike", "9sj7En4")
or die(mysql_error());
```

4. Test the value of `$connection`. If it's true, the connection to MySQL was made, and a variable is created to hold a message:

```
if ($connection) {
    $msg = "success!";
}
```

NOTE

If a connection cannot be made, the script will end with the `die()` function.

---

5. Close your PHP block, then add HTML:

```
?>
<HTML>
<HEAD>
<TITLE>MySQL Connection</TITLE>
</HEAD>
<BODY>
```

6. Print the message string:

```
<? echo "$msg"; ?>
```

7. Add some more HTML so that the document is valid:

```
</BODY>
</HTML>
```

8. Save the file with the name `db_connect.php` and place this file in the document root of your Web server.

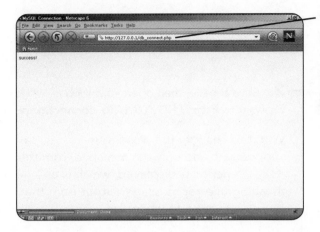

9. Open your Web browser and type **http://127.0.0.1/db_connect.php**

If you entered the correct username and password, you should have a successful result.

Breaking Your Connection Script

Anytime you work with databases, you will have errors. It's inevitable. That's why I want to show you some common errors and how to handle them fairly gracefully.

You'll make a modification to the db_connect.php script that causes it to fail on connection, simply by changing the username.

1. Change the username to buffy (unless buffy is a real user!) so that the connection line reads as follows:

```
$connection = mysql_connect("localhost", "buffy", "9sj7En4") or
die(mysql_error());
```

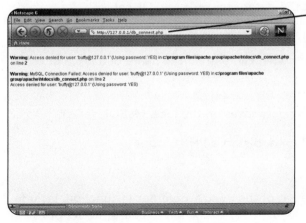

2. Save the file, then open your Web browser to **http://127.0.01/db_connect.php**

That is some kind of nasty response! At least it tells you exactly what is wrong, and several times over: user buffy couldn't connect to MySQL. You can suppress one of the ugly warnings and just go with the message from the die() function by placing a @ before the mysql_connect() function name. Try it.

1. Add a @ before the `mysql_connect()` function, keeping the bad username:

```
$connection = @mysql_connect("localhost", "buffy", "9sj7En4")
or die(mysql_error());
```

2. Save the file, then open your Web browser to **http://127.0.0.1/db_connect.php**

With this change, the warning is suppressed, and only the message from the `die()` function is displayed, which is a meaningful error message output from the `mysql_error()` function.

If you can keep nasty errors and warnings to a minimum, it will make the overall user experience much more pleasant if your database decides to render itself unavailable during peak Web-surfing hours.

Listing Databases on a Server

Now that you've successfully used PHP to make a connection to MySQL, familiarize yourself with some of the built-in MySQL–related functions. In this section, you'll use the following functions:

- **`mysql_list_dbs()`** Used to list the databases on a MySQL server.

- **`mysql_num_rows()`** Returns the number of rows in a result set.

- **`mysql_tablename()`** Despite its name, can extract the name of a table or a database from a result.

The goal of this script is to list all the databases on the local MySQL server.

1. Open a new file in your text editor and start a PHP block:

```
<?
```

2. Create a variable to hold the result of the `mysql_connect()` function. Include the @ to suppress warnings, as well as the `die()` function to cause the script to end and a message to display if the connection fails:

```
$connection = @mysql_connect("localhost", "spike", "9sj7En4")
or die(mysql_error());
```

3. Create a variable to hold the result of the `mysql_list_dbs()` function. Include the @ to suppress warnings, as well as the `die()` function to cause the script to end and a message to display if the script can't get the list:

```
$dbs = @mysql_list_dbs($connection) or die(mysql_error());
```

> **NOTE**
>
> The only argument necessary for the `mysql_list_dbs()` function is the link identifier for the current connection.

4. You'll be looping through a result and dynamically populating a bullet list. Start that bullet list outside the loop:

```
$db_list = "<ul>";
```

5. Start a counter. You'll need it for your loop:

```
$i = 0;
```

6. Begin a `while` loop. This loop will continue for as long as the value of $i is less than the number of rows in the $dbs result value:

```
while ($i < mysql_num_rows($dbs)) {
```

7. Once you're within the `while` loop, get the name of the database reflected in the current row of the result:

```
$db_names[$i] = mysql_tablename($dbs, $i);
```

> **NOTE**
>
> The variable $i is replaced by its value, so during the first loop this line would be something like `$db_names[0] = mysql_tablename($dbs, 0);`
>
> Counting starts at 0, not 1, so this would reflect the first row in the result. As the counter increments, so does the row number.

8. Add the current database name to the bullet list:

```
$db_list .= "<li>$db_names[$i]";
```

9. Increment your count before you close the `while` loop:

```
$i++;
```

10. Close the `while` loop, the bullet list, and your PHP block:

```
}
$db_list .= "</ul>";
?>
```

11. Add this HTML:

```
<HTML>
<HEAD>
<TITLE>MySQL Databases</TITLE>
</HEAD>
<BODY>
<P><strong>Databases on localhost</strong>:</P>
```

12. Print the message string:

```
<? echo "$db_list"; ?>
```

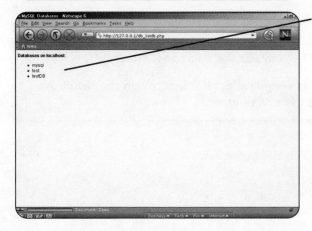

13. Add some more HTML so that the document is valid:

```
</BODY>
</HTML>
```

14. Save the file with the name `db_listdb.php`. Your code should look something like this:

15. Place this file in the document root of your Web server, then open your Web browser and type **http://127.0.0.1/db_listdb.php**

Your list may vary, depending on how much you played around with things in the first chapter, but you should at least see the MySQL system database (`mysql`) and the database created in Chapter 1 (`testDB`). Next you'll add another loop to this script to print the tables within each database.

Listing Tables in a Database

A few additions to the `db_listdb.php` script are all you need to list the tables in the databases as well. Here is the only new function you'll see:

* **`mysql_list_tables()`** Used to list tables within a MySQL database.

The goal of this script is to list all of the databases, including the tables within those databases, on the local MySQL server.

1. Open a new file in your text editor and start a PHP block:

```
<?
```

2. Add the connection information as you have been:

```
$connection = @mysql_connect("localhost", "spike", "9sj7En4")
or die(mysql_error());
```

3. Create a variable to hold the result of the `mysql_list_dbs()` function. Include the @ to suppress warnings, as well as the `die()` function to cause the script to end and a message to display if the script can't get the list:

```
$dbs = @mysql_list_dbs($connection) or die(mysql_error());
```

4. You'll be looping through a result and dynamically populating a bullet list. Start that bullet list outside the loop:

```
$db_list = "<ul>";
```

5. Start a counter. You'll need it for your loop:

```
$db_num = 0;
```

NOTE

Use `$db_num` instead of `$i` as the counter because at one point in this script, you'll have two counters going at the same time.

---

6. Begin a `while` loop. This loop will continue for as long as the value of `$db_num` is less than the number of rows in the `$dbs` result value:

```
while ($db_num < mysql_num_rows($dbs)) {
```

7. Once you're within the `while` loop, get the name of the database reflected in the current row of the result:

```
$db_names[$db_num] = mysql_tablename($dbs, $db_num);
```

8. Add the current database name to the bullet list:

```
$db_list .= "<li>$db_names[$db_num]";
```

9. Create a variable to hold the result of the `mysql_list_tables()` function. Include the `@` to suppress warnings, as well as the `die()` function to cause the script to end and a message to display if the script can't get the list:

```
$tables = @mysql_list_tables($db_names[$db_num]) or
die(mysql_error());
```

NOTE

The only argument necessary for the `mysql_list_tables()` function is the name of the current database.

---

10. You'll be looping through a result and dynamically populating a bullet list. Start that bullet list outside the loop:

```
$table_list = "<ul>";
```

11. Start a counter. You'll need it for your second loop:

```
$table_num = 0;
```

12. Begin a `while` loop. This loop will continue for as long as the value of `$table_num` is less than the number of rows in the `$tables` result value.

```
while ($table_num < mysql_num_rows($tables)) {
```

13. Once you're within the `while` loop, get the name of the table reflected in the current row of the result:

```
$table_names[$table_num] = mysql_tablename($tables, $table_num);
```

14. Add the current table name to the bullet list:

```
$table_list .= "<li>$table_names[$table_num]";
```

15. Increment your count before you close the `while` loop:

```
$table_num++;
```

16. Close the inner `while` loop and the bullet list of tables:

```
}
$table_list .= "</ul>";
```

17. Add the value of `$table_list` to `$db_list`, and then increment your count before you close the outer `while` loop:

```
$db_list .= "$table_list";
$db_num++;
}
```

18. Close the bullet list of databases, then your PHP block:

```
$db_list .= "</ul>";
?>
```

19. Add this HTML:

```
<HTML>
<HEAD>
<TITLE>MySQL Tables</TITLE>
</HEAD>
<BODY>
<P><strong>Databases and tables on localhost</strong>:</P>
```

20. Print the message string:

```
<? echo "$db_list"; ?>
```

21. Add some more HTML so that the document is valid:

```
</BODY>
</HTML>
```

22. Save the file with the name `db_listtables.php`.

Your code should look something like this:

```
<?
//connection code
$connection = @mysql_connect("localhost", "spike", "9sj7En4")
or die(mysql_error());

//get database list
$dbs = @mysql_list_dbs($connection) or die(mysql_error());

//start first bullet list
```

```php
$db_list = "<ul>";
$db_num = 0;

//loop through results of function
while ($db_num < mysql_num_rows($dbs)) {

    //get database names and make each a bullet point
    $db_names[$db_num] = mysql_tablename($dbs, $db_num);
    $db_list .= "<li>$db_names[$db_num]";
    //get table names and start another bullet list
    $tables = @mysql_list_tables($db_names[$db_num]) or
    die(mysql_error());
    $table_list = "<ul>";
    $table_num = 0;

    //loop through results of function
    while ($table_num < mysql_num_rows($tables)) {
    //get table names and make each a bullet point
    $table_names[$table_num] = mysql_tablename($tables,
    $table_num);
    $table_list .= "<li>$table_names[$table_num]";
    $table_num++;
    }
    //close inner bullet list and increment number to continue loop
    $table_list .= "</ul>";
    $db_list .= "$table_list";
    $db_num++;
}
//close outer bullet list
$db_list .= "</ul>";
?>
<HTML>
<HEAD>
<TITLE>MySQL Tables</TITLE>
</HEAD>
<BODY>
<P><strong>Databases and tables on localhost</strong>:</P>
<? echo "$db_list"; ?>
</BODY>
</HTML>
```

It's time to see if this script lists the databases on your server, including their tables, so place this file in the document root of your Web server and open your Web browser to **http://127.0.0.1/db_listtables.php.**

Because all privileges on all tables were granted to the test user, you should see a list of all tables and databases, including those reserved by the system. Your mileage may vary, depending on your server setup and your databases and tables.

In the next section, you'll attempt to create new databases on your server.

Creating a New Database

The complex elements of the previous scripts are nowhere to be found in this next script. The goal of this script is to create a new database on the MySQL server.

1. Open a new file in your text editor and start a PHP block:

```
<?
```

2. Create a variable to hold the name of the new database:

```
$new_db = "testDB2";
```

3. Add the connection information as you have been:

```
$connection = @mysql_connect("localhost", "spike", "9sj7En4")
or die(mysql_error());
```

4. Create a variable to hold the result of the mysql_create_db() function. Include the @ to suppress warnings, as well as the die() function to cause the script to end and a message to display if the creation of the database fails:

```
$result = @mysql_create_db($new_db, $connection) or
die(mysql_error());
```

> **NOTE**
>
> The `mysql_create_db()` function requires a database name and the link identifier for the current connection.

5. Test the value of `$result`. If it's true, the database was created, and a variable is created to hold a message:

```
if ($result) {
    $msg = "<P>Database has been created!</P>";
}
```

> **NOTE**
>
> If the database cannot be created, the script will end with the `die()` function.

6. Close your PHP block, then add HTML:

```
?>
<HTML>
<HEAD>
<TITLE>Create a MySQL Database</TITLE>
</HEAD>
<BODY>
```

7. Print the message string:

```
<? echo "$msg"; ?>
```

8. Add some more HTML so that the document is valid:

```
</BODY>
</HTML>
```

9. Save the file with the name `db_createdb.php` and place this file in the document root of your Web server.

10. Open your Web browser and type **http://127.0.0.1/db_createdb.php**

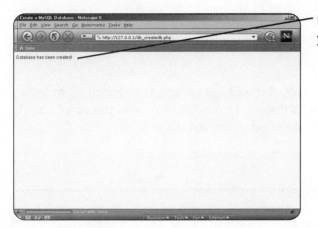

If the database creation was successful, you'll see this message.

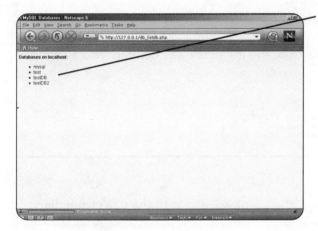

Verify that the new database is present by opening your Web browser to **http://127.0.01/db_listdb.php**. You should see your new database in the list.

In the next section, you'll drop (delete) the database you just created.

Deleting a Database

The goal of this script is to delete a database on the MySQL server.

1. Open a new file in your text editor and start a PHP block:

```
<?
```

2. Create a variable to hold the name of the database you want to delete:

```
$drop_db = "testDB2";
```

3. Add the connection information as you have been:

```
$connection = @mysql_connect("localhost", "spike", "9sj7En4")
or die(mysql_error());
```

4. Create a variable to hold the result of the `mysql_drop_db()` function. Include the @ to suppress warnings, as well as the `die()` function to cause the script to end and a message to display if the deletion of the database fails:

```
$result = @mysql_drop_db($drop_db, $connection) or
die(mysql_error());
```

NOTE

The `mysql_drop_db()` function requires a database name and the link identifier for the current connection.

---

5. Test the value of `$result`. If it's true, the database was deleted, and a variable is created to hold a message:

```
if ($result) {
    $msg = "<P>Database has been dropped!</P>";
}
```

NOTE

If the database cannot be deleted, the script will end with the `die()` function.

---

6. Close your PHP block and add HTML:

```
?>
<HTML>
<HEAD>
<TITLE>Drop a MySQL Database</TITLE>
</HEAD>
<BODY>
```

7. Print the message string:

```
<? echo "$msg"; ?>
```

8. Add some more HTML so that the document is valid:

```
</BODY>
</HTML>
```

9. Save the file with the name db_dropdb.php and place this file in the document root of your Web server.

10. Open your Web browser and type **http://127.0.0.1/db_dropdb.php**

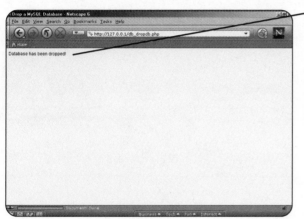

If the database deletion was successful, you'll see this message.

In the next chapter, you'll create a database table for keeps, and you'll eventually populate that table with some data.

12

Creating a Database Table

You have this great database server and only a table called
`test_table` sitting in a database called `testDB`. Where's the fun?
In this chapter, you'll learn how to do the following:

- Plan for a database table
- Recognize the pitfalls of certain data types
- Recognize the importance of unique fields
- Follow a two-step process for table creation
- Create a table to hold your personal music catalog

Planning for Your Tables

Creating a table is easy—it's the planning that takes some brainpower. To create a simple table, you only need to give it a name. But that would make for a boring table, since it wouldn't contain any columns (fields) and couldn't hold any data. So besides the name, you should know the number of fields and the types of fields you'd like to have in your table.

Basic MySQL Data Types

All fields in a table are given a particular data type definition. The data type defines the type of data that's allowed in the field. With some data type definitions, you must also define the maximum length you wish to allow in the field, but others are assumed to have one specific length for its particular type.

It's very important to define fields appropriately. For example, if you have a field to hold the name of a recording, and it's a 50-character `varchar` field, yet you try to stuff a 100-character string into the field, your string will truncate at 50 characters.

Not only is it important to define the fields correctly so that the data fits inside the fields, but if you define a field with an incorrect SQL syntax, the table won't be created, period. For example, if you want to use the text data type for a field, you cannot specify a length: it's automatically assumed to have a particular length.

Table 12.1 shows some of the more common types you will use. For a complete list, please read the MySQL manual.

Defining Your Fields

The overall goal of this chapter is to create a table to hold data from your own personal music collection. Take a moment to think about the kinds of things you'd want to know: the title and artist, obviously, and maybe the record label, the date it was acquired, and your own personal notes regarding the recording. I thought about what I wanted for my own table, which I've decided to call `my_music`.

In the next section, you'll create a sequence of forms that will take your table information and send it to your MySQL database. In the first step, you'll submit the name of the table and the number of fields you want to include. The second step will display additional form fields so that you can define the properties of your table columns. A third step will send the request to MySQL, verify that the table was created, and display a "Success!" message.

Table 12.1   Some MySQL Data Types

Data Type	Definition
TINYINT	A very small integer that can be signed or unsigned. If signed, the allowable range is from –128 to 127. If unsigned, the allowable range is from 0 to 255.
SMALLINT	A small integer that can be signed or unsigned. If signed, the allowable range is from –32768 to 32767. If unsigned, the allowable range is from 0 to 65535.
MEDIUMINT	A medium-sized integer that can be signed or unsigned. If signed, the allowable range is from –8388608 to 8388607. If unsigned, the allowable range is from 0 to 16777215.
INT	A normal-sized integer that can be signed or unsigned. If signed, the allowable range is from –2147483648 to 2147483647. If unsigned, the allowable range is from 0 to 4294967295.
BIGINT	A large integer that can be signed or unsigned. If signed, the allowable range is from –2147483648 to 2147483647. If unsigned, the allowable range is from 0 to 18446744073709551615.
FLOAT	A floating point number that cannot be unsigned. You can define the display length (M) and the number of decimals (D). This is not required and will default to 10,2, where 2 is the number of decimals. Decimal precision can go to 24 places for a FLOAT.
DATE	A date in YYYY-MM-DD format, between 1000-01-01 and 9999-12-31. For example, December 30, 1973 would be stored as 1973-12-30.
DATETIME	A date in YYYY-MM-DD format, between 1000-01-01 and 9999-12-31. For example, December 30, 1973 would be stored as 1973-12-30.
TIMESTAMP	A timestamp between midnight, January 1, 1970 and sometime in 2037. You can define multiple lengths to the TIMESTAMP field, which directly correlates to what is stored in it. The default length for TIMESTAMP is 14, which stores YYYYMMDDHHMMSS. This looks like the DATETIME format above, only without the hyphens between numbers; 3:30 in the afternoon on December 30, 1973 would be stored as 19731230153000. Other definitions of TIMESTAMP are 12 (YYMMDDHHMMSS), 8 (YYYYMMDD), and 6 (YYMMDD).
CHAR	A fixed-length string between 1 and 255 characters in length, right-padded with spaces to the specified length when stored. Defining a length is not required, but the default is 1.
VARCHAR	A variable-length string between 1 and 255 characters in length. You must define a length when creating a VARCHAR field.
BLOB or TEXT	A field with a maximum length of 65535 characters. BLOBs are "Binary Large Objects" and are used to store large amounts of binary data, such as images or other types of files. Fields defined as TEXT also hold large amounts of data; the difference between the two is that sorts and comparisons on stored data are case sensitive on BLOBs and case insensitive in TEXT fields. You do not specify a length with BLOB or TEXT.
ENUM	An enumeration (list). When defining an ENUM, you are creating a list of items from which the value must be selected (or it can be NULL). For example, if you wanted your field to contain either "A" or "B" or "C," you would define your ENUM as ENUM ('A', 'B', 'C') and only those values (or NULL) could ever populate that field. ENUMs can have 65535 different values.

Table 12.2   Fields for my_music

Field Name	Description
id	Creates a unique ID number for the entry
format	Is it a CD, cassette, or even an LP?
title	The title of the recording
artist_fn	The artist's first name
artist_ln	The artist's last name or the name of the group
rec_label	The record label
my_notes	My own thoughts about the recording
date_acq	Date acquired

The Importance of Unique Fields

Using unique ID numbers not only helps you keep track of your data, but down the road, helps you attempt to establish relationships between multiple tables. In the my_music table, there will be an ID field (see Table 12.2). Using this field as the unique field, instead of the title field, will allow you to have two recordings in your table that have the same name. For example, if you own the album *Strange Fire* by Indigo Girls, you could have two entries in your table: one for the version released in 1987 and one for the version rereleased in 1989.

Without using a unique identifier, you would have to pick only one version to put in your table, and your table wouldn't be very accurate. I hope this simple example conveys the importance of having a unique identifier in each record in your table. The usage of the unique identifier will become more apparent throughout the remainder of this book as you create more database-driven elements.

A Two-Step Form Sequence

A two-step form sequence for creating a database table might seem like overkill. After all, you saw a basic table-creation SQL statement in Chapter 1, when you created test_table:

```
create table test_table (test_id int, test_note text);
```

When using a PHP script to create a table, all you're doing is sending the exact same query to MySQL. However, you can tie a pretty ribbon around the process (creating a form-based interface) and call it an administrative interface!

In the process of creating the administrative interface, you'll start with an HTML form, then create a PHP script that takes information from that form and dynamically creates another form. Finally, you'll create a script that sends the actual SQL query.

Step 1: Number of Fields

This HTML form will contain two input fields: one for the name of the table and one for the number of fields you want your table to contain.

1. Open a new file in your text editor and type the following HTML:

```
<HTML>
<HEAD>
<TITLE>Create a Database Table: Step 1</TITLE>
</HEAD>
<BODY>
<H1>Step 1: Name and Number</H1>
```

2. Begin your form. Assume that the method is POST and the action is a script called do_showfielddef.php:

```
<FORM METHOD="POST" ACTION="do_showfielddef.php">
```

3. Create an input field for the table name with a text label:

```
<P><strong>Table Name:</strong><br>
<INPUT TYPE="text" NAME="table_name" SIZE=30></P>
```

4. Create an input field for the number of fields in the table with a text label:

```
<P><strong>Number of Fields:</strong><br>
<INPUT TYPE="text" NAME="num_fields" SIZE=5></P>
```

5. Add a submit button, then close your form and add some more HTML so that the document is valid:

```
<P><INPUT TYPE="submit" NAME="submit" VALUE="Go to Step 2"></P>
</FORM>
</BODY>
</HTML>
```

6. Save the file with the name `show_createtable.html` and place this file in the document root of your Web server.

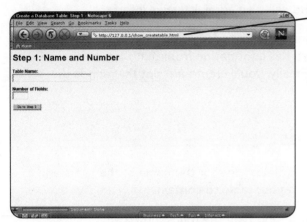

7. Open your Web browser and type **http://127.0.0.1/show_createtable.html**

In the next section, you'll follow step 2 of the process, and create the script that dynamically creates another form based on the values of `$_POST[table_name]` and `$_POST[num_fields]`.

Step 2: Defining Your Fields

In step 1, you created variables to hold the name of the table (`$_POST[table_name]`) and the number of fields you want to place in the table (`$_POST[num_fields]`). In this step, you'll create a PHP script to display additional form elements needed for further definition of the fields: name, type, and length.

1. Open a new file in your text editor and start a PHP block:

```
<?
```

2. Check that values were actually entered for `$_POST[table_name]` and `$_POST[num_fields]`. If they weren't, direct the user back to the form and exit the script:

```
if ((!$_POST[table_name]) || (!$_POST[num_fields])) {
    header( "Location: http://127.0.0.1/show_createtable.html");
    exit;
}
```

3. Start building a string called $form_block, starting with the form action and method. Assume that the method is POST and the action is a script called do_createtable.php. Remember to escape your quotation marks!

```
$form_block = "
<FORM METHOD=\"POST\" ACTION=\"do_createtable.php\">
```

NOTE

Since the script is creating the next form on-the-fly (dynamically), build one big string so that you can echo just the string after the complicated parsing has taken place. This way you won't be stuck with a half-built page that won't display if an error occurs.

---

4. Add a hidden field to hold the value of $_POST[table_name], which you'll use at the end of the sequence just to show the user that the proper table has been created:

```
<INPUT TYPE=\"hidden\" NAME=\"table_name\"
VALUE=\"$_POST[table_name]\">
```

5. Display your form in an HTML table so that fields line up nicely. Start with a row of column headings, and close the $form_block string for now:

```
<TABLE CELLSPACING=5 CELLPADDING=5>
<TR>
<TH>FIELD NAME</TH><TH>FIELD TYPE</TH><TH>FIELD LENGTH</TH></TR>";
```

6. Start a for loop to handle the creation of the form fields. Like a while loop, a for loop continues for as long as a condition is true. In this case, the for loop starts out with the variable $i having a value of 0, and it continues for as long as $i is less than the value of $_POST[num_fields]. After each loop, $i is incremented by 1:

```
for ($i = 0; $i < $_POST[num_fields]; $i++) {
```

7. Within the for loop, you'll add to the original $form_block. You'll add one row for each field you want to have in your database table. Start with the table row tag and a table data cell containing an input type for the field name:

```
$form_block .= "
<TR>
<TD ALIGN=CENTER><INPUT TYPE=\"text\" NAME=\"field_name[]\"
SIZE=\"30\"></TD>
```

> **NOTE**
>
> The use of brackets (the [ ]) after `field_name` in your input field indicates an array. For each field you define in this form, you'll be adding a value to the `$_POST[field_name]` array.
>
> An array holds many variables in numbered slots, beginning with 0. Slots are added automatically as the array grows. For example, if you are creating a database table with six fields, the `$_POST[field_name]` array will be made up of six field name variables: `$_POST[field_name][0]`, `$_POST[field_name][1]`, `$_POST[field_name][2]`, `$_POST[field_name][3]`, `$_POST[field_name][4]`, and `$_POST[field_name][5]`.

8. In the next table data cell, create a drop-down list containing some common field types:

```
<TD ALIGN=CENTER>
<SELECT NAME=\"field_type[]\">
    <OPTION VALUE=\"char\">char</OPTION>
    <OPTION VALUE=\"date\">date</OPTION>
    <OPTION VALUE=\"float\">float</OPTION>
    <OPTION VALUE=\"int\">int</OPTION>
    <OPTION VALUE=\"text\">text</OPTION>
    <OPTION VALUE=\"varchar\">varchar</OPTION>
</SELECT>
</TD>
```

9. In the final table data cell, create a text field for the length of the field, and close your table row. Also close the `$form_block` string because you're done with it for now:

```
<TD ALIGN=CENTER><INPUT TYPE=\"text\" NAME=\"field_length[]\"
SIZE=\"5\"></TD>
</TR>";
```

10. Close the `for` loop:

```
}
```

11. Add the final chunk of HTML to the `$form_block` string. You'll add one row that holds the submit button, and then close your table and form:

```
$form_block .= "
<TR>
```

```
<TD ALIGN=CENTER COLSPAN=3><INPUT TYPE=\"submit\" VALUE=\"Create
Table\"></TD>
</TR>
</TABLE>
</FORM>";
```

12. Close the PHP block and type the following HTML:

```
?>
<HTML>
<HEAD>
<TITLE>Create a Database Table: Step 2</TITLE>
</HEAD>
<BODY>
```

13. Add a nice heading so that the user knows what he's viewing. Mingle HTML and PHP to include the value of the $_POST[table_name] variable:

```
<H1>Define fields for <? echo "$_POST[table_name]"; ?></H1>
```

14. Display the contents of $form_block:

```
<? echo "$form_block"; ?>
```

15. Add some more HTML so that the document is valid:

```
</BODY>
</HTML>
```

16. Save the file with the name do_showfielddef.php and place this file in the document root of your Web server.

Your code should look something like this:

```
<?
//validate important input
if ((!$_POST[table_name]) || (!$_POST[num_fields])) {
    header( "Location: http://127.0.0.1/show_createtable.html");
    exit;
}

//begin creating form for display
$form_block = "
<FORM METHOD=\"POST\" ACTION=\"do_createtable.php\">
<INPUT TYPE=\"hidden\" NAME=\"table_name\"
VALUE=\"$_POST[table_name]\">
```

```
<TABLE CELLSPACING=5 CELLPADDING=5>
<TR>
<TH>FIELD NAME</TH><TH>FIELD TYPE</TH><TH>FIELD LENGTH</TH></TR>";

//count from 0 until you reach the number of fields
for ($i = 0; $i < $_POST[num_fields]; $i++) {
    //add to the form, one row for each field
    $form_block .= "
    <TR>
    <TD ALIGN=CENTER><INPUT TYPE=\"text\" NAME=\"field_name[]\"
SIZE=\"30\"></TD>
    <TD ALIGN=CENTER>
    <SELECT NAME=\"field_type[]\">
    <OPTION VALUE=\"char\">char</OPTION>
    <OPTION VALUE=\"date\">date</OPTION>
    <OPTION VALUE=\"float\">float</OPTION>
    <OPTION VALUE=\"int\">int</OPTION>
    <OPTION VALUE=\"text\">text</OPTION>
    <OPTION VALUE=\"varchar\">varchar</OPTION>
    </SELECT>
    </TD>
    <TD ALIGN=CENTER><INPUT TYPE=\"text\" NAME=\"field_length[]\"
SIZE=\"5\"></TD>
    </TR>";
}

//finish up the form
$form_block .= "
<TR>
<TD ALIGN=CENTER COLSPAN=3><INPUT TYPE=\"submit\" VALUE=\"Create
Table\"></TD>
</TR>
</TABLE>
</FORM>";
?>
<HTML>
<HEAD>
<TITLE>Create a Database Table: Step 2</TITLE>
</HEAD>
<BODY>
<H1>Define fields for <? echo "$_POST[table_name]"; ?></H1>
<? echo "$form_block"; ?>
```

```
</BODY>
</HTML>
```

In the next section, you'll go from step 1 to step 2, preparing to create the table.

Starting the Table Creation Process

You should be able to go from step 1 (naming the table and providing the number of fields) to step 2 (defining the fields) without any problems. Let's try it out.

1. Open your Web browser to **http://127.0.0.1/show_createtable.html**

2. In the Table Name field, type **my_music**.

3. In the Number of Fields field, type **8**.

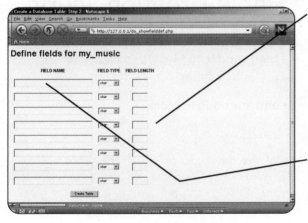

4. Click the Go to Step 2 button. You should see this form.

There are eight rows, corresponding to the eight fields you want to create in the my_music table. Populate those fields, but hold off on pressing the Create Table button, since you haven't created the script yet!

5. In the first row, type **id** for the Field Name, select int from the Field Type drop-down menu, and specify a Field Length of **5**.

6. In the second row, type **format** for the Field Name, select char from the Field Type drop-down menu, and specify a Field Length of **2**.

7. In the third row, type **title** for the Field Name, select varchar from the Field Type drop-down menu, and specify a Field Length of **150**.

8. In the fourth row, type **artist_fn** for the Field Name, select varchar from the Field Type drop-down menu, and specify a Field Length of **100**.

9. In the fifth row, type **artist_ln** for the Field Name, select varchar from the Field Type drop-down menu, and specify a Field Length of **100**.

10. In the sixth row, type **rec_label** for the Field Name, select varchar from the Field Type drop-down menu, and specify a Field Length of **50**.

11. In the seventh row, type **my_notes** for the Field Name and select text from the Field Type drop-down menu.

12. In the eighth row, type **date_acq** for the Field Name and select date from the Field Type drop-down menu.

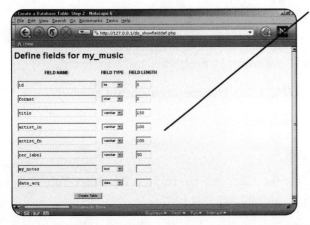

The completed form should look like this.

In the next section, you'll create the back-end script for this form so that you can click that button and create the table.

Creating the Table-Creation Script

This script will build a SQL statement and then send it to MySQL to create the my_music table.

1. Open a new file in your text editor and start a PHP block:

```
<?
```

2. Create a variable to hold the name of the database on which the table should reside:

```
$db_name = "testDB";
```

3. Add the connection information as you have been:

```
$connection = @mysql_connect("localhost", "spike", "9sj7En4")
or die(mysql_error());
```

4. Create a variable to hold the result of the mysql_select_db() function. Include the @ to suppress warnings, as well as the die() function to cause the script to end and a message to display if the selection of the database fails:

```
$db = @mysql_select_db($db_name, $connection) or die(mysql_error());
```

NOTE

The mysql_select_db() function requires a database name and the link identifier for the current connection.

---

5. Start building the query by placing the initial syntax in a variable called $sql:

```
$sql = "CREATE TABLE $_POST[table_name] (";
```

6. Create a for loop to create the remainder of the SQL statement. The loop should repeat for the number of fields contained as elements in the $_POST[field_name] array:

```
for ($i = 0; $i < count($_POST[field_name]); $i++) {
```

NOTE

The count() function counts the number of elements in an array.

---

7. For each new field, you'll need to add the field name and type to the SQL statement:

```
$sql .= $_POST[field_name][$i]." ".$_POST[field_type][$i];
```

8. Since some field definitions will have a specific length and others will not, start an if…else block to handle this aspect. If a length is present, it must go inside parentheses, followed by a comma to start the next field definition:

```
if ($_POST[field_length][$i] != "") {
    $sql .= " (".$_POST[field_length][$i]."),";
```

9. If no length is present, just print the comma to separate the field definitions. Then close the if…else block:

```
} else {
    $sql .= ",";
}
```

10. Close the for loop:

```
}
```

11. The SQL statement held in $sql still needs some help. It should have an extraneous comma at the end of it, and the parentheses must be closed. Use the substr() function to return the entire string, with the exception of the last character:

```
$sql = substr($sql, 0, -1);
```

NOTE

The 0 in the `substr()` argument list tells the function to begin at the first character, and the –1 tells the function to stop at the next-to-last character.

---

12. Close the parentheses:

```
$sql .= ")";
```

13. Create a variable to hold the result of the `mysql_query()` function. Include the @ to suppress warnings, as well as the `die()` function to cause the script to end and a message to display if the query fails:

```
$result = mysql_query($sql,$connection) or die(mysql_error());
```

NOTE

The `mysql_query()` function requires a SQL statement and the link identifier for the current connection.

---

14. Test the value of `$result`. If it's true, the query was successful, and a variable is created to hold a message:

```
if ($result) {
    $msg = "<P>".$_POST[table_name]." has been created!</P>";
}
```

NOTE

If a connection cannot be made, the script will end with the `die()` function.

---

15. Close your PHP block and add HTML:

```
?>
<HTML>
<HEAD>
<TITLE>Create a Database Table: Step 3</TITLE>
</HEAD>
<BODY>
```

16. Add a nice heading so that the user knows what he's viewing. Mingle HTML and PHP to include the value of the $_POST[db_name] variable:

```
<h1>Adding table to <? echo "$db_name"; ?>...</h1>
```

17. Print the message string:

```
<? echo "$msg"; ?>
```

18. Add some more HTML so that the document is valid:

```
</BODY>

</HTML>
```

19. Save the file with the name db_createtable.php and place this file in the document root of your Web server.

Your code should look something like this:

```
<?
//indicate the database you want to use
$db_name = "testDB";
//connect to database
$connection = @mysql_connect("localhost", "spike", "9sj7En4")
or die(mysql_error());
$db = @mysql_select_db($db_name, $connection) or
die(mysql_error());
//start creating the SQL statement
$sql = "CREATE TABLE $_POST[table_name] (";

//continue the SQL statement for each new field
for ($i = 0; $i < count($_POST[field_name]); $i++) {
   $sql .= $_POST[field_name][$i]." ".$_POST[field_type][$i];

   if ($_POST[field_length][$i] != "") {
      $sql .= " (".$_POST[field_length][$i]."),";
   } else {
      $sql .= ",";
   }
}
//clean up the end of the string
$sql = substr($sql, 0, -1);
$sql .= ")";

//execute the query
```

```
$result = mysql_query($sql,$connection) or die(mysql_error());

//get a good message for display upon success
if ($result) {
    $msg = "<P>".$_POST[table_name]." has been created!</P>";
}
?>
<HTML>
<HEAD>
<TITLE>Create a Database Table: Step 3</TITLE>
</HEAD>
<BODY>
<h1>Adding table to <? echo "$db_name"; ?>...</h1>
<? echo "$msg"; ?>
</BODY>
</HTML>
```

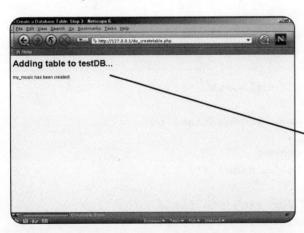

Go on to the next step, where you get to click a button and create a table.

Create That Table!

You should still have your Web browser opened to the field definition form with the fields complete and ready for submission. Go ahead and click on the Create Table button. If everything goes smoothly, you'll see this response.

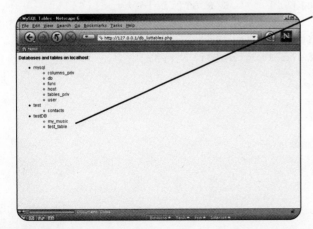

To prove that the my_music table has really been created on the testDB database, access the db_listtables.php script you created in the previous chapter. You should see this.

In the next chapter, you'll create an HTML form interface to a script that adds entries to the my_music table.

13

Inserting Data into a Table

The my_music database table is just sitting there, waiting for you to add information about your music collection. In this chapter, you'll learn how to do the following:

- Create an administrative interface for adding a record
- Create a script to insert the record into your table

Creating the Record Addition Form

The HTML form will contain an input field for each column in the `my_music` database table. In the previous chapter, you created eight fields, which correspond to eight columns. Your record addition interface should have a space for each of these fields.

NOTE

Use the database field names as the value of the NAME attribute in the HTML form fields. Also, where appropriate, use the size of the database field as the value of the MAXLENGTH attribute in the HTML form fields.

---

1. Open a new file in your text editor and type the following HTML:

```
<HTML>
<HEAD>
<TITLE>Add a Record</TITLE>
</HEAD>
<BODY>
<H1>Adding a Record to my_music</H1>
```

2. Begin your form. Assume that the method is POST and the action is a script called `do_addrecord.php`:

```
<FORM METHOD="POST" ACTION="do_addrecord.php">
```

3. Begin an HTML table to assist in layout. Start a new table row and table data cell, and then create an input field for the ID, with a text label:

```
<TABLE CELLSPACING=3 CELLPADDING=3>
<TR>
<TD VALIGN=TOP>
<P><STRONG>ID:</STRONG><BR>
<INPUT TYPE="text" NAME="id" SIZE=5 MAXLENGTH=5></P>
```

4. Create an input field for the date acquired with a text label. Close the table data cell after the input field:

```
<P><STRONG>Date Acquired (YYYY-MM-DD):</STRONG><BR>
<INPUT TYPE="text" NAME="date_acq" SIZE=10 MAXLENGTH=10></P>
</TD>
```

> **NOTE**
>
> The date type used in MySQL uses the YYYY-MM-DD format. An example of a date using this format is 2002-03-02 (March 2, 2002).

5. In a new table data cell, create a set of radio buttons to select the format of the recording. Close the table data cell and the table row after the set of radio buttons:

```
<TD VALIGN=TOP>
<P><STRONG>Format:</STRONG><BR>
<INPUT TYPE="radio" NAME="format" VALUE="CD" checked> CD
<INPUT TYPE="radio" NAME="format" VALUE="CS"> cassette
<INPUT TYPE="radio" NAME="format" VALUE="LP"> LP
</P>
</TD>
</TR>
```

6. Start a new table row and table data cell, and then create an input field for the title with a text label. Close the table data cell after the input field:

```
<TR>
<TD VALIGN=TOP>
<P><STRONG>Title:</STRONG><BR>
<INPUT TYPE="text" NAME="title" SIZE=35 MAXLENGTH=150></P>
</TD>
```

7. In a new table data cell, create an input field for the record label information with a text label. Close the table data cell and the table row after the input field:

```
<TD VALIGN=TOP>
<P><STRONG>Record Label:</STRONG><BR>
<INPUT TYPE="text" NAME="rec_label" SIZE=35 MAXLENGTH=50></P>
</TD>
</TR>
```

8. Start a new table row and table data cell, and then create an input field for the artist's first name with a text label. Close the table data cell after the input field:

```
<TR>
<TD VALIGN=TOP>
<P><STRONG>Artist's First Name:</STRONG><BR>
<INPUT TYPE="text" NAME="artist_fn" SIZE=35 MAXLENGTH=100></P>
</TD>
```

9. In a new table data cell, create an input field for the artist's last name (or group name) with a text label. Close the table data cell and the table row after the input field:

```
<TD VALIGN=TOP>
<P><STRONG>Artist's Last Name (or Group Name):</STRONG><BR>
<INPUT TYPE="text" NAME="artist_ln" SIZE=35 MAXLENGTH=100></P>
</TD>
</TR>
```

10. Start a new table row and a table data cell that spans two columns. Create a textarea field with a text label to hold your notes regarding the recording:

```
<TR>
<TD VALIGN=TOP COLSPAN=2 ALIGN=CENTER>
<P><STRONG>My Notes:</STRONG><BR>
<TEXTAREA NAME="my_notes" COLS=35 ROWS=5 WRAP=virtual>
</TEXTAREA></P>
```

11. Add a submit button, and then close the table data cell, the table row, and the table itself:

```
<P><INPUT TYPE="SUBMIT" NAME="submit" VALUE="Add Record"></P>
</TD>
</TR>
</TABLE>
```

12. Close your form and add some more HTML so that the document is valid:

```
</FORM>
</BODY>
</HTML>
```

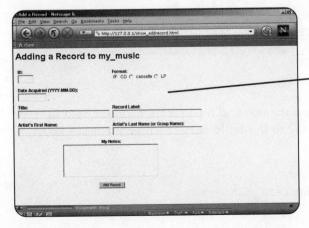

13. Save the file with the name `show_addrecord.html` and place this file in the document root of your Web server.

14. Open your Web browser and type **http://127.0.0.1/show_addrecord.html**

In the next section, you'll create the script that takes the form input, creates a SQL statement, and adds the record to the database table.

Creating the Record Addition Script

The script you'll create for a record addition is a lot simpler than the script for table creation!

1. Open a new file in your text editor and start a PHP block:

```
<?
```

2. Check that values were actually entered for $_POST[id], $_POST[format], and $_POST[title]. If they weren't, direct the user back to the form and exit the script:

```
if ((!$_POST[id]) || (!$_POST[format]) || (!$_POST[title])) {
    header( "Location: http://127.0.0.1/show_addrecord.html");
    exit;
}
```

NOTE

You can have as many (or as few) required fields as you'd like.

---

3. Create a variable to hold the name of the database on which the table resides:

```
$db_name = "testDB";
```

4. Create a variable to hold the name of the table you're populating with this script:

```
$table_name = "my_music";
```

5. Add the connection information as you have been:

```
$connection = @mysql_connect("localhost", "spike", "9sj7En4")
or die(mysql_error());
```

6. Select the database as you have learned:

```
$db = @mysql_select_db($db_name, $connection) or
die(mysql_error());
```

7. Create the SQL statement. The first parenthetical statement gives the names of the fields to populate (in order), and the second parenthetical statement sends the actual strings:

```
$sql = "INSERT INTO $table_name (id, format, title, artist_fn,
artist_ln, rec_label, my_notes, date_acq) VALUES ('$_POST[id]',
'$_POST[format]', '$_POST[title]', '$_POST[artist_fn]',
'$_POST[artist_ln]', '$_POST[rec_label]',
'$_POST[my_notes]','$_POST[date_acq]')";
```

8. Create a variable to hold the result of the `mysql_query()` function, as you have learned:

```
$result = @mysql_query($sql,$connection) or die(mysql_error());
```

9. Close your PHP block and add HTML:

```
?>
<HTML>
<HEAD>
<TITLE>Add a Record</TITLE>
</HEAD>
<BODY>
```

10. Add a nice heading so that the user knows what he's viewing. Mingle HTML and PHP to include the value of the `$table_name` variable:

```
<H1>Adding a Record to <? echo "$table_name"; ?></H1>
```

11. Next, you'll re-create the layout used in `show_addrecord.html`, only it won't contain form fields. Instead, you'll mingle HTML and PHP to show the values that were entered. Start a new table row and table data cell, and then display a text label and value for ID:

```
<TABLE CELLSPACING=3 CELLPADDING=3>
<TR>
<TD VALIGN=TOP>
<P><STRONG>ID:</STRONG><BR>
<? echo "$_POST[id]"; ?></P>
```

12. Display a text label and value for the date acquired, and then close the table data cell:

```
<P><STRONG>Date Acquired (YYYY-MM-DD):</STRONG><BR>
<? echo "$_POST[date_acq]"; ?></P>
</TD>
```

13. Display a text label and the format of the recording, and then close the table data cell and table row:

```
<TD VALIGN=TOP>
<P><STRONG>Format:</STRONG><BR>
<? echo "$_POST[format]"; ?>
</P>
</TD>
</TR>
```

14. Start a new table row and table data cell, display a text label and value for the title, and close the table data cell:

```
<TR>
<TD VALIGN=TOP>
<P><STRONG>Title:</STRONG><BR>
<? echo "$_POST[title]"; ?></P>
</TD>
```

15. In a new table data cell, display a text label and value for the record label information, and then close the table data cell and table row:

```
<TD VALIGN=TOP>
<P><STRONG>Record Label:</STRONG><BR>
<? echo "$_POST[rec_label]"; ?></P>
</TD>
</TR>
```

16. Start a new table row and table data cell, and then create an input field for the artist's first name with a text label. Close the table data cell after the input field:

```
<TR>
<TD VALIGN=TOP>
<P><STRONG>Artist's First Name:</STRONG><BR>
<? echo "$_POST[artist_fn]"; ?></P>
</TD>
```

17. In a new table data cell, display a text label and value for the artist's last name (or group name), and then close the table data cell and table row:

```
<TD VALIGN=TOP>
<P><STRONG>Artist's Last Name (or Group Name):</STRONG><BR>
<? echo "$_POST[artist_ln]"; ?></P>
</TD>
</TR>
```

18. Start a new table row and a table data cell that spans two columns. Display a text label and value for your notes regarding the recording:

```
<TR>
<TD VALIGN=TOP COLSPAN=2 ALIGN=CENTER>
<P><STRONG>My Notes:</STRONG><BR>
<? echo stripslashes($_POST[my_notes]); ?></P>
```

NOTE

The `stripslashes()` function will remove any slashes automatically added to your form data, which is turned on by default in PHP. It will add slashes where necessary to escape special characters such as single quotes and double quotes. You can turn it off by modifying your `php.ini` file, but if you leave it on, it's one less thing you have to worry about.

---

19. Add a link back to the original form, and then close the table data cell, the table row, and the table itself:

```
<P><a href="show_addrecord.html">Add Another</a></P>
</TD>
</TR>
</TABLE>
```

20. Add some more HTML so that the document is valid:

```
</BODY>
</HTML>
```

21. Save the file with the name `do_addrecord.php` and place it in the document root of your Web server.

Your code should look something like this:

```
<?
//check for required fields
if ((!$_POST[id]) || (!$_POST[format]) || (!$_POST[title])) {
    header( "Location: http://127.0.0.1/show_addrecord.html");
    exit;
}

//set up database and table names
$db_name = "testDB";
```

```
$table_name = "my_music";

//connect to MySQL and select database to use
$connection = @mysql_connect("localhost", "spike", "9sj7En4")
or die(mysql_error());
$db = @mysql_select_db($db_name, $connection) or
die(mysql_error());

//create SQL statement and issue query
$sql = "INSERT INTO $table_name (id, format, title, artist_fn,
artist_ln, rec_label, my_notes, date_acq) VALUES ('$_POST[id]',
'$_POST[format]', '$_POST[title]', '$_POST[artist_fn]',
'$_POST[artist_ln]', '$_POST[rec_label]',
'$_POST[my_notes]','$_POST[date_acq]')";

$result = @mysql_query($sql,$connection) or die(mysql_error());
?>
<HTML>
<HEAD>
<TITLE>Add a Record</TITLE>
</HEAD>
<BODY>
<H1>Adding a Record to <? echo "$table_name"; ?></H1>
<TABLE CELLSPACING=3 CELLPADDING=3>
<TR>
<TD VALIGN=TOP>
<P><STRONG>ID:</STRONG><BR>
<? echo "$_POST[id]"; ?></P>
<P><STRONG>Date Acquired (YYYY-MM-DD):</STRONG><BR>
<? echo "$_POST[date_acq]"; ?></P>
</TD>
<TD VALIGN=TOP>
<P><STRONG>Format:</STRONG><BR>
<? echo "$_POST[format]"; ?>
</P>
</TD>
</TR>
<TR>
<TD VALIGN=TOP>
<P><STRONG>Title:</STRONG><BR>
<? echo "$_POST[title]"; ?></P>
</TD>
```

```
<TD VALIGN=TOP>
<P><STRONG>Record Label:</STRONG><BR>
<? echo "$_POST[rec_label]"; ?></P>
</TD>
</TR>
<TR>
<TD VALIGN=TOP>
<P><STRONG>Artist's First Name:</STRONG><BR>
<? echo "$_POST[artist_fn]"; ?></P>
</TD>
<TD VALIGN=TOP>
<P><STRONG>Artist's Last Name (or Group Name):</STRONG><BR>
<? echo "$_POST[artist_ln]"; ?></P>
</TD>
</TR>
<TR>
<TD VALIGN=TOP COLSPAN=2 ALIGN=CENTER>
<P><STRONG>My Notes:</STRONG><BR>
<? echo stripslashes($_POST[my_notes]); ?></P>
<P><a href="show_addrecord.html">Add Another</a></P>
</TD>
</TR>
</TABLE>
</BODY>
</HTML>
```

Go on to the next step, where you get to click a button and add a record.

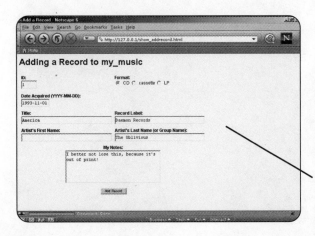

Populating Your Table

Now the fun begins! If you didn't close your Web browser after the first part of this chapter, show_addrecord.html should still be visible in your browser window. If it's not, open **http://127.0.0.1/show_addrecord.html** now.

Complete the addition form for an album you have lying around. Here's an example from my collection.

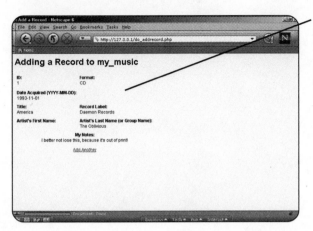

Click the Add Record button, and you should see a confirmation screen.

Add several of your own recordings to the database table. Unless you changed the script on your own, the only required fields are ID, format, and title.

NOTE

In later chapters, you'll learn to make modifications to your table so that the ID field really is unique and increments automatically so that you don't have to keep entering a number and hoping it works.

14

Selecting and Displaying Data

By now, you've happily and repeatedly populated the my_music table with all the items in your music collection—or at least a few. In this chapter, you'll learn how to do the following:

⬤ Select records from a table using the SQL ORDER BY clause

⬤ Format and display records from a database table

Planning and Creating Your Administrative Menu

You could just write one script that says "Select all my data; I don't care about the order," but that would be boring. In this chapter, you'll see four ways to select records from the my_music table. To facilitate easy navigation, create an administration menu—fancy words for "a list of links to scripts."

1. Open a new file in your text editor and type the following HTML:

```
<HTML>
<HEAD>
<TITLE>My Menu</TITLE>
</HEAD>
<BODY>
<H1>My Menu</H1>
<P><strong>My Music</strong></P>
```

2. Start a bullet list and create the first link to a script called sel_byid.php. This script will display the records ordered by ID number:

```
<ul>
<li><a href="sel_byid.php">ordered by ID</a>
```

3. Add a link to a script called sel_bydateacq.php. This script will display the records ordered by date acquired. The most recently acquired item will be listed first:

```
<li><a href="sel_bydateacq.php">ordered by date acquired</a> (most
recent first)
```

4. Add a link to a script called sel_bytitle.php. This script will display the records ordered by title:

```
<li><a href="sel_bytitle.php">ordered by title</a>
```

5. Add a link to a script called sel_byartist.php. This script will display the records ordered by artist:

```
<li><a href="sel_byartist.php">ordered by artist</a>
```

6. Close the bullet list, and then add some HTML so that the document is valid:

```
</ul>
</BODY>
</HTML>
```

7. Save the file with the name `my_menu.html` and place this file in the document root of your Web server.

8. Open your Web browser and type **http://127.0.0.1/my_menu.html**

In the next sections, you'll create the scripts that do all the aforementioned selecting.

Selecting Data from the my_music Table

The next four sections contain scripts that are variations on a theme: selecting and displaying data. A large portion of the scripts is exactly the same, but repetition makes perfection, I was always told.

The only new function in these scripts is the `mysql_fetch_array()` function. This function takes the result of a SQL query and places the rows in array format. Using a simple `while` loop, you can extract and display these elements.

Hang on to your hat, and start with the first script, which just returns the results ordered by their ID number.

Displaying Records Ordered by ID

One of the required fields in the record addition script is ID. In this script, you'll select all the records in the `my_music` table, ordered by the ID number. The default value of the `ORDER BY` clause is `ASC` (ascending), so the records will be returned with ID 1 first, followed by 2, 3, and so on.

1. Open a new file in your text editor and start a PHP block:

```
<?
```

2. Create a variable to hold the name of the database on which the table resides:

```
$db_name = "testDB";
```

3. Create a variable to hold the name of the table you're selecting from, using this script:

```
$table_name = "my_music";
```

4. Add the connection information as you have been:

```
$connection = @mysql_connect("localhost", "spike", "9sj7En4")
or die(mysql_error());
```

5. Select the database as you have learned:

```
$db = @mysql_select_db($db_name, $connection) or
die(mysql_error());
```

6. Create the SQL statement:

```
$sql = "SELECT id, format, title, artist_fn, artist_ln, rec_label,
my_notes, date_acq FROM $table_name ORDER BY id";
```

TIP

Since you're selecting all the fields, you could use a * in the SQL statement instead of naming all the fields. In this case, the line would look like this:

```
$sql = "SELECT * FROM $table_name ORDER BY id";
```

---

7. Create a variable to hold the result of the mysql_query() function, as you have learned:

```
$result = @mysql_query($sql,$connection) or die(mysql_error());
```

8. Start the while loop. The while loop will create an array called $row for each record in the result set ($result):

```
while ($row = mysql_fetch_array($result)) {
```

9. Get the individual elements of the record, and give them good names. Add the stripslashes() function around any free text field which may have had slashes added to it:

```
$id = $row['id'];
$format = $row['format'];
$title = stripslashes($row['title']);
$artist_fn = stripslashes($row['artist_fn']);
$artist_ln = stripslashes($row['artist_ln']);
```

```
$rec_label = stripslashes($row['rec_label']);
$my_notes = stripslashes($row['my_notes']);
$date_acq = $row['date_acq'];
```

10. Do a little formatting with the artists' names. Since some artists have only a first name, some artists use both first and last names, and group names are thrown into the artist_ln field, start an if…else block to deal with this. Start by looking for groups:

```
if ($artist_fn != "") {
```

11. Create a variable called $artist_fullname, which will contain a string with $artist_fn, followed by a space, followed by $artist_ln, all within the trim() function:

```
$artist_fullname = trim("$artist_fn $artist_ln");
```

NOTE

The trim() function gets rid of extraneous space at the beginning and end of a string.

---

12. Continue the block, assigning the trimmed value of $artist_ln to $artist_fullname:

```
} else {
    $artist_fullname = trim("$artist_ln");
}
```

13. Do a little more formatting. If you didn't enter a date in the date_acq field, MySQL will enter a default value of 0000-00-00. Create an if block that looks for this value and then replaces it with something more friendly:

```
if ($date_acq == "0000-00-00") {
    $date_acq = "[unknown]";
}
```

14. Create a variable called $display_block to hold all the formatted records. The formatting in this block places the title of the recording in bold, followed by the artist's name in parentheses. Next comes a line break, then your notes, and then an emphasized parenthetical statement that holds the date acquired and format:

```
$display_block .= "
<P><strong>$title</strong> ($artist_fullname)<br>
$my_notes <em>(acquired: $date_acq, format: $format)</em></P>";
```

15. Close the `while` loop, then your PHP block:

```
}
?>
```

16. Add this HTML:

```
<HTML>
<HEAD>
<TITLE>My Music (Ordered by ID)</TITLE>
</HEAD>
<BODY>
<H1>My Music: Ordered by ID</H1>
```

17. Display the results:

```
<? echo "$display_block"; ?>
```

18. Add a link back to the main menu, and then add some more HTML to make a valid document:

```
<P><a href="my_menu.html">Return to Menu</a></P>
</BODY>
</HTML>
```

19. Save the file with the name `sel_byid.php` and place this file in the document root of your Web server.

20. Open your Web browser and type **http://127.0.0.1/my_menu.html**

21. Click on the link called ordered by ID.

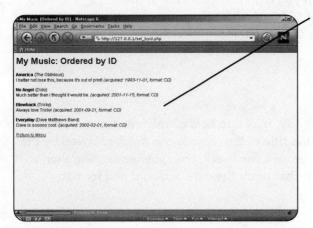

Your records will be different from mine, but you should see a screen like the following, where the records are ordered by internal ID number.

In the next section, you'll create the script that displays results ordered by date acquired.

Displaying Records Ordered by Date Acquired

Although it isn't a required field, the record addition script has a space for the date the recording made its way into your music collection. In this script, you'll select all the records in the my_music table, ordered by this date, with the most recent acquisition appearing first in the list.

1. Open a new file in your text editor and start a PHP block:

```
<?
```

2. Create a variable to hold the name of the database on which the table resides:

```
$db_name = "testDB";
```

3. Create a variable to hold the name of the table you're selecting from, using this script:

```
$table_name = "my_music";
```

4. Add the connection information as you have been:

```
$connection = @mysql_connect("localhost", "spike", "9sj7En4")
or die(mysql_error());
```

5. Select the database as you have learned:

```
$db = @mysql_select_db($db_name, $connection) or
die(mysql_error());
```

6. Create the SQL statement, now using the wildcard to select all of the fields:

```
$sql = "SELECT * FROM $table_name ORDER BY date_acq DESC";
```

7. Create a variable to hold the result of the mysql_query() function, as you have learned:

```
$result = @mysql_query($sql,$connection) or die(mysql_error());
```

8. Start the while loop. The while loop will create an array called $row for each record in the result set ($result):

```
while ($row = mysql_fetch_array($result)) {
```

9. Get the individual elements of the record, and give them good names. Add the `stripslashes()` function around any free text field which may have had slashes added to it:

```
$id = $row['id'];
$format = $row['format'];
$title = stripslashes($row['title']);
$artist_fn = stripslashes($row['artist_fn']);
$artist_ln = stripslashes($row['artist_ln']);
$rec_label = stripslashes($row['rec_label']);
$my_notes = stripslashes($row['my_notes']);
$date_acq = $row['date_acq'];
```

10. Do a little formatting with the artists' names. Since some artists have only a first name, some artists use both first and last names, and group names are thrown into the `artist_ln` field, start an if...else block to deal with this. Start by looking for groups:

```
if ($artist_fn != "") {
```

11. Create a variable called `$artist_fullname`, which will contain a string with `$artist_fn`, followed by a space, followed by `$artist_ln`, all within the `trim()` function:

```
$artist_fullname = trim("$artist_fn $artist_ln");
```

NOTE

The `trim()` function gets rid of extraneous space at the beginning and end of a string.

---

12. Continue the block, assigning the trimmed value of `$artist_ln` to `$artist_fullname`:

```
} else {
    $artist_fullname = trim("$artist_ln");
}
```

13. Do a little more formatting. If you didn't enter a date in the `date_acq` field, MySQL will enter a default value of 0000-00-00. Create an `if` block that looks for this value and then replaces it with something more friendly:

```
if ($date_acq == "0000-00-00") {
    $date_acq = "[unknown]";
}
```

14. Create a variable called $display_block to hold all the formatted records. The formatting in this block places the title of the recording in bold, followed by the artist's name in parentheses. Next comes a line break, then your notes, and then an emphasized parenthetical statement that holds the date acquired and format:

```
$display_block .= "
<P><strong>$title</strong> ($artist_fullname)<br>
$my_notes <em>(acquired: $date_acq, format: $format)</em></P>";
```

15. Close the `while` loop, then your PHP block:

```
}
?>
```

16. Add this HTML:

```
<HTML>
<HEAD>
<TITLE>My Music (Ordered by Date Acquired)</TITLE>
</HEAD>
<BODY>
<H1>My Music: Ordered by Date Acquired</H1>
```

17. Display the results:

```
<? echo "$display_block"; ?>
```

18. Add a link back to the main menu, and then add some more HTML to make a valid document:

```
<P><a href="my_menu.html">Return to Menu</a></P>
</BODY>
</HTML>
```

19. Save the file with the name `sel_bydateacq.php` and place this file in the document root of your Web server.

20. Open your Web browser and type **http://127.0.0.1/my_menu.html**

21. Click on the link called ordered by date acquired.

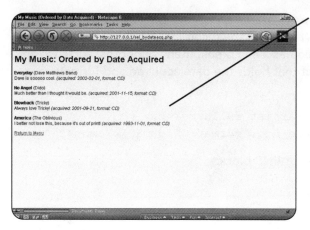

Your records will be different from mine, but you should see a screen like this one, where the records are ordered by the date the recordings were acquired. Those without dates would appear at the end of the list.

In the next section, you'll create the script that displays results ordered by title.

Displaying Records Ordered by Title

As you might imagine, the recording title is a required field in the record addition script. In this script, you'll select all the records in the my_music table, ordered alphabetically by title.

1. Open a new file in your text editor and start a PHP block:

```
<?
```

2. Create a variable to hold the name of the database on which the table resides:

```
$db_name = "testDB";
```

3. Create a variable to hold the name of the table you're selecting from, using this script:

```
$table_name = "my_music";
```

4. Add the connection information as you have been:

```
$connection = @mysql_connect("localhost", "spike", "9sj7En4")
or die(mysql_error());
```

5. Select the database as you have learned:

```
$db = @mysql_select_db($db_name, $connection) or
die(mysql_error());
```

6. Create the SQL statement, using the wildcard to select all fields:

```
$sql = "SELECT * FROM $table_name ORDER BY title";
```

7. Create a variable to hold the result of the `mysql_query()` function, as you have learned:

```
$result = @mysql_query($sql,$connection) or die(mysql_error());
```

8. Start the `while` loop. The `while` loop will create an array called `$row` for each record in the result set (`$result`):

```
while ($row = mysql_fetch_array($result)) {
```

9. Get the individual elements of the record, and give them good names. Add the `stripslashes()` function around any free text field which may have had slashes added to it:

```
$id = $row['id'];
$format = $row['format'];
$title = stripslashes($row['title']);
$artist_fn = stripslashes($row['artist_fn']);
$artist_ln = stripslashes($row['artist_ln']);
$rec_label = stripslashes($row['rec_label']);
$my_notes = stripslashes($row['my_notes']);
$date_acq = $row['date_acq'];
```

10. Do a little formatting with the artists' names. Since some artists have only a first name, some artists use both first and last names, and group names are thrown into the `artist_ln` field, start an `if...else` block to deal with this. Start by looking for groups:

```
if ($artist_fn != "") {
```

11. Create a variable called `$artist_fullname`, which will contain a string with `$artist_fn`, followed by a space, followed by `$artist_ln`, all within the `trim()` function:

```
$artist_fullname = trim("$artist_fn $artist_ln");
```

NOTE

The `trim()` function gets rid of extraneous space at the beginning and end of a string.

---

12. Continue the block, assigning the trimmed value of `$artist_ln` to `$artist_fullname`:

```
} else {
    $artist_fullname = trim("$artist_ln");
}
```

13. Do a little more formatting. If you didn't enter a date in the `date_acq` field, MySQL will enter a default value of 0000-00-00. Create an `if` block that looks for this value and then replaces it with something more friendly:

```
if ($date_acq == "0000-00-00") {
    $date_acq = "[unknown]";
}
```

14. Create a variable called `$display_block` to hold all the formatted records. The formatting in this block places the title of the recording in bold, followed by the artist's name in parentheses. Next comes a line break, then your notes, and then an emphasized parenthetical statement that holds the date acquired and format:

```
$display_block .= "
<P><strong>$title</strong> ($artist_fullname)<br>
$my_notes <em>(acquired: $date_acq, format: $format)</em></P>
";
```

15. Close the `while` loop, then your PHP block:

```
}
?>
```

16. Add this HTML:

```
<HTML>
<HEAD>
<TITLE>My Music (Ordered by Title)</TITLE>
</HEAD>
<BODY>
<H1>My Music: Ordered by Title</H1>
```

17. Display the results:

```
<? echo "$display_block"; ?>
```

18. Add a link back to the main menu, and then add some more HTML to make a valid document:

```
<P><a href="my_menu.html">Return to Menu</a></P>
</BODY>
</HTML>
```

19. Save the file with the name `sel_bytitle.php` and place this file in the document root of your Web server.

20. Open your Web browser and type **http://127.0.0.1/my_menu.html**

21. Click on the link called ordered by title.

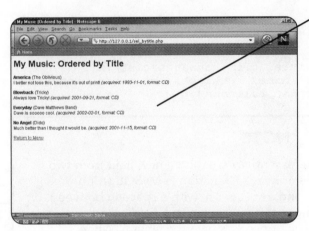

Your records will be different from mine, but you should see a screen like this one, where the records are ordered by title of the recording.

In the next section, you'll create the script that displays results ordered by artist name.

Displaying Records Ordered by Artist

This script is a bit trickier because you have to take into consideration issues associated with artist names: some have only a first name, some have first and last names, and group names are thrown into the `artist_ln` field as well. In this script, you'll select all the records in the `my_music` table, ordered alphabetically by the full name of the artist.

1. Open a new file in your text editor and start a PHP block:

```
<?
```

2. Create a variable to hold the name of the database on which the table resides:

```
$db_name = "testDB";
```

3. Create a variable to hold the name of the table you're selecting from, using this script:

```
$table_name = "my_music";
```

4. Add the connection information as you have been:

```
$connection = @mysql_connect("localhost", "spike", "9sj7En4")
or die(mysql_error());
```

5. Select the database as you have learned:

```
$db = @mysql_select_db($db_name, $connection) or
die(mysql_error());
```

6. Create the SQL statement. Go back to the method that names all the fields in the SELECT statement:

```
$sql = "SELECT id, format, title, trim(concat(artist_fn,
' ',artist_ln)) as artist_fullname, rec_label, my_notes, date_acq
FROM $table_name ORDER BY artist_fullname";
```

NOTE

Within this SQL statement, you're essentially creating a new field from two fields that already exist, using the concat() function (a MySQL string function) to combine artist_fn and artist_ln, with a space in between. Using as artist_fullname assigns this new value to a field called artist_fullname. For example, suppose you own the album "White Ladder" by David Gray. The artist's first name ("David") and last name ("Gray") would go in their respective areas of the form, but would be output as one string ("David Gray").

The trim() function still strips the white space. The phrase trim(concat(artist_fn,' ',artist_ln)) as artist_fullname replaces the if...else block usually seen within the while loop in previous scripts.

---

7. Create a variable to hold the result of the mysql_query() function, as you have learned:

```
$result = @mysql_query($sql,$connection) or die(mysql_error());
```

8. Start the while loop. The while loop will create an array called $row for each record in the result set ($result):

```
while ($row = mysql_fetch_array($result)) {
```

9. Get the individual elements of the record, and give them good names. Remember, you have a new field called `artist_fullname`. Add the `stripslashes()` function around any free text field which may have had slashes added to it:

```
$id = $row['id'];
$format = $row['format'];
$title = stripslashes($row['title']);
$artist_fullname = stripslashes($row['artist_fullname']);
$rec_label = stripslashes($row['rec_label']);
$my_notes = stripslashes($row['my_notes']);
$date_acq = $row['date_acq'];
```

10. If you didn't enter a date in the `date_acq` field, MySQL will enter a default value of 0000-00-00. Create an `if` block that looks for this value and then replaces it with something more friendly:

```
if ($date_acq == "0000-00-00") {
    $date_acq = "[unknown]";
}
```

11. Create a variable called `$display_block`, to hold all the formatted records. The formatting in this block places the title of the recording in bold, followed by the artist's name in parentheses. Next comes a line break, then your notes, and then an emphasized parenthetical statement that holds the date acquired and format:

```
$display_block .= "
<P><strong>$title</strong> ($artist_fullname)<br>
$my_notes <em>(acquired: $date_acq, format: $format)</em></P>";
```

12. Close the `while` loop, then your PHP block:

```
}
?>
```

13. Add this HTML:

```
<HTML>
<HEAD>
<TITLE>My Music (Ordered by Artist)</TITLE>
</HEAD>
<BODY>
<H1>My Music: Ordered by Artist</H1>
```

14. Display the results:

```
<? echo "$display_block"; ?>
```

15. Add a link back to the main menu, and then add some more HTML to make a valid document:

```
<P><a href="my_menu.html">Return to Menu</a></P>
</BODY>
</HTML>
```

16. Save the file with the name `sel_byartist.php` and place this file in the document root of your Web server.

17. Open your Web browser and type **http://127.0.0.1/my_menu.html**

18. Click on the link called ordered by artist.

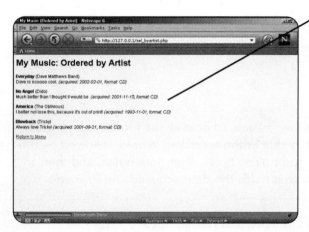

Your records will be different from mine, but you should see a screen like this one, where the records are ordered by the name of the artist.

The next chapters will give you a break from database work, as you learn a bit about user authentication, cookies, and sessions.

PART V

User Authentication and Tracking

15

Database-Driven User Authentication

Everyone has secrets they don't want to share with the entire world. But some secrets *can* be shared—with certain people. In this chapter, you'll learn how to do the following:

- Create a database table for authorized users

- Create a login form and script sequence that authenticates users before displaying any secrets

Why Authenticate Anyone?

When initially developing a Web site, you might want to restrict access to certain members of your development team. If your corporate Web site contains sensitive financial data, you might want to restrict your financial statements to a particular list of investors. Or maybe you just don't want people poking around in your personal things.

A common type of user authentication is *database-driven*, in which usernames and passwords are kept in a database table and accessed via a login form and script. In the next section, you'll create this database table and add some users to it.

Creating the User Table

In Chapter 12, "Creating a Database Table," you followed a two-step table-creation process. You'll be able to use that same process to create the authorized users table.

1. Open your Web browser to **http://127.0.0.1/show_createtable.html**

2. In the Table Name field, type **auth_users**.

3. In the Number of Fields field, type **4**.

4. Click on the Go to Step 2 button. You should see a form with four rows, corresponding to the four fields which will be in the `auth_users` table.

5. In the first row, type **f_name** for the Field Name, select `varchar` from the Field Type drop-down menu, and specify a Field Length of **50**. This field will hold the user's first name.

6. In the second row, type **l_name** for the Field Name, select `varchar` from the Field Type drop-down menu, and specify a Field Length of **50**. This field will hold the user's last name.

7. In the third row, type **username** for the Field Name, select `varchar` from the Field Type drop-down menu, and specify a Field Length of **25**. This field will hold the user's username.

8. In the fourth row, type **password** for the Field Name, select `varchar` from the Field Type drop-down menu, and specify a Field Length of **100**. This field will hold a hash of the password.

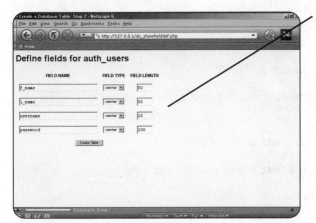

The completed form should look like this.

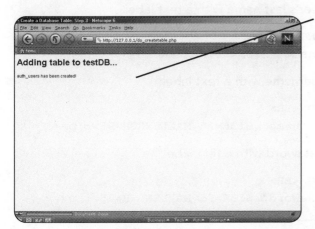

Click on the Create Table button. You should see a confirmation screen.

In the next section, you'll create a record addition form and script and add users to the auth_users table.

Adding Users to Your Table

An empty auth_users table does you no good. In this section, you'll create a simple record addition form and script, similar to those you created in Chapter 13, "Inserting Data into a Table."

Creating the User Addition Form and Script

The HTML form will contain an input field for each column in the auth_users table.

1. Open a new file in your text editor and type the following HTML:

```
<HTML>
<HEAD>
```

```
<TITLE>Add a User</TITLE>
</HEAD>
<BODY>
<H1>Adding a Record to auth_users</H1>
```

2. Begin your form. Assume that the method is POST and the action is a script called do_adduser.php:

```
<FORM METHOD="POST" ACTION="do_adduser.php">
```

3. Create an input field for the user's first name with a text label:

```
<P><STRONG>First Name:</STRONG><BR>
<INPUT TYPE="text" NAME="f_name" SIZE=25 MAXLENGTH=50></p>
```

4. Create an input field for the user's last name with a text label.

```
<P><STRONG>Last Name:</STRONG><BR>
<INPUT TYPE="text" NAME="l_name" SIZE=25 MAXLENGTH=50></p>
```

5. Create an input field for the username with a text label:

```
<P><STRONG>Username:</STRONG><BR>
<INPUT TYPE="text" NAME="username" SIZE=25 MAXLENGTH=25></p>
```

6. Create an input field for the password with a text label.

```
<P><STRONG>Password:</STRONG><BR>
<INPUT TYPE="text" NAME="password" SIZE=25 MAXLENGTH=25></p>
```

NOTE

The MAXLENGTH of the password form field is 25, while the database field maximum length is 100. This discrepancy in length takes into consideration the encryption that will occur. A 25-character plain-text password, such as that entered in this form field, will be probably be longer than 25 characters when encrypted. Since only the encrypted password is stored in the database, the greater maximum length will handle the extra data.

---

7. Add a submit button, then close your form and add some more HTML so that the document is valid:

```
<P><INPUT TYPE="SUBMIT" NAME="submit" VALUE="Add User"></P>
</FORM>
</BODY>
</HTML>
```

8. Save the file with the name `show_adduser.html` and place this file in the document root of your Web server.

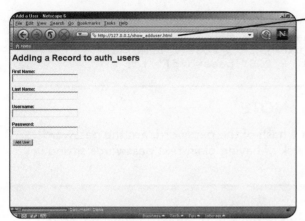

9. Open your Web browser and type **http://127.0.0.1/show_adduser.html**

You will see a form for adding a user, with four fields for name and password information as well as a submit button. Next, you will create the back-end script for the record-addition form.

1. Open a new file in your text editor and start a PHP block:

```
<?
```

2. Check that values were actually entered for all four fields. If they weren't, direct the user back to the form and exit the script:

```
if ((!$_POST[f_name]) || (!$_POST[l_name]) || (!$_POST[username])
|| (!$_POST[password])) {
   header( "Location: http://127.0.0.1/show_adduser.html");
   exit;
}
```

3. Create a variable to hold the name of the database on which the table resides:

```
$db_name = "testDB";
```

4. Create a variable to hold the name of the table you're populating with this script:

```
$table_name = "auth_users";
```

5. Add the connection information as you have been:

```
$connection = @mysql_connect("localhost", "spike", "9sj7En4")
or die(mysql_error());
```

6. Select the database as you have learned:

```
$db = @mysql_select_db($db_name, $connection) or die(mysql_error());
```

7. Create the SQL statement. The first parenthetical statement gives the names of the fields to populate (in order), and the second parenthetical statement sends the actual strings:

```
$sql = "INSERT INTO $table_name (f_name, l_name, username,
password) VALUES ('$_POST[f_name]', '$_POST[l_name]',
'$_POST[username]', password('$_POST[password]'))";
```

NOTE

The `password()` function inserts a hash of the password, not the password itself. This alleviates the security risk of having plain-text passwords sitting in your database.

---

8. Create a variable to hold the result of the `mysql_query()` function, as you have learned:

```
$result = @mysql_query($sql,$connection) or die(mysql_error());
```

9. Close your PHP block, then add HTML:

```
?>
<HTML>
<HEAD>
<TITLE>Add a User</TITLE>
</HEAD>
<BODY>
<H1>Added to auth_users:</H1>
```

10. Mingle HTML and PHP to show the values entered for each field, starting with the first-name field:

```
<P><STRONG>First Name:</STRONG><BR>
<? echo "$_POST[f_name]"; ?></p>
<P><STRONG>Last Name:</STRONG><BR>
<? echo "$_POST[l_name]"; ?></p>
<P><STRONG>Username:</STRONG><BR>
<? echo "$_POST[username]"; ?></p>
<P><STRONG>Password:</STRONG><BR>
<? echo "$_POST[password]"; ?></p>
```

11. Add a link back to the original form:

```
<P><a href="show_adduser.html">Add Another</a></p>
```

12. Add some more HTML so that the document is valid:

```
</BODY>
</HTML>
```

13. Save the file with the name do_adduser.php and place this file in the document root of your Web server.

Your code should look like this:

```
<?
//check for required fields
if ((!$_POST[f_name]) || (!$_POST[l_name]) || (!$_POST[username])
|| (!$_POST[password])) {
   header( "Location: http://127.0.0.1/show_adduser.html");
   exit;
}
//set up the names of the database and table
$db_name = "testDB";
$table_name = "auth_users";

//connect to the server and select the database
$connection = @mysql_connect("localhost", "spike", "9sj7En4")
or die(mysql_error());
$db = @mysql_select_db($db_name, $connection) or
die(mysql_error());

//create and issue query
$sql = "INSERT INTO $table_name (f_name, l_name, username,
password)
VALUES ('$_POST[f_name]', '$_POST[l_name]', '$_POST[username]',
password('$_POST[password]'))";
$result = @mysql_query($sql,$connection) or die(mysql_error());
?>
<HTML>
<HEAD>
<TITLE>Add a User</TITLE>
</HEAD>
<BODY>
<H1>Added to auth_users:</H1>
<P><STRONG>First Name:</STRONG><BR>
<? echo "$_POST[f_name]"; ?></p>

<P><STRONG>Last Name:</STRONG><BR>
```

```
<? echo "$_POST[l_name]"; ?></p>

<P><STRONG>Username:</STRONG><BR>
<? echo "$_POST[username]"; ?></p>

<P><STRONG>Password:</STRONG><BR>
<? echo "$_POST[password]"; ?></p>

<P><a href="show_adduser.html">Add Another</a></p>

</BODY>
</HTML>
```

Next you'll test this by adding some sample users to your table.

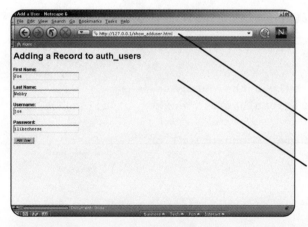

Adding Some Users

The next examples are based on fake users on my server. Your results will vary, depending on what you enter in your table. To get to the user addition form, open your Web browser and type **http://127.0.0.1/ show_adduser.html**.

In my user addition form, I typed information for a user named Joe Webby, with a username of joe and a password of ilikecheese.

After I clicked on the Add User button, the confirmation screen was displayed.

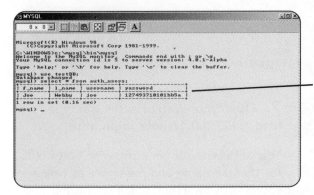

To see an example of how the password hash is stored, use the command-line interface to the MySQL Monitor to view your record. In the example, notice how the password entry says `127493710101bb5a`, not ilikecheese.

Continue adding some users on your own, until you have a nice family of users.

Creating the Login Form

The HTML form will contain just two fields: username and password. Both are required.

1. Open a new file in your text editor and type the following HTML:

```
<HTML>
<HEAD>
<TITLE>Login</TITLE>
</HEAD>
<BODY>
<H1>Login to Secret Area</H1>
```

2. Begin your form. Assume that the method is POST and the action is a script called do_authuser.php:

```
<FORM METHOD="POST" ACTION="do_authuser.php">
```

3. Create an input field for the username with a text label:

```
<P><STRONG>Username:</STRONG><BR>
<INPUT TYPE="text" NAME="username" SIZE=25 MAXLENGTH=25></p>
```

4. Create an input field for the password with a text label.

```
<P><STRONG>Password:</STRONG><BR>
<INPUT TYPE="text" NAME="password" SIZE=25 MAXLENGTH=25></p>
```

5. Add a submit button, then close your form and add some more HTML so that the document is valid:

```
<P><INPUT TYPE="SUBMIT" NAME="submit" VALUE="Login"></P>
</FORM>
```

```
</BODY>
</HTML>
```

6. Save the file with the name `show_login.html` and place this file in the document root of your Web server.

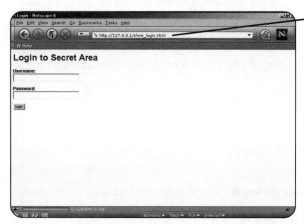

7. Open your Web browser and type **http://127.0.0.1/show_login.html**

You will see the login form, with text fields for the username and password as well as a submit button. Next, you'll create the back-end script for the login form.

Creating the Authentication Script

The goal of this script is to match the username and password entered in the form with a username and password (in the same record) in the `auth_users` table.

1. Open a new file in your text editor and start a PHP block:

```
<?
```

2. Check that values were actually entered for both. If they weren't, direct the user back to the form and exit the script:

```
if ((!$_POST[username]) || (!$_POST[password])) {
    header("Location: http://127.0.0.1/show_login.html");
    exit;
}
```

3. Create a variable to hold the name of the database on which the table resides:

```
$db_name = "testDB";
```

4. Create a variable to hold the name of the table you're populating with this script:

```
$table_name = "auth_users";
```

5. Add the connection information as you have been:

```
$connection = @mysql_connect("localhost", "spike", "9sj7En4")
or die(mysql_error());
```

6. Select the database as you have learned:

```
$db = @mysql_select_db($db_name, $connection) or
die(mysql_error());
```

7. Create the SQL statement. The statement is looking for all fields in a record where the username in the table matches the username entered in the form, and the password hash in the table matches a hash of the password entered in the form:

```
$sql = "SELECT * FROM $table_name WHERE username =
'$_POST[username]' AND password = password('$_POST[password]')";
```

8. Create a variable to hold the result of the `mysql_query()` function, as you have learned:

```
$result = @mysql_query($sql,$connection) or die(mysql_error());
```

9. Check for any results from the query by counting the number of rows returned in the result set:

```
$num = mysql_num_rows($result);
```

10. Start an `if...else` block to deal with your result. If the number of returned rows is more than 1, a match was found. Create a variable to hold an appropriate message:

```
if ($num != 0) {
$msg = "<P>Congratulations, you're authorized!</p>";
```

11. If the number of returned rows is 0, no matches were found. In that case, direct the user back to the login form, and then close the `if...else` block:

```
} else {
header("Location: http://127.0.0.1/show_login.html");
exit;
}
```

12. Close your PHP block and add HTML:

```
?>
<HTML>
<HEAD>
<TITLE>Secret Area</TITLE>
</HEAD>
<BODY>
```

13. Display the message:

```
<? echo "$msg"; ?>
```

14. Add some more HTML so that the document is valid:

```
</BODY>
</HTML>
```

15. Save the file with the name `do_authuser.php` and place this file in the document root of your Web server.

Your code should look like this:

```
<?
//check for required fields
if ((!$_POST[username]) || (!$_POST[password])) {
    header( "Location: http://127.0.0.1/show_login.html");
    exit;
}

//setup names of database and table to use
$db_name = "testDB";
$table_name = "auth_users";

//connect to server and select database
$connection = @mysql_connect("localhost", "spike", "9sj7En4")
or die(mysql_error());
$db = @mysql_select_db($db_name, $connection) ©Ú
die(mysql_error());

//build and issue the query
$sql = "SELECT * FROM $table_name WHERE username =
'$_POST[username]' AND password = password('$_POST[password]')";

$result = @mysql_query($sql,$connection) or die(mysql_error());

//get the number of rows in the result set
$num = mysql_num_rows($result);

//print a message or redirect elsewhere, based on result
if ($num != 0) {
    $msg = "<P>Congratulations, you're authorized!</p>";
} else {
```

```
        header("Location: http://127.0.0.1/show_login.html");
        exit;
}
?>
<HTML>
<HEAD>
<TITLE>Secret Area</TITLE>
</HEAD>
<BODY>
<? echo "$msg"; ?>
</BODY>
</HTML>
```

Next, you get to test the login form!

Trying to Authenticate Yourself

In this section, you'll attempt to log in as one of the users you added to the auth_users table. Your results will vary, depending on the usernames and passwords you're using. To get to the login form, open your Web browser and type **http://127.0.0.1/show_login.html**.

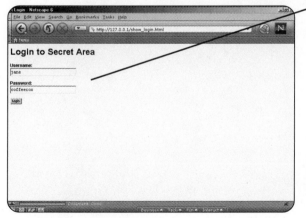

I first tried to break the authentication routine by entering a bad username and a bad password.

After I clicked on the Login button, I was directed back to the login page, since both the username and password were invalid.

NOTE
Any combination of bad username and bad password will cause the authentication to fail.

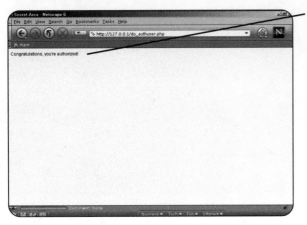

Then I entered correct values in the Username and Password fields, and after I clicked on the Login button, I saw the success message.

In the next chapter, you'll be introduced to cookies, and you'll see how to use them in an authentication scheme or just for general user tracking.

16

Using Cookies

Cookies are great little tools, but they get a bad rap in the press when nasty people misuse them. These little bits of text will make your development life much easier if you use them properly. In this chapter, you'll learn how to do the following:

- Set a cookie
- Extract data from a cookie
- Amend your user authentication routines to use a cookie

What's a Cookie?

Cookies are pieces of text that are sent to a user's Web browser. Cookies can help you create shopping carts, user communities, and personalized sites. It's not recommended that you store sensitive data in a cookie, but you can store a unique identification string that will match a user with data held securely in a database.

Take the shopping example. Suppose you assign an identification variable to a user so that you can track what he does when he visits your site. First, the user logs in, and you send a cookie with variables designed to say, "This is Joe, and Joe is allowed to be here." While Joe is surfing around your site, you can say, "Hello, Joe!" on each and every page. If Joe clicks through your catalog and chooses 14 different items to buy, you can keep track of these items and display them all in a bunch when Joe goes to the checkout area.

Setting Cookies

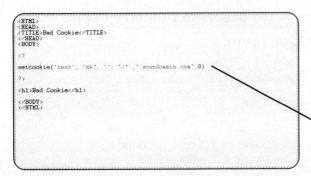

```
<HTML>
<HEAD>
<TITLE>Bad Cookie</TITLE>
</HEAD>
<BODY>

<?

setcookie("test", "ok", "", "/" ,".yourdomain.com",0)

?>

<h1>Bad Cookie</h1>

</BODY>
</HTML>
```

Before you start setting cookies, determine how you will use them and at what point you will set them. Whatever cookies you decide to set, remember that you absolutely must set a cookie before sending any other content to the browser because a cookie is actually part of the header information.

If you heed this warning, you won't spend hours wondering why you're getting "Cannot add header information" errors. This sample code does just that.

It produces this error.

Anytime you see this error, assume that you've sent *something* to the Web browser. This can include white space, a line break, or text you can actually see.

The `setcookie()` function, used to set one cookie at a time, expects six arguments:

- **Name**. Holds the name of the variable that will be kept in the global `$_COOKIE` and will be accessible in subsequent scripts.

- **Value**. The value of the variable passed in the name parameter.

- **Expiration**. Sets a specific time at which the cookie value will no longer be accessible. Cookies without a specific expiration time will expire when the Web browser closes.

- **Path**. Determines for which directories the cookie is valid. If a single slash is in the path parameter, the cookie is valid for all files and directories on the Web server. If a specific directory is named, this cookie is valid only for pages within that directory.

- **Domain**. Cookies are valid only for the host and domain that set them. If no domain is specified, the default value is the host name of the server that generated the cookie. The domain parameter must have at least two periods in the string in order to be valid.

- **Security**. If the security parameter is 1, the cookie will only be transmitted via HTTPS, which is to say, over a secure Web server.

This next line is an example of a cookie called `id` with a value of `55sds809892jjsj2`. This particular cookie will expire in four hours (the current time plus 14,400 seconds), and it is valid for any page below the document root on the domain `yourdomain.com`.

```
setcookie("id", "55sds809892jjsj2", time()+14400, "/"
,".yourdomain.com",0);
```

In the next section, I'll give you a cheat sheet for common values of time. Then you'll move into using cookie variables.

Counting Time

If you want to specify an expiration date or time, the easiest way to do that is to tell PHP to count forward for you, and then place a value in the expiration slot within the `setcookie()` function. This value should be a UNIX time integer (the number of seconds since January 1, 1970), which you can get using the `time()` function with additional seconds added to it.

Setting an expiration date on your cookies builds in some extra assurances of the validity of your users. If you set your cookie without a time limit, it will automatically expire when the user closes their browser. This is helpful when users are sharing computers; you don't want the next user to have all the access afforded by the previous user's cookie. Similarly, you may want to set a cookie for only 15 minutes if you are building an online store that allows you to receive a discount on everything purchased in the first 15 minutes of your users' visits.

Table 16.1 shows some common uses of `time()+n` within the `setcookie()` function.

Table 16.1   Common Times

Value	Definition
`time()+60`	One minute from the current time
`time()+900`	15 minutes from the current time
`time()+1800`	30 minutes from the current time
`time()+3600`	One hour from the current time
`time()+14400`	Four hours from the current time
`time()+43200`	12 hours from the current time
`time()+86400`	24 hours from the current time
`time()+259200`	Three days from the current time
`time()+604800`	One week from the current time
`time()+2592000`	30 days from the current time

Setting a Test Cookie

The goal of this little script is just to set a test cookie, and then print a message to the screen. Before you start, ensure that you do not have any personal firewall settings blocking incoming cookies. Also, modify your Web browser preferences to prompt you before setting cookies. This is the only way to watch a cookie as the server attempts to send it to your browser.

1. Open a new file in your text editor and start a PHP block, then create a set of variables called $cookie_name, $cookie_value, $cookie_expire, and $cookie_domain, and give them the following values:

```
<?
$cookie_name = "test_cookie";
$cookie_value = "test string!";
```

```
$cookie_expire = time()+86400;
$cookie_domain = "127.0.0.1";
```

> ## NOTE
>
> Substitute your own domain name for the value of `$cookie_domain`, if you are not using 127.0.0.1 (`localhost`) as your domain.

2. Use the `setcookie()` function to set this test cookie, and then close the PHP block:

```
setcookie($cookie_name, $cookie_value, $cookie_expire, "/" ,
$cookie_domain, 0);
?>
```

3. Type the following HTML:

```
<HTML>
<HEAD>
<TITLE>Set Test Cookie</TITLE>
</HEAD>
<BODY>
<h1>Mmmmmmmmm...cookie!</h1>
</BODY>
</HTML>
```

4. Save the file with the name `setcookie.php` and place this file in the document root of your Web server.

5. Open your Web browser and type **http://127.0.0.1/setcookie.php**

You should see a dialog box prompting you to accept the cookie. The actual dialog box will differ from browser to browser.

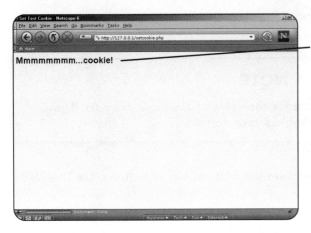

6. Click on OK to accept the cookie.

You should see the HTML text.

Using Cookie Variables

There's an element to using cookies that most people forget about until they spend a few hours trying to debug something that isn't even wrong (I've done this). When a Web browser accepts a cookie, you can't extract its value until the next HTTP request is made.

In other words, if you set a cookie called name with a value of Julie on page 1, you can't extract that value until the user reaches page 2 (or page 5 or page 28—just some other page that isn't the page on which the cookie is initially set).

Using Cookies with Authentication

In the authentication script in the previous chapter, you had a login form and a results page. However, the authentication was valid only for the results page because it dynamically displayed the secret content (in this case, a "Congratulations!" message). If you want to require authentication for a series of static pages, you have to make some minor adjustments.

1. Open do_authuser.php in your text editor.

2. Scroll down to the if...else block that deals with the result of the authentication. Add a block that sets a cookie:

```
if ($num != 0) {
$cookie_name = "auth";
$cookie_value = "ok";
$cookie_expire = "0";
$cookie_domain = "127.0.0.1";
setcookie($cookie_name, $cookie_value, $cookie_expire, "/" ,
$cookie_domain, 0);
```

NOTE

The `setcookie()` function will send a cookie called `auth` with a value of `ok`. It will expire at the end of the browser session and will be valid for all directories on 127.0.0.1. Use your own domain name if appropriate.

---

3. Delete this line:

```
$msg = "<P>Congratulations, you're authorized!</p>";
```

4. Add this string:

```
$display_block = "
<p><strong>Secret Menu:</strong></p>
<ul>
<li><a href=\"secretA.php\">secret page A</a>
<li><a href=\"secretB.php\">secret page B</a>
</ul>";
```

NOTE

Don't worry; you'll create these pages soon enough.

---

5. Scroll until you see the following:

```
<? echo "$msg"; ?>
```

6. Replace it with this:

```
<? echo "$display_block"; ?>
```

7. Save the file.

Your new code should look like this:

```
<?
//check for required fields
if ((!$_POST[username]) || (!$_POST[password])) {
    header("Location: http://127.0.0.1/show_login.html");
    exit;
}

//setup names of database and table to use
```

```php
$db_name = "testDB";
$table_name = "auth_users";
//connect to server and select database
$connection = @mysql_connect("127.0.0.1", "spike", "9sj7En4")
or die(mysql_error());

$db = @mysql_select_db($db_name, $connection) or
die(mysql_error());

//build and issue query
$sql = "SELECT * FROM $table_name WHERE username =
'$_POST[username]' AND password = password('$_POST[password]')";

$result = @mysql_query($sql) or die (mysql_error());

//get the number of rows in the result set
$num = mysql_numrows($result);

//print a message and set a cookie if authorized,
//or redirect elsewhere if unauthorized
if ($num != 0) {
    $cookie_name = "auth";
    $cookie_value = "ok";
    $cookie_expire = "0";
    $cookie_domain = "127.0.0.1";
    setcookie($cookie_name, $cookie_value, $cookie_expire, "/" ,
$cookie_domain, 0);

    $display_block = "
    <p><strong>Secret Menu:</strong></p>
    <ul>
    <li><a href=\"secretA.php\">secret page A</a>
    <li><a href=\"secretB.php\">secret page B</a>
    </ul>";
} else {
    header("Location: http://127.0.0.1/show_login.html");
    exit;
}
?>
<HTML>
<HEAD>
```

```
<TITLE>Secret Area</TITLE>
</HEAD>
<BODY>
<? echo "$display_block"; ?>
</BODY>
</HTML>
```

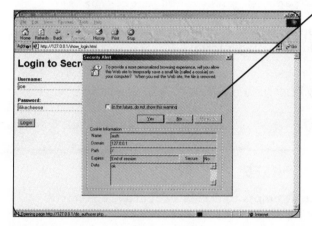

Open your Web browser and type **http://127.0.0.1/show_login.html** to get to the login form, and then enter a valid username and password. If you still have your preferences set to warn before accepting cookies, you'll see a dialog box with cookie information in it. Again, this dialog box differs from browser to browser.

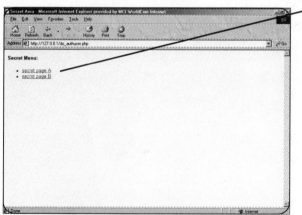

After you click on Yes (or OK, depending on the dialog box), the new menu will display.

Checking for the Authentication Cookie

The secret menu contains links to two files: `secretA.php` and `secretB.php`. By adding a snippet of code to the beginning of these pages, you'll be able to check for an authorized user.

1. Open a new file in your text editor and start a PHP block:

```
<?
```

2. Start an `if...else` block to check the value of `$_COOKIE[auth]`. The value must be `ok` for the user to be an authorized user:

```
if ($_COOKIE[auth] == "ok") {
```

3. Create a value to hold a success message:

```
$msg = "<P>Welcome to secret page A, authorized user!</p>";
```

4. Continue the `if...else` statement to account for an unauthorized visitor. An unauthorized user will be redirected to the login form:

```
} else {
    header( "Location: http://127.0.0.1/show_login.html");
    exit;
}
```

NOTE

A unauthorized visitor is one who attempts to access `secretA.php` directly without going through the authentication process.

---

5. Close the PHP block and type the following HTML:

```
?>
<HTML>
<HEAD>
<TITLE>Secret Page A</TITLE>
</HEAD>
<BODY>
```

6. Display the message:

```
<? echo "$msg"; ?>
```

7. Add some more HTML so that the document is valid:

```
</BODY>
</HTML>
```

8. Save the file with the name `secretA.php` and place this file in the document root of your Web server.

The contents of `secretB.php` should be nearly identical to `secretA.php`, so create another file just like `secretA.php`, only changing "A" to "B" in the messaging.

It's time for some tests. Unless your browser crashed, you should still be logged in (the `auth` cookie hasn't expired), and you should have the secret menu in front of you.

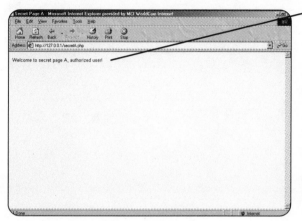

1. Click on the link for secret page A. You should see the success message.

Now exit completely out of your Web browser. This includes closing all browser windows and your mail client (if it's integrated). The `auth` cookie should now have expired (there's nothing to see; it just goes away).

2. Reopen your Web browser, and attempt to directly access `secretB.php` by typing **http://127.0.0.1/secretB.php**

3. Because you are not an authorized user anymore, you should be redirected to the login screen. Go ahead and log back in as an authorized user, and accept the cookie.

4. Click on the link for secret page B.

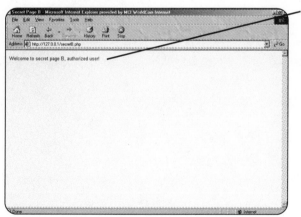

You should see the success message now.

Thus concludes a brief, yet useful, introduction to user authentication.

17

Session Basics

Sessions are like cookies on steroids. Using sessions, you can maintain user-specific information without setting multiple cookies or even using a database. In this chapter, you'll learn how to do the following:

- Start a session
- Add a variable to the $_SESSION superglobal
- Enable a per-user access count
- Maintain user preferences throughout multiple pages

Before You Begin…Check php.ini

Before you start working with sessions, check a value in your `php.ini` file. Look for this section of text and read it carefully:

```
; Argument passed to save_handler. In the case of files, this is
the path
; where data files are stored. Note: Windows users have to change
this
; variable in order to use PHP's session functions.
session.save_path = /tmp
```

To reiterate, you must modify the value of `session.save_path` so that the file can be written to a directory that exists. This change primarily affects Windows users, and the modification is simple: enter a directory name after the = for `session.save_path`.

For example, my `php.ini` file on Windows contains this:

```
session.save_path = c:\Windows\Temp
```

After making the change, restart Apache so that the changes take effect. If you are using Linux/UNIX, `/tmp` is a standard directory, and you can leave this alone unless you want to change it for some compelling reason.

What's a Session?

In terms of time, a *session* is the amount of time during which a user visits a site. In the programming world, a session is kind of like a big blob that can hold all sorts of variables and values.

- This blob has an identification string, such as `940f8b05a40d5119c030c9c7745aead9`.

- This identification string is automatically sent to the user when a session is initiated, in a cookie called `PHPSESSID`.

- On the server side, a matching temporary file is created with the same name (`940f8b05a40d5119c030c9c7745aead9`).

Understanding Session Variables

Session variables (and their values) are stored in the temporary session file on the Web server. Since these values and variables are not kept in a database, no additional system resources are required to connect to and extract information from database tables. You can access session variables through the `$_SESSION` superglobal.

For example, a temporary session file might contain the following:

```
count|s:7:"76";
valid|s:7:"yes";
```

In this example, `count` and `valid` are the names of the session variables and 76 and yes are their respective values. However, to out the variable in the session, you must first explicitly add it to the `$_SESSION` superglobal. Once it is added, you can extract the value (using `$_SESSION[count]` or `$_SESSION[valid]`, in this example).

When you attempt to retrieve a session variable, the sequence goes something like this (say you're trying to get the value of `$_SESSION[count]`):

1. The PHP parser gets the value of `PHPSESSID` from the user cookie.

2. The PHP parser finds a matching temporary session file.

3. Inside the session file, the PHP parser looks for `count` and then finds its value (say, 76).

4. `$_SESSION[count]` is equal to 76.

Next, you'll start your own per-user counter script using a session.

Starting a Session

Starting a session is a snap. You just call the `session_start()` function, and PHP takes care of the rest—sending the cookie and creating the temporary file.

1. Open a new file in your text editor and start a PHP block:

```
<?
```

2. Call the `session_start()` function:

```
session_start();
```

> ### NOTE
>
> The `session_start()` function actually performs several important tasks. First, it checks to see if a session has been started for the current user, and it starts one if necessary. It also alerts the PHP engine that session variables and other session-related functions will be used within the specific script.
>
> Because of the dual purpose of `session_start()`, use it at the beginning of all session-related scripts.

3. Create a string to hold a message:

```
$msg = "started a session....";
```

4. Close the PHP block:

```
?>
```

5. Type the following HTML:

```
<HTML>
<HEAD>
<TITLE>Start a Session</TITLE>
</HEAD>
<BODY>
```

6. Display the message string:

```
<? echo "$msg"; ?>
```

7. Add some more HTML so that the document is valid:

```
</BODY>
</HTML>
```

8. Save the file with the name `session.php` and place this file in the document root of your Web server.

9. Open your Web browser and type **http://127.0.0.1/session.php**

If you still have your preferences set to warn before accepting cookies, you'll see a dialog box like this one (or one appropriate to your browser).

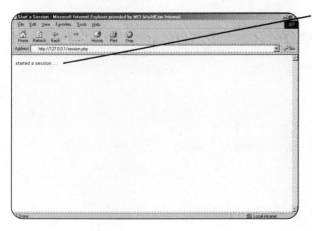

After you click on OK, the message will display.

How inspiring was that? In the next section, you'll register an actual value and watch it change during the course of your session.

Registering and Modifying Session Variables

The goal of this script is to register a variable and change its value during the course of a user session.

1. Open a new file in your text editor, start a PHP block, and call the `session_start()` function:

```
<?
session_start();
```

2. Register a variable called `count`:

```
session_register('count');
```

NOTE

Now, for as long as this session exists, a variable called `$_SESSION[count]` will be available. Currently, the variable has no value.

---

3. Increment the value of `$_SESSION[count]` to account for the current access:

```
$_SESSION[count]++;
```

4. Create a string to hold a message, including the value of `$_SESSION[count]`:

```
$msg = "<P>You've been here $_SESSION[count] times. Thanks!</p>";
```

5. Close the PHP block and type the following HTML:

```
?>
<HTML>
<HEAD>
<TITLE>Count Me!</TITLE>
</HEAD>
<BODY>
```

6. Display the message string:

```
<? echo "$msg"; ?>
```

7. Add some more HTML so that the document is valid:

```
</BODY>
</HTML>
```

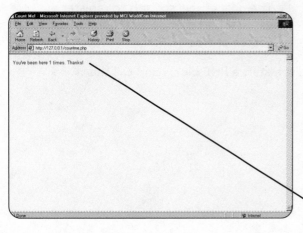

8. Save the file with the name `countme.php` and place this file in the document root of your Web server.

9. Open your Web browser and type **http://127.0.0.1/countme.php**

Unless you closed your Web browser between the last script and now, your old session will still be active and you won't see the cookie approval dialog box. You should just see this.

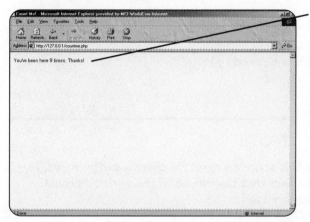

Reload the page several times, and watch how the counter increments by 1 after each reload. For example, I reloaded the page eight times and finally saw this.

In the next section, you'll handle more than just an access count: you'll set and display user preferences during a user session.

Managing User Preferences with Sessions

Moving beyond the simple access counter, you can use sessions to manage your users' preferences when they visit your site. In this three-step example, you'll start a session, ask a user for his font family and base font size preferences, display those preferences on subsequent pages, and allow the user to change his mind and reset the values.

Starting a Session and Registering Defaults

In this script, you'll start a session and register the font_family and font_size variables. The displayed HTML will be a form that allows you to change your preferences.

1. Open a new file in your text editor, start a PHP block, and call the session_start() function:

```
<?
session_start();
```

2. Start an if...else block to check for any previous values for font_family and font_size. If values are not present in the current session, assign default values and add them:

```
if ((!$_SESSION[font_family]) || (!$_SESSION[font_size])) {
    $font_family = "sans-serif";
    $font_size = "10";
    $_SESSION[font_family] = $font_family;
    $_SESSION[font_size] = $font_size;
```

3. If previous values do exist, extract the values from the $_SESSION superglobal.

```
} else {
   $font_family = $_SESSION[font_family];
   $font_size = $_SESSION[font_size];
}
```

NOTE

Since the user will come back to this script to reset his display preferences, you have to take into account the fact that the values of the variables must always be extracted from the session itself.

If you simply added the variables to a session without checking for previous values, each time the page were loaded the value of these variables would be overwritten as an empty string.

---

4. Close the PHP block and type the following HTML:

```
?>
<HTML>
<HEAD>
<TITLE>My Display Preferences</TITLE>
```

5. Create a style sheet block, starting with the opening <STYLE> tag:

```
<STYLE type="text/css">
```

6. Add a style sheet entry for the BODY, P, and A tags. Mingle HTML and PHP to display the current values of $font_family and $font_size:

```
BODY, P, A {font-family:<? echo "$font_family"; ?>;font-size:<?
echo "$font_size"; ?>pt;font-weight:normal;}
```

7. Add a style sheet entry for the H1 tag. Mingle HTML and PHP to display the value of $font_family and a modified value of $font_size (base value plus 4):

```
H1 {font-family:<? echo "$font_family"; ?>;font-size:<? echo
$font_size + 4; ?>pt;font-weight:bold;}
```

8. Close the </STYLE> tag and continue with the HTML, adding a heading and beginning a form. Assume that the form method is POST and the action is session02.php:

```
</STYLE>
</HEAD>
```

```
<BODY>
<H1>Set Your Display Preferences</H1>
<FORM METHOD="POST" ACTION="session02.php">
```

9. Create a set of radio buttons from which the user can choose a new font family:

```
<P>Pick a Font Family:<br>
<input type="radio" name="sel_font_family" value="serif"> serif
<input type="radio" name="sel_font_family" value="sans-serif"
checked> sans-serif
<input type="radio" name="sel_font_family" value="Courier">
Courier
<input type="radio" name="sel_font_family" value="Wingdings">
Wingdings
</p>
```

10. Create a set of radio buttons from which the user can choose a new base font size:

```
<P>Pick a Base Font Size:<br>
<input type="radio" name="sel_font_size" value="8"> 8pt
<input type="radio" name="sel_font_size" value="10" checked> 10pt
<input type="radio" name="sel_font_size" value="12"> 12pt
<input type="radio" name="sel_font_size" value="14"> 14pt
</p>
```

11. Add a submit button and close the form:

```
<P><input type="submit" name="submit" value="Set Display
Preferences"></p>
</FORM>
```

12. Add some more HTML so that the document is valid:

```
</BODY>
</HTML>
```

13. Save the file with the name session01.php and place this file in the document root of your Web server.

Your entire code should look like this:

```
<?
//start a session
session_start();


//check for stored values and register defaults
```

```
if ((!$_SESSION[font_family]) || (!$_SESSION[font_size])) {
    $font_family = "sans-serif";
    $font_size = "10";
    $_SESSION[font_family] = $font_family;
    $_SESSION[font_size] = $font_size;
} else {
    //extract from $_SESSION superglobal if exist
    $font_family = $_SESSION[font_family];
    $font_size = $_SESSION[font_size];
}
?>
<HTML>
<HEAD>
<TITLE>My Display Preferences</TITLE>

<STYLE type="text/css">
BODY, P, A {font-family:<? echo "$font_family"; ?>;font-size:<?
echo "$font_size"; ?>pt;font-weight:normal;}
H1 {font-family:<? echo "$font_family"; ?>;font-size:<? echo
$font_size + 4; ?>pt;font-weight:bold;}
</STYLE>
</HEAD>
<BODY>
<H1>Set Your Display Preferences</H1>
<FORM METHOD="POST" ACTION="session02.php">

<P>Pick a Font Family:<br>
<input type="radio" name="sel_font_family" value="serif"> serif
<input type="radio" name="sel_font_family" value="sans-serif"
checked> sans-serif
<input type="radio" name="sel_font_family" value="Courier">
Courier
<input type="radio" name="sel_font_family" value="Wingdings">
Wingdings
</p>

<P>Pick a Base Font Size:<br>
<input type="radio" name="sel_font_size" value="8"> 8pt
<input type="radio" name="sel_font_size" value="10" checked> 10pt
<input type="radio" name="sel_font_size" value="12"> 12pt
<input type="radio" name="sel_font_size" value="14"> 14pt
```

```
</p>

<P><input type="submit" name="submit" value="Set Display
Preferences"></p>
</FORM>
</BODY>
</HTML>
```

Now open your Web browser and type **http://127.0.0.1/session01.php**.

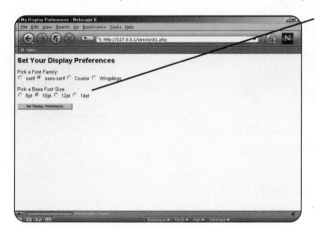

Unless you closed your Web browser between the last script and now, your old session will still be active and you won't see the cookie approval dialog box. You should just see what's in the figure.

In the next section, you'll create the script that handles the preference changes.

Making Preference Changes

In this script, you'll assign the new values for font_family and font_size and display a confirmation that the changes have been made.

1. Open a new file in your text editor, start a PHP block, and call the session_start() function:

```
<?
session_start();
```

2. Start an if...else block to check for the posted values for font_family and font_size. If values are present, add them in the session.

```
if (($_POST[sel_font_family]) && ($_POST[sel_font_size])) {
    $font_family = $_POST[sel_font_family];
    $font_size = $_POST[sel_font_size];
    $_SESSION[font_family] = $font_family;
    $_SESSION[font_size] = $font_size;
```

3. Continue the block to check for previously stored values for `font_family` and `font_size`, but only if the posted values are not present.

```
} else if (((!$_POST[sel_font_family]) &&
(!$_POST[sel_font_size])) && ($_SESSION[font_family]) &&
($_SESSION[font_size])) {
    $font_family = $_SESSION[font_family];
    $font_size = $_SESSION[font_size];
    $_SESSION[font_family] = $font_family;
    $_SESSION[font_size] = $font_size;
```

4. Finally, if values are not present from the form or from a previous session, define and add some defaults:

```
} else {
    $font_family = "sans-serif";
    $font_size = "10";
    $_SESSION[font_family] = $font_family;
    $_SESSION[font_size] = $font_size;
}
```

5. Close the PHP block and type the following HTML:

```
?>
<HTML>
<HEAD>
<TITLE>My Display Preferences</TITLE>
```

6. Create a style sheet block, starting with the opening `<STYLE>` tag:

```
<STYLE type="text/css">
```

7. Add a style sheet entry for the `BODY`, `P`, and `A` tags. Mingle HTML and PHP to display the current value of `$font_family` and `$font_size`:

```
BODY, P, A {font-family:<? echo "$font_family"; ?>;font-size:<?
echo "$font_size"; ?>pt;font-weight:normal;}
```

8. Add a style sheet entry for the `H1` tag. Mingle HTML and PHP to display the value of `$font_family` and a modified value of `$font_size` (base value plus 4):

```
H1 {font-family:<? echo "$font_family"; ?>;font-size:<? echo
$font_size + 4; ?>pt;font-weight:bold;}
```

9. Close the `</STYLE>` tag and continue with the HTML, displaying the values of the two registered session variables:

```
</STYLE>
</HEAD>
<BODY>
<H1>Your Preferences Have Been Set</H1>
<P>As you can see, your selected font family is now <? echo
"$font_family"; ?>, with a base size of <? echo "$font_size" ?>
pt.</p>
```

10. Provide a link back to `session01.php` in case the user wants to change preferences again, then add some more HTML so that the document is valid:

```
<P>Please feel free to <a href="session01.php">change your
preferences</a> again.</p>
</BODY>
</HTML>
```

11. Save the file with the name `session02.php` and place this file in the document root of your Web server.

Your entire code should look like this:

```
<?
//start a session
session_start();

//check for posted values and register defaults
if (($_POST[sel_font_family]) && ($_POST[sel_font_size])) {
   $font_family = $_POST[sel_font_family];
   $font_size = $_POST[sel_font_size];
   $_SESSION[font_family] = $font_family;
   $_SESSION[font_size] = $font_size;
//check for stored values, extract from $_SESSION superglobal and
register
} else if (((!$_POST[sel_font_family]) &&
(!$_POST[sel_font_size])) && ($_SESSION[font_family]) &&
($_SESSION[font_size])) {
   $font_family = $_SESSION[font_family];
   $font_size = $_SESSION[font_size];
   $_SESSION[font_family] = $font_family;
   $_SESSION[font_size] = $font_size;
//register defaults
} else {
```

```
    $font_family = "sans-serif";
    $font_size = "10";
    $_SESSION[font_family] = $font_family;
    $_SESSION[font_size] = $font_size;
}
?>
<HTML>
<HEAD>
<TITLE>My Display Preferences</TITLE>
<STYLE type="text/css">
BODY, P, A {font-family:<? echo "$font_family"; ?>;font-size:<?
echo "$font_size"; ?>pt;font-weight:normal;}
H1 {font-family:<? echo "$font_family"; ?>;font-size:<? echo
$font_size + 4; ?>pt;font-weight:bold;}
</STYLE>
</HEAD>
<BODY>
<H1>Your Preferences Have Been Set</H1>
<P>As you can see, your selected font family is now <? echo
"$font_family"; ?>, with a base size of <? echo "$font_size" ?>
pt.</p>
<P>Please feel free to <a href="session01.php">change your
preferences</a> again.</p>
</BODY>
</HTML>
```

Unless you closed your Web browser between the last script and now, you should still be staring at the font family and font size selection form.

1. Select sans-serif for the font family.

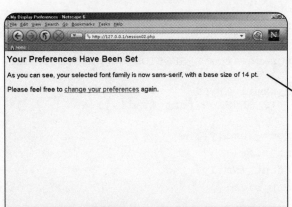

2. Select 14 pt for the base font size.

3. Click on the Set Display Preferences button.

The page is displayed using your selected font family and base font size, and the changes are confirmed.

Displaying Changes

This is getting fun! With your Web browser still open to the confirmation screen for the initial preference changes, click on the Change Your Preferences link.

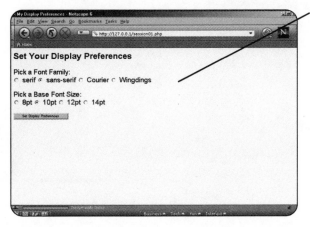

The selection form is also displayed using your new font family and base font size.

1. Select Courier for the font family.

2. Select 8 pt for the base font size.

3. Click on the Set Display Preferences button.

The page is displayed using your selected font family and base font size, and the changes are confirmed. Click on the Change Your Preferences link, and the selection form is displayed using your new font family and base font size.

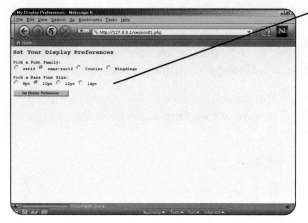

Continue changing the font family and sizes, and you'll quickly discover which preferences you like and which are simply annoying!

PART VI

Creating Your Own Contact Management System

18

Planning Your System

The first step in good application design is having a plan. Although improvisation along the way is sometimes a good thing, it's best to start with a solid foundation and a series of goals. The next several chapters will help you create a contact management system—an online address book. In this chapter, you'll learn how to do the following:

- Define administrative tasks and create a menu
- Modify the table-creation script sequence to account for primary keys and auto-incrementing fields
- Define and create the `my_contacts` table

Planning and Creating the Administration Menu

Not only will you be able to view data within your system, but you'll also be able to add, modify, and delete contacts. A menu would be good—one that provides links to all your action scripts and adds some authentication to the mix so that only you can see the data. Now create all that in one script!

1. Open a new file in your text editor and start a PHP block:

```
<?
```

2. Start a session, or continue a session if a session currently exists:

```
session_start();
```

3. Start an if...else block that checks for the value of the $_POST[op] variable, which is a hidden variable in the login form you'll soon create:

```
if ($_POST[op] == "ds") {
```

4. If the value of $_POST[op] is ds, the user has completed the form. Start another if...else block that checks the validity of the username and password entered by the user:

```
if (($_POST[username] != "admin") || ($_POST[password] !=
"abc123")) {
```

NOTE

You can use any username and password you'd like. This script checks that the username is admin and that the password is abc123.

---

5. If either the username or password is incorrect, create a variable called $msg to hold an error message:

```
$msg = "<P><font color=\"#FF0000\"><strong>Bad Login - Try Again</
strong></font></P>";
```

6. Create a variable called $show_form, and give it a value of yes. This value will be checked later in the script to determine what to display:

```
$show_form = "yes";
```

7. Continue the if...else statement:

```
} else {
```

8. If the user makes it this far, the username and password are correct. Create a variable called $valid, with a value of yes, and then add the session variable called valid, with a value of $valid:

```
$valid = "yes";
$_SESSION[valid] = $valid;
```

9. Create a variable called $show_menu, and give it a value of yes. This value will be checked later in the script to determine what to display:

```
$show_menu = "yes";
```

10. Close the inner if...else block:

```
}
```

11. Continue the outer if...else block:

```
} else {
```

12. If the user is within this section of the outer if...else block, he has reached this script without going through the form. Check for the value of $_SESSION[valid], and determine what to show—menu or form:

```
if ($_SESSION[valid] == "yes") {
    $show_menu = "yes";
} else {
    $show_form = "yes";
}
```

13. Close the outer if...else block:

```
}
```

14. Create the form block, which will be shown if the user has not logged in or if the login is incorrect. Start by creating the variable and printing a header:

```
$form_block = "
<h1>Login</h1>
```

15. Start the form. In this case, the method is POST and the action is a variable called $_SERVER[PHP_SELF]:

```
<form method=POST action=\"$_SERVER[PHP_SELF]\">
```

NOTE

$_SERVER[PHP_SELF] is a global variable whose value is equal to the name of the current script. By using $_SERVER[PHP_SELF] as a form action, you're essentially saying, "When the submit button is clicked, reload me!"

---

16. Print the value of $msg:

```
$msg
```

NOTE

If the login is incorrect, $msg will contain a value, and that value will be printed in this space. If $msg was not created or a value was not given, nothing will print, so it doesn't hurt anything by being present.

---

17. Create input fields for the username and password with text labels:

```
<P><strong>username:</strong><br>
<input type=\"text\" name=\"username\" size=15 maxlength=25></P>
<P><strong>password:</strong><br>
<input type=\"password\" name=\"password\" size=15 maxlength=25></P>
```

18. Add the hidden field for op:

```
<input type=\"hidden\" name=\"op\" value=\"ds\">
```

19. Add the submit button, and close the form and string:

```
<P><input type=\"submit\" name=\"submit\" value=\"login\"></P>
</FORM>";
```

20. Create the menu block, which will be shown if a user has logged in and is valid. Start by creating the variable and printing a header:

```
$menu_block = "
<h1>My Contact Administration System</h1>
```

21. Add several menu items, and then close the string:

```
<P><strong>Administration</strong>
<ul>
```

```
<li><a href=\"show_addcontact.php\">Add a Contact</a>
<li><a href=\"pick_modcontact.php\">Modify a Contact</a>
<li><a href=\"pick_delcontact.php\">Delete a Contact</a>
</ul>

<P><strong>View Records</strong>
<ul>
<li><a href=\"show_contactsbyname.php\">Show Contacts, Ordered by
Name</a>
</ul>";
```

22. Use an if…else block to perform a final check to see which should be displayed—$form_block or $menu_block. Whichever should be displayed should be the value of a new variable called $display_block:

```
if ($show_form == "yes") {
    $display_block = $form_block;
} else if ($show_menu == "yes") {
    $display_block = $menu_block;
}
```

23. Close your PHP block and add HTML:

```
?>
<HTML>
<HEAD>
<TITLE>My Contact Management System</TITLE>
</HEAD>
<BODY>
```

24. Display the results:

```
<? echo "$display_block"; ?>
```

25. Add some more HTML to make a valid document:

```
</BODY>
</HTML>
```

26. Save the file with the name contact_menu.php and place this file in the document root of your Web server.

You just created a heck of a lot of code. It should look something like this:

```
<?
//start a session
```

```php
session_start();

//check if user is coming from a form
if ($_POST[op] == "ds") {

    //check username and password
    if (($_POST[username] != "admin") || ($_POST[password] !=
"abc123")) {

        //handle bad login
        $msg = "<P><font color=\"#FF0000\"><strong>Bad Login - Try
Again</strong></font></P>";
        $show_form = "yes";
    } else {

        //handle good login
        $valid = "yes";
        $_SESSION[valid] = $valid;
        $show_menu = "yes";

    }
} else {

    //determine what to show
    if ($valid == "yes") {
        $show_menu = "yes";
    } else {
    $show_form = "yes";
    }
}

//build form block
$form_block = "
<h1>Login</h1>
<form method=POST action=\"$_SERVER[PHP_SELF]\">
$msg
<P><strong>username:</strong><br>
<input type=\"text\" name=\"username\" size=15 maxlength=25></P>
<P><strong>password:</strong><br>
<input type=\"password\" name=\"password\" size=15 maxlength=25>
</P>
<input type=\"hidden\" name=\"op\" value=\"ds\">
```

```
<P><input type=\"submit\" name=\"submit\" value=\"login\"></P>
</FORM>";

//build menu block
$menu_block = "
<h1>My Contact Administration System</h1>
<P><strong>Administration</strong>
<ul>
<li><a href=\"show_addcontact.php\">Add a Contact</a>
<li><a href=\"pick_modcontact.php\">Modify a Contact</a>
<li><a href=\"pick_delcontact.php\">Delete a Contact</a>
</ul>

<P><strong>View Records</strong>
<ul>
<li><a href=\"show_contactsbyname.php\">Show Contacts, Ordered by
Name</a>
</ul>";

//assign the block to show to the $display_block variable
if ($show_form == "yes") {
    $display_block = $form_block;
} else if ($show_menu == "yes") {
    $display_block = $menu_block;
}
?>
<HTML>
<HEAD>
<TITLE>My Contact Management System</TITLE>
</HEAD>
<BODY>
<? echo "$display_block"; ?>
</BODY>
</HTML>
```

Logging In to the Administration Menu

Now try to log in to the administration menu using the hard-coded username and password from the script.

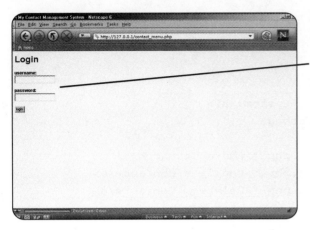

1. Open your Web browser and type **http://127.0.0.1/contact_menu.php**

You will see the login form with text fields for the username and password as well as a submit button.

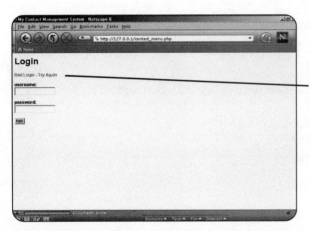

2. Type a bad username and/or a bad password in the appropriate fields, and then click on the login button.

You will see the login form again, with a red error message displayed.

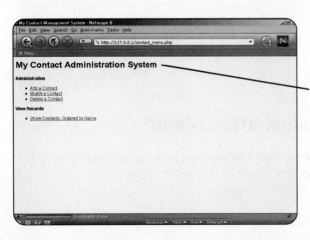

3. Type the correct username (**admin**) and the correct password (**abc123**), and then click on the login button.

You will see the Administrative Menu for your contact management system.

In the next section, you'll take a step back and create the my_contacts table so that you can perform all the tasks listed in this fancy administration menu!

Defining the my_contacts Table

Take a moment to think about the kinds of things you'd want in a contact management system: names, addresses, telephone numbers of all sorts, e-mail addresses, and maybe even the person's birthday.

I thought about what I wanted for my own table, which I've decided to call `my_contacts`. This information appears in Table 18.1.

Table 18.1 Fields for my_contacts

Field Name	Description
id	Creates a unique ID number for the entry
f_name	The person's first name
l_name	The person's last name
address1	First line of the address
address2	Second line of the address
address3	Third line of the address
postcode	Zip or postal code
country	Country in which the person resides
prim_tel	Primary telephone number
sec_tel	Secondary telephone number
email	E-mail address
birthday	The person's birthday

In the next section, you'll modify the table-creation scripts from Chapter 12, "Creating a Database Table." You'll also add the ability to name primary keys and auto-incrementing fields.

Modifying the Table-Creation Scripts

With a few minor modifications to two of the three scripts in the table-creation sequence from Chapter 12, you can add check boxes to the form to handle primary keys and auto-incrementing fields. These types of fields are incredibly useful for ID fields.

1. Open `do_showfielddef.php` in your text editor, find the section of `$form_block` that prints table headings, and add the following before the end of the row:

```
<TH>PRIMARY KEY?</TH><TH>AUTO-INCREMENT?</TH>
```

2. In the `$form_block` within the `for` loop, the next-to-last line prints a text field with a name of `field_length[]`. After that line, and before the end of the table row, put these two lines:

```
<TD ALIGN=CENTER><INPUT TYPE=\"checkbox\" NAME=\"primary[]\"
VALUE=\"Y\"></TD>
<TD ALIGN=CENTER><INPUT TYPE=\"checkbox\"
NAME=\"auto_increment[]\" VALUE=\"Y\"></TD>
```

3. Save this file.

Your modified code for this script should look something like this:

```
<?
//validate important input
if ((!$_POST[table_name]) || (!$_POST[num_fields])) {
    header( "Location: http://127.0.0.1/show_createtable.html");
    exit;
}
//begin creating form for display
$form_block = "
<FORM METHOD=\"POST\" ACTION=\"do_createtable.php\">
<INPUT TYPE=\"hidden\" NAME=\"table_name\"
VALUE=\"$_POST[table_name]\">
<TABLE CELLSPACING=5 CELLPADDING=5>
<TR>
<TH>FIELD NAME</TH><TH>FIELD TYPE</TH><TH>FIELD LENGTH</
TH><TH>PRIMARY KEY?</TH><TH>AUTO-INCREMENT?</TH></TR>";

//count from 0 until you reach the number of fields
for ($i = 0; $i <$_POST[num_fields]; $i++) {
    //add to the form, one row for each field
    $form_block .= "
    <TR>
    <TD ALIGN=CENTER><INPUT TYPE=\"text\" NAME=\"field_name[]\"
SIZE=\"30\"></TD>
    <TD ALIGN=CENTER>
    <SELECT NAME=\"field_type[]\">
```

```
        <OPTION VALUE=\"char\">char</OPTION>
        <OPTION VALUE=\"date\">date</OPTION>
        <OPTION VALUE=\"float\">float</OPTION>
        <OPTION VALUE=\"int\">int</OPTION>
        <OPTION VALUE=\"text\">text</OPTION>
        <OPTION VALUE=\"varchar\">varchar</OPTION>
    </SELECT>
    </TD>
    <TD ALIGN=CENTER><INPUT TYPE=\"text\" NAME=\"field_length[]\"
SIZE=\"5\"></TD>
    <TD ALIGN=CENTER><INPUT TYPE=\"checkbox\" NAME=\"primary[]\"
VALUE=\"Y\"></TD>
    <TD ALIGN=CENTER><INPUT TYPE=\"checkbox\"
NAME=\"auto_increment[]\" VALUE=\"Y\"></TD>
    </TR>";
}


//finish up the form
$form_block .= "
<TR>
<TD ALIGN=CENTER COLSPAN=3><INPUT TYPE=\"submit\" VALUE=\"Create
Table\"></TD>
</TR>
</TABLE>
</FORM>";
?>
<HTML>
<HEAD>
<TITLE>Create a Database Table: Step 2</TITLE>
</HEAD>
<BODY>
<H1>Define fields for <? echo "$_POST[table_name]"; ?></H1>
<? echo "$form_block"; ?>
</BODY>
</HTML>
```

Next, you will modify the final part of the table-creation script.

1. Open do_createtable.php in your text editor.

2. Within the for loop, the first line appends text to the $sql variable, which holds the SQL statement for table creation. Since you've added two check boxes for additional elements of the SQL statement, you need to check for them. Start by creating an `if…else` block that checks whether the `auto_increment` check box has been checked:

```
if ($_POST[auto_increment][$i] == "Y") {
```

3. If the `auto_increment` check box has been checked, create a variable to hold additional SQL options:

```
$additional = "NOT NULL auto_increment";
```

NOTE

When you define a field as `auto_increment`, it must also be defined as `NOT NULL`.

4. If the `auto_increment` check box hasn't been checked, create the variable but do not place any text in it, and then close the block. This will assist in resetting the value of the string to an empty value as the looping continues:

```
} else {
    $additional = "";
}
```

5. Create an `if…else` block that checks whether the primary key check box has been checked:

```
if ($_POST[primary][$i] == "Y") {
```

6. If the primary key check box has been checked, append the primary key syntax to the `$additional` variable:

```
$additional .= ", primary key (".$_POST[field_name][$i].")";
```

NOTE

The syntax for naming a field as a primary key is separated by a comma from the initial field definition. It looks something like this: `primary key (field_name)`

7. If the primary key check box hasn't been checked, append an empty value to the `$additional` value, and then close the block:

```
} else {
   $additional = "";
}
```

8. The last change is to the pre-existing loop that checks for field length and creates part of the SQL statement. Find the line that looks like this:

```
$sql .= " (".$_POST[field_length][$i]."),";
```

9. Change the line so that it looks like the following. This ensures that the `$additional` string is placed in the proper section of the SQL statement:

```
$sql .= " (".$_POST[field_length][$i].") $additional ,";
```

10. Similarly, find a line that looks like this:

```
$sql .= ",";
```

11. Change the line so that it looks like the following:

```
$sql .= " $additional ,";
```

12. Save the file.

Your modified code for this script should look something like this:

```
<?
//indicate the database you want to use
$db_name = "testDB";

//connect to database
$connection = @mysql_connect("localhost", "spike", "9sj7En4")
   or die(mysql_error());
$db = @mysql_select_db($db_name, $connection) or
die(mysql_error());

//start creating the SQL statement
$sql = "CREATE TABLE $_POST[table_name] (";

//continue the SQL statement for each new field
for ($i = 0; $i < count($_POST[field_name]); $i++) {
   $sql .= $_POST[field_name][$i]." ".$_POST[field_type][$i];

   if ($_POST[auto_increment][$i] == "Y") {
```

```
        $additional = "NOT NULL auto_increment";
    } else {
    $additional = "";
    }

    if ($_POST[primary][$i] == "Y") {
        $additional .= ", primary key (".$_POST[field_name][$i].")";
    } else {
        $additional = "";
    }

    if ($_POST[field_length][$i] != "") {
        $sql .= " (".$_POST[field_length][$i].") $additional ,";
    } else {
        $sql .= " $additional ,";
    }

}

//clean up the end of the string
$sql = substr($sql, 0, -1);
$sql .= ")";

//execute the query
$result = mysql_query($sql,$connection) or die(mysql_error());

//get a good message for display upon success
if ($result) {
    $msg = "<P>".$_POST[table_name]." has been created!</P>";
}
?>
<HTML>
<HEAD>
<TITLE>Create a Database Table: Step 3</TITLE>
</HEAD>
<BODY>
<h1>Adding table to <? echo "$db_name"; ?>...</h1>
<? echo "$msg"; ?>
</BODY>
</HTML>
```

In the next section, you'll use these new scripts to create the my_contacts table.

Creating the my_contacts Table

It's time to create the my_contacts table, complete with one primary key and auto-incrementing field!

1. Open your Web browser and type **http://127.0.0.1/show_createtable.html**

2. In the Table Name field, type **my_contacts**.

3. In the Number of Fields field, type **12**.

4. Click on the Go to Step 2 button.

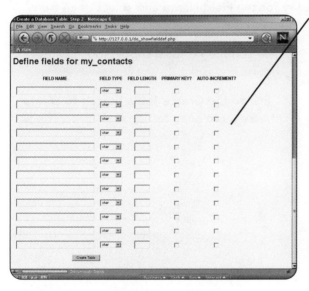

You will see a form with 12 rows, corresponding to the 12 fields you want to create in the my_contacts table. Populate the fields in these next steps:

1. In the first row, type **id** for the Field Name, select int from the Field Type drop-down menu, check the check box for Primary Key, and check the check box for Auto-Increment.

2. In the second row, type **f_name** for the Field Name, select varchar from the Field Type drop-down menu, and specify a Field Length of **75**.

3. In the third row, type **l_name** for the Field Name, select varchar from the Field Type drop-down menu, and specify a Field Length of **75**.

4. In the fourth row, type **address1** for the Field Name, select varchar from the Field Type drop-down menu, and specify a Field Length of **100**.

5. In the fifth row, type **address2** for the Field Name, select varchar from the Field Type drop-down menu, and specify a Field Length of **100**.

6. In the sixth row, type **address3** for the Field Name, select varchar from the Field Type drop-down menu, and specify a Field Length of **100**.

7. In the seventh row, type **postcode** for the Field Name, select varchar from the Field Type drop-down menu, and specify a Field Length of **25**.

8. In the eighth row, type **country** for the Field Name, select varchar from the Field Type drop-down menu, and specify a Field Length of **100**.

9. In the ninth row, type **prim_tel** for the Field Name, select varchar from the Field Type drop-down menu, and specify a Field Length of **35**.

10. In the tenth row, type **sec_tel** for the Field Name, select varchar from the Field Type drop-down menu, and specify a Field Length of **35**.

11. In the eleventh row, type **email** for the Field Name, select varchar from the Field Type drop-down menu, and specify a Field Length of **100**.

12. In the twelfth row, type **birthday** for the Field Name and select date from the Field Type drop-down menu.

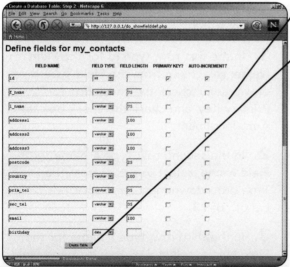

The completed form should look like the figure.

Click on the Create Table button to create the my_contacts table.

Congratulations! The table has been created. In the next chapter, you'll create the record addition interface for this table. You'll be well on your way to creating a contact management system!

19

Adding Contacts

You're one step down the development path: you have the my_contacts table all created, waiting for contacts to be added. In this chapter, you'll learn how to do the following:

- Create an administrative interface for adding a record
- Create a script to insert the record into your table
- Require session-based authentication before the script can be viewed or the record can be added

Creating the Record-Addition Form

The HTML form will contain an input field for each column in the `my_contacts` table. In the previous chapter, you created 12 fields, which correspond to 12 columns. Your record-addition interface should have a space for each of these fields, except the ID field, which can be left blank.

NOTE

Because the ID field is an auto-incrementing field, if you add a record and leave the field blank, MySQL will place the next-highest number in that field.

---

1. Open a new file in your text editor and start a PHP block:

```
<?
```

2. Start a session, or continue a session if a session currently exists:

```
session_start();
```

3. Start an if...else block that checks the value of `$_SESSION[valid]` and performs a particular action based on the result. If the value is not `yes`, the user didn't go through the proper authentication channels:

```
if ($_SESSION[valid] != "yes") {
```

4. Send the user back to the login form, and exit this script:

```
header("Location: http://127.0.0.1/contact_menu.php");
exit;
```

5. Close your PHP block, then type this HTML to start building the record-addition form:

```
?>
<HTML>
<HEAD>
<TITLE>My Contact Management System: Add a Contact</TITLE>
</HEAD>
<BODY>
<h1>My Contact Management System</h1>
<h2><em>Add a Contact</em></h2>
```

6. Begin your form. Assume that the method is POST and the action is a script called do_addcontact.php:

```
<FORM METHOD="POST" ACTION="do_addcontact.php">
```

7. Begin an HTML table to assist in layout. Start a new table row, add two column headings, and then close that row:

```
<table cellspacing=3 cellpadding=5>
<tr>
<th>NAME & ADDRESS INFORMATION</th>
<th>OTHER CONTACT/PERSONAL INFORMATION</th>
</tr>
```

8. Start a new table row and table data cell, and then create an input field for the person's first name with a text label:

```
<tr>
<td valign=top>
<P><STRONG>First Name:</STRONG><BR>
<INPUT TYPE="text" NAME="f_name" SIZE=35 MAXLENGTH=75></P>
```

9. In the same table data cell, create an input field for the person's last name with a text label:

```
<P><STRONG>Last Name:</STRONG><BR>
<INPUT TYPE="text" NAME="l_name" SIZE=35 MAXLENGTH=75></P>
```

10. In the same table data cell, create an input field for the person's address (first line) with a text label:

```
<P><STRONG>Address Line 1:</STRONG><BR>
<INPUT TYPE="text" NAME="address1" SIZE=35 MAXLENGTH=100></P>
```

11. In the same table data cell, create an input field for the person's address (second line) with a text label:

```
<P><STRONG>Address Line 2:</STRONG><BR>
<INPUT TYPE="text" NAME="address2" SIZE=35 MAXLENGTH=100></P>
```

12. In the same table data cell, create an input field for the person's address (third line) with a text label:

```
<P><STRONG>Address Line 3:</STRONG><BR>
<INPUT TYPE="text" NAME="address3" SIZE=35 MAXLENGTH=100></P>
```

13. In the same table data cell, create an input field for the person's zip/postal code with a text label:

```
<P><STRONG>Zip/Postal Code:</STRONG><BR>
<INPUT TYPE="text" NAME="postcode" SIZE=35 MAXLENGTH=25></P>
```

14. In the same table data cell, create an input field for the person's country with a text label. Close the table data cell after this input field:

```
<P><STRONG>Country:</STRONG><BR>
<INPUT TYPE="text" NAME="country" SIZE=35 MAXLENGTH=100></P>
</td>
```

15. In a new table data cell, create an input field for the person's primary telephone number with a text label:

```
<td valign=top>
<P><STRONG>Primary Telephone Number:</STRONG><BR>
<INPUT TYPE="text" NAME="prim_tel" SIZE=35 MAXLENGTH=35></P>
```

16. In the same table data cell, create an input field for the person's secondary telephone number with a text label:

```
<P><STRONG>Secondary Telephone Number:</STRONG><BR>
<INPUT TYPE="text" NAME="sec_tel" SIZE=35 MAXLENGTH=35></P>
```

17. In the same table data cell, create an input field for the person's e-mail address with a text label:

```
<P><STRONG>E-mail Address:</STRONG><BR>
<INPUT TYPE="text" NAME="email" SIZE=35 MAXLENGTH=100></P>
```

18. In the same table data cell, create an input field for the person's birthday with a text label. Close the table data cell and the table row after this input field:

```
<P><STRONG>Birthday (YYYY-MM-DD):</STRONG><BR>
<INPUT TYPE="text" NAME="birthday" SIZE=10 MAXLENGTH=10></P>
</td>
</tr>
```

NOTE

The date type used in MySQL uses the YYYY-MM-DD format. An example of a date using this format is 2002-03-20 (March 20, 2002).

19. Start a new table row and table data cell that spans two columns. Inside, add a submit button as well as a link back to the main menu. Close the table data cell, the table row, and the table itself:

```
<tr>
<td align=center colspan=2><br>
<P><INPUT TYPE="SUBMIT" NAME="submit" VALUE="Add Contact to
System"></P>
<p><a href="contact_menu.php">Return to Main Menu</a></p>

</TD>
</TR>
</TABLE>
```

20. Close your form and add some more HTML so that the document is valid:

```
</FORM>
</BODY>
</HTML>
```

21. Save the file with the name show_addcontact.php, then place this file in the document root of your Web server.

Your code should look something like this:

```
<?
//start a session
session_start();

//validate user to see if they are allowed to be here
if ($_SESSION[valid] != "yes") {
    header("Location: http://127.0.0.1/contact_menu.php");
    exit;
}
?>
<HTML>
<HEAD>
<TITLE>My Contact Management System: Add a Contact</TITLE>
</HEAD>
<BODY>
<h1>My Contact Management System</h1>
<h2><em>Add a Contact</em></h2>
<FORM METHOD="POST" ACTION="do_addcontact.php">
```

```html
<table cellspacing=3 cellpadding=5>
<tr>
<th>NAME & ADDRESS INFORMATION</th>
<th>OTHER CONTACT/PERSONAL INFORMATION</th>
</tr>
<tr>
<td valign=top>
<P><STRONG>First Name:</STRONG><BR>
<INPUT TYPE="text" NAME="f_name" SIZE=35 MAXLENGTH=75></P>
<P><STRONG>Last Name:</STRONG><BR>
<INPUT TYPE="text" NAME="l_name" SIZE=35 MAXLENGTH=75></P>
<P><STRONG>Address Line 1:</STRONG><BR>
<INPUT TYPE="text" NAME="address1" SIZE=35 MAXLENGTH=100></P>
<P><STRONG>Address Line 2:</STRONG><BR>
<INPUT TYPE="text" NAME="address2" SIZE=35 MAXLENGTH=100></P>
<P><STRONG>Address Line 3:</STRONG><BR>
<INPUT TYPE="text" NAME="address3" SIZE=35 MAXLENGTH=100></P>
<P><STRONG>Zip/Postal Code:</STRONG><BR>
<INPUT TYPE="text" NAME="postcode" SIZE=35 MAXLENGTH=25></P>
<P><STRONG>Country:</STRONG><BR>
<INPUT TYPE="text" NAME="country" SIZE=35 MAXLENGTH=100></P>
</td>
<td valign=top>
<P><STRONG>Primary Telephone Number:</STRONG><BR>
<INPUT TYPE="text" NAME="prim_tel" SIZE=35 MAXLENGTH=35></P>
<P><STRONG>Secondary Telephone Number:</STRONG><BR>
<INPUT TYPE="text" NAME="sec_tel" SIZE=35 MAXLENGTH=35></P>
<P><STRONG>E-mail Address:</STRONG><BR>
<INPUT TYPE="text" NAME="email" SIZE=35 MAXLENGTH=100></P>
<P><STRONG>Birthday (YYYY-MM-DD):</STRONG><BR>
<INPUT TYPE="text" NAME="birthday" SIZE=10 MAXLENGTH=10></P>
</td>
</tr>
<tr>
<td align=center colspan=2><br>
<P><INPUT TYPE="SUBMIT" NAME="submit" VALUE="Add Contact to
System"></P>
<p><a href="contact_menu.php">Return to Main Menu</a></p>
</TD>
</TR>
</TABLE>
```

```
</FORM>
</BODY>
</HTML>
```

In the next section, you'll create the script that takes the form input, creates a SQL statement, and adds the record to the database table.

Creating the Record-Addition Script

This script will add your record to the `my_contacts` table, taking into consideration the auto-incrementing ID field.

1. Open a new file in your text editor and start a PHP block:

```
<?
```

2. Start an `if...else` block that checks for values in `$_POST[f_name]` and `$_POST[1_name]`. If they don't have values, direct the user back to the form and exit the script:

```
if ((!$_POST[f_name]) || (!$_POST[1_name])) {
    header( "Location: http://127.0.0.1/show_addcontact.php");
    exit;
```

> ### NOTE
> You can have as many (or as few) required fields as you'd like.

3. If the required fields have values, start a session, or continue a session if one currently exists. Then close the block:

```
} else {
    session_start();
}
```

4. Start an `if...else` block that checks the value of `$_SESSION[valid]` and performs a particular action based on the result. If the value is not `yes`, the user didn't go through the proper authentication channels:

```
if ($_SESSION[valid] != "yes") {
```

5. Send the user back to the login form, and exit this script:

```
header("Location: http://127.0.0.1/contact_menu.php");
exit;
}
```

6. Create a variable to hold the name of the database on which the table resides:

```
$db_name = "testDB";
```

7. Create a variable to hold the name of the table you're populating with this script:

```
$table_name = "my_contacts";
```

8. Add the connection information as you have been:

```
$connection = @mysql_connect("localhost", "spike", "9sj7En4")
or die(mysql_error());
```

9. Select the database as you have learned:

```
$db = @mysql_select_db($db_name, $connection) or
die(mysql_error());
```

10. Create the SQL statement. The first parenthetical statement gives the names of the fields to populate (in order), and the second parenthetical statement sends the actual strings:

```
$sql = "INSERT INTO $table_name (id, f_name, l_name, address1,
address2, address3, postcode, country, prim_tel, sec_tel, email,
birthday) VALUES ('', '$_POST[f_name]', '$_POST[l_name]',
'$_POST[address1]', '$_POST[address2]', '$_POST[address3]',
'$_POST[postcode]', '$_POST[country]', '$_POST[prim_tel]',
'$_POST[sec_tel]', '$_POST[email]', '$_POST[birthday]')";
```

> **NOTE**
>
> Leaving a blank slot for the ID field will ensure that the field auto-increments on its own.

11. Create a variable to hold the result of the `mysql_query()` function, as you have learned:

```
$result = @mysql_query($sql,$connection) or die(mysql_error());
```

12. Close your PHP block and add this HTML:

```
?>
<HTML>
<HEAD>
<TITLE>My Contact Management System: Contact Added</TITLE>
</HEAD>
<BODY>
<h1>My Contact Management System</h1>
<h2><em>Add a Contact - Contact Added</em></h2>
```

13. Add a confirmation statement. Mingle HTML and PHP to include the value of the $table_name variable:

```
<P>The following information was successfully added to
<? echo "$table_name"; ?></P>
```

14. Next, you'll re-create the layout used in show_addcontact.php, only it won't contain form fields. Instead, you'll mingle HTML and PHP to show the values that were entered.

```
<table cellspacing=3 cellpadding=5>
<tr>
<th>NAME & ADDRESS INFORMATION</th>
<th>OTHER CONTACT/PERSONAL INFORMATION</th>
</tr>
<tr>
<td valign=top>
<P><STRONG>First Name:</STRONG><BR>
<? echo "$_POST[f_name]"; ?></P>
<P><STRONG>Last Name:</STRONG><BR>
<? echo "$_POST[l_name]"; ?></P>
<P><STRONG>Address Line 1:</STRONG><BR>
<? echo "$_POST[address1]"; ?></P>
<P><STRONG>Address Line 2:</STRONG><BR>
<? echo "$_POST[address2]"; ?></P>
<P><STRONG>Address Line 3:</STRONG><BR>
<? echo "$_POST[address3]"; ?></P>
<P><STRONG>Zip/Postal Code:</STRONG><BR>
<? echo "$_POST[postcode]"; ?></P>
<P><STRONG>Country:</STRONG><BR>
<? echo "$_POST[country]"; ?></P>
</td>
```

```
<td valign=top>
<P><STRONG>Primary Telephone Number:</STRONG><BR>
<? echo "$_POST[prim_tel]"; ?></P>
<P><STRONG>Secondary Telephone Number:</STRONG><BR>
<? echo "$_POST[sec_tel]"; ?></P>
<P><STRONG>E-mail Address:</STRONG><BR>
<? echo "$_POST[email]"; ?></P>
<P><STRONG>Birthday (YYYY-MM-DD):</STRONG><BR>
<? echo "$_POST[birthday]"; ?></P>
</td>
</tr>
```

15. Start a new table row and table data cell that spans two columns. Inside, add a link back to the main menu. Close the table data cell, the table row, and the table itself:

```
<tr>
<td align=center colspan=2><br>
<p><a href="contact_menu.php">Return to Main Menu</a></p>
</TD>
</TR>
</TABLE>
```

16. Add some more HTML so that the document is valid:

```
</BODY>
</HTML>
```

17. Save the file with the name do_addcontact.php and place this file in the document root of your Web server.

Your code should look something like this:

```
<?
//check for required form variables
if ((!$_POST[f_name]) || (!$_POST[l_name])) {
    header( "Location: http://127.0.0.1/show_addcontact.php");
    exit;
} else {
    //if form variables are present, start a session
    session_start();
}

//check for validity of user
```

```
if ($_SESSION[valid] != "yes") {
   header("Location: http://127.0.0.1/contact_menu.php");
   exit;
}


//set up table and database names
$db_name = "testDB";
$table_name = "my_contacts";

//connect to server and select database
$connection = @mysql_connect("localhost", "spike", "9sj7En4")
or die(mysql_error());

$db = @mysql_select_db($db_name, $connection) or
die(mysql_error());

//build and issue query
$sql = "INSERT INTO $table_name (id, f_name, l_name, address1,
address2, address3, postcode, country, prim_tel, sec_tel, email,
birthday)
VALUES  ('', '$_POST[f_name]', '$_POST[l_name]',
'$_POST[address1]', '$_POST[address2]', '$_POST[address3]',
'$_POST[postcode]', '$_POST[country]', '$_POST[prim_tel]',
'$_POST[sec_tel]', '$_POST[email]', '$_POST[birthday]')";

$result = @mysql_query($sql,$connection) or die(mysql_error());
?>
<HTML>
<HEAD>
<TITLE>My Contact Management System: Contact Added</TITLE>
</HEAD>
<BODY>
<h1>My Contact Management System</h1>
<h2><em>Add a Contact - Contact Added</em></h2>
<P>The following information was successfully added to
<? echo "$table_name"; ?></P>
<table cellspacing=3 cellpadding=5>
<tr>
<th>NAME & ADDRESS INFORMATION</th>
<th>OTHER CONTACT/PERSONAL INFORMATION</th>
</tr>
<tr>
```

```
<td valign=top>
<P><STRONG>First Name:</STRONG><BR>
<? echo "$_POST[f_name]"; ?></P>
<P><STRONG>Last Name:</STRONG><BR>
<? echo "$_POST[l_name]"; ?></P>
<P><STRONG>Address Line 1:</STRONG><BR>
<? echo "$_POST[address1]"; ?></P>
<P><STRONG>Address Line 2:</STRONG><BR>
<? echo "$_POST[address2]"; ?></P>
<P><STRONG>Address Line 3:</STRONG><BR>
<? echo "$_POST[address3]"; ?></P>
<P><STRONG>Zip/Postal Code:</STRONG><BR>
<? echo "$_POST[postcode]"; ?></P>
<P><STRONG>Country:</STRONG><BR>
<? echo "$_POST[country]"; ?></P>
</td>
<td valign=top>
<P><STRONG>Primary Telephone Number:</STRONG><BR>
<? echo "$_POST[prim_tel]"; ?></P>
<P><STRONG>Secondary Telephone Number:</STRONG><BR>
<? echo "$_POST[sec_tel]"; ?></P>
<P><STRONG>E-mail Address:</STRONG><BR>
<? echo "$_POST[email]"; ?></P>
<P><STRONG>Birthday (YYYY-MM-DD):</STRONG><BR>
<? echo "$_POST[birthday]"; ?></P>
</td>
</tr>
<tr>
<td align=center colspan=2><br>
<p><a href="contact_menu.php">Return to Main Menu</a></p>
</TD>
</TR>
</TABLE>
</BODY>
</HTML>
```

Go on to the next step and start adding contacts!

Populating Your Table

To start populating the `my_contacts` table, open `http://127.0.0.1/contact_menu.php`. If you've already logged in, you'll see your administrative menu. Otherwise, log in using the username (`admin`) and password (`abc123`).

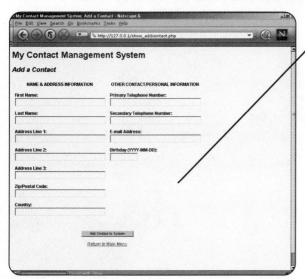

1. Select the Add a Contact menu item.

You will see a blank form with numerous fields for adding contact information as well as a submit button and a link back to the Main Menu.

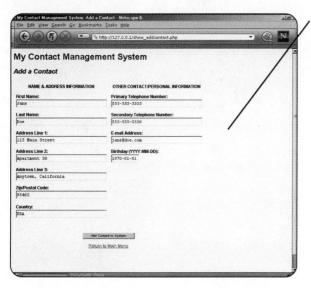

2. Complete the form. Only two fields are required (unless you changed that on your own): first name and last name. The figure shows a sample contact.

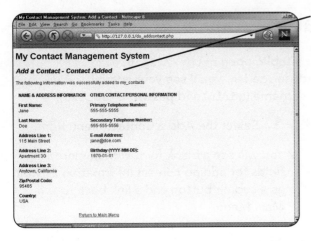

3. Click on the Add Contact to System button. You should see a confirmation screen.

Add several of your own contacts to the system. Feel free to make some mistakes because in the next chapter, you'll create a set of record-modification scripts.

20
Modifying Contacts

Now that you have contacts in your database table, you need a simple way to modify information. People move, change e-mail accounts—you'll need to update your records sometimes. In this chapter, you'll learn how to do the following:

- Create an administrative interface for modifying a record
- Create a script to update the record in your table
- Require session-based authentication before the script can be viewed or the record can be modified

Creating the Record-Selection Form

You have a number of entries in the my_contacts table, so you'll need a quick way to select a single record for modification. The next script will create a drop-down menu of all the people in your database, from which you can select one record to modify.

1. Open a new file in your text editor and start a PHP block.

```
<?
```

2. Start a session, or continue a session if one currently exists:

```
session_start();
```

3. Start an *if...else* block that checks the value of $_SESSION[valid] and performs a particular action based on the result. If the value is not yes, the user didn't go through the proper authentication channels:

```
if ($_SESSION[valid] != "yes") {
```

4. Send the user back to the login form, and exit this script:

```
header("Location: http://127.0.0.1/contact_menu.php");
exit;
}
```

5. Create a variable to hold the name of the database on which the table resides:

```
$db_name = "testDB";
```

6. Create a variable to hold the name of the table you're populating with this script:

```
$table_name = "my_contacts";
```

7. Add the connection information as you have been:

```
$connection = @mysql_connect("localhost", "spike", "9sj7En4")
or die(mysql_error());
```

8. Select the database as you have learned:

```
$db = @mysql_select_db($db_name, $connection) or die(mysql_error());
```

9. Create the SQL statement. You want to select just the ID number, first name, and last name of each record in the table:

```
$sql = "SELECT id, f_name, l_name FROM $table_name ORDER BY l_name";
```

10. Create a variable to hold the result of the `mysql_query()` function, as you have learned:

```
$result = @mysql_query($sql,$connection) or die(mysql_error());
```

11. Check for results using the `mysql_num_rows()` function:

```
$num = @mysql_num_rows($result);
```

12. Check the value returned by the `mysql_num_rows()` function, and create a variable called `$display_block` to hold an error message if the number is less than 1 (in other words, if there are no rows returned, and therefore no records in the table).

```
if ($num < 1) {
    $display_block = "<P><em>Sorry! No results.</em></p>";
```

13. Continue the `if...else` block, so the script continues if the count of rows is one or more:

```
} else {
```

14. Start the `while` loop. The `while` loop will create an array called `$row` for each record in the result set (`$result`):

```
while ($row = mysql_fetch_array($result)) {
```

15. Get the individual elements of the record, and give them good names:

```
$id = $row['id'];
$f_name = $row['f_name'];
$l_name = $row['l_name'];
```

16. Create a variable called `$option_block`, which will contain the individual elements in the drop-down menu:

```
$option_block .= "<option value=\"$id\">$l_name, $f_name</option>";
```

17. Close the `while` loop:

```
}
```

18. Create a variable called `$display_block`, which will hold the form. While this same variable was used to hold an error message in Step 12, it will not be used at that point unless there is an error. If there is an error, the script will never get to this step, so you have no worries about over-writing variables and can begin your form. For the form, assume that the method is POST and the action is a script called show_modcontact.php:

```
$display_block = "
<FORM METHOD=\"POST\" ACTION=\"show_modcontact.php\">
```

19. Create a text label for the drop-down menu:

```
<P><strong>Contact:</strong>
```

20. Start the drop-down menu:

```
<select name=\"id\">
```

21. Place the $option_block string inside the <select> </select> tag pair. It should contain at least one <option> element:

```
$option_block
```

22. Finish the drop-down menu:

```
</select>
```

23. Add a submit button:

```
<INPUT TYPE=\"SUBMIT\" NAME=\"submit\" VALUE=\"Select this
Contact\"></P>
```

24. Close your form, the string, the if...else block, and the PHP block:

```
</form>";
}
?>
```

25. Add this HTML:

```
<HTML>
<HEAD>
<TITLE>My Contact Management System: Modify a Contact</TITLE>
</HEAD>
<BODY>
<h1>My Contact Management System</h1>
<h2><em>Modify a Contact - Select from List</em></h2>
<P>Select a contact from the list below, to modify the contact's
record.</P>
```

26. Display the contents of $display_block:

```
<? echo "$display_block"; ?>
```

27. Add a link back to the main menu:

```
<br><p><a href="contact_menu.php">Return to Main Menu</a></p>
```

28. Add some more HTML so that the document is valid:

```
</BODY>
</HTML>
```

29. Save the file with the name `pick_modcontact.php` and place this file in the document root of your Web server.

Your code should look something like this:

```
<?
//start a session
session_start();

//check validity of user
if ($_SESSION[valid] != "yes") {
    header("Location: http://127.0.0.1/contact_menu.php");
    exit;
}

//set up table and database names
$db_name = "testDB";
$table_name = "my_contacts";

//connect to server and select database
$connection = @mysql_connect("localhost", "spike", "9sj7En4")
or die(mysql_error());
$db = @mysql_select_db($db_name, $connection) or
die(mysql_error());

//build and issue query
$sql = "SELECT id, f_name, l_name FROM $table_name ORDER BY
l_name";
$result = @mysql_query($sql,$connection) or die(mysql_error());

//check the number of results
$num = @mysql_num_rows($result);

if ($num < 1) {
    //if there are no results, display message
```

```
    $display_block = "<P><em>Sorry! No results.</em></p>";
} else {
    //if results are found, loop through them
    //and make a form selection block
    while ($row = mysql_fetch_array($result)) {
        $id = $row['id'];
        $f_name = $row['f_name'];
        $l_name = $row['l_name'];
        $option_block .= "<option value=\"$id\">$l_name, $f_name</
option>";
    }

    //create the entire form block
    $display_block = "
<FORM METHOD=\"POST\" ACTION=\"show_modcontact.php\">
<P><strong>Contact:</strong>
<select name=\"id\">
$option_block
</select>
<INPUT TYPE=\"SUBMIT\" NAME=\"submit\" VALUE=\"Select this
Contact\"></P>
</form>";
}
?>
<HTML>
<HEAD>
<TITLE>My Contact Management System: Modify a Contact</TITLE>
</HEAD>
<BODY>
<h1>My Contact Management System</h1>
<h2><em>Modify a Contact - Select from List</em></h2>
<P>Select a contact from the list below, to modify the contact's
record.</P>
<? echo "$display_block"; ?>
<br>
<p><a href="contact_menu.php">Return to Main Menu</a></p>
</BODY>
</HTML>
```

In the next section, you'll create the record-modification form, which looks strikingly similar to the record-addition form.

Creating the Record-Modification Form

The record-modification form is based on the record-addition form created in the previous chapter. The difference lies in the pre-population of values in the form fields. In other words, if there's already data in a record, you can see what you have before you change it.

1. Open a new file in your text editor and start a PHP block:

```
<?
```

2. Start an if...else block that checks for a value for $_POST[id], the one variable sent from the record-selection form. If a value doesn't exist, direct the user back to the selection form, and exit the script:

```
if (!$_POST[id]) {
    header( "Location: http://127.0.0.1/pick_modcontact.php");
    exit;
```

3. If the required field has a value, start a session, or continue a session if one currently exists. Then close the block:

```
} else {
    session_start();
}
```

4. Start an if...else block that checks the value of $_SESSION[valid] and performs a particular action based on the result. If the value is not yes, the user didn't go through the proper authentication channels:

```
if ($_SESSION[valid] != "yes") {
```

5. Send the user back to the login form, and exit this script:

```
header("Location: http://127.0.0.1/contact_menu.php");
exit;
}
```

6. Create a variable to hold the name of the database on which the table resides:

```
$db_name = "testDB";
```

7. Create a variable to hold the name of the table you're populating with this script:

```
$table_name = "my_contacts";
```

8. Add the connection information as you have been:

```
$connection = @mysql_connect("localhost", "spike", "9sj7En4")
or die(mysql_error());
```

9. Select the database as you have learned:

```
$db = @mysql_select_db($db_name, $connection) or
die(mysql_error());
```

10. Create the SQL statement. You want to select all the fields in the database except ID for the record with an ID equal to the value of $_POST[id]:

```
$sql = "SELECT f_name, l_name, address1, address2, address3,
postcode, country, prim_tel, sec_tel, email, birthday FROM
$table_name WHERE id = '$_POST[id]'";
```

11. Create a variable to hold the result of the mysql_query() function, as you have learned:

```
$result = @mysql_query($sql,$connection) or die(mysql_error());
```

12. Start the while loop. The while loop will create an array called $row for each record in the result set ($result):

```
while ($row = mysql_fetch_array($result)) {
```

13. Get the individual elements of the record, and give them good names:

```
$f_name = $row['f_name'];
$l_name = $row['l_name'];
$address1 = $row['address1'];
$address2 = $row['address2'];
$address3 = $row['address3'];
$postcode = $row['postcode'];
$country = $row['country'];
$prim_tel = $row['prim_tel'];
$sec_tel = $row['sec_tel'];
$email = $row['email'];
$birthday = $row['birthday'];
```

NOTE

Now that you have the current values for the selected record, you will use them later in the script to populate the form fields.

---

14. Close the `while` loop, then your PHP block:

```
}
?>
```

15. Type this HTML to start building the record-modification form:

```
<HTML>
<HEAD>
<TITLE>My Contact Management System: Modify a Contact</TITLE>
</HEAD>
<BODY>
<h1>My Contact Management System</h1>
<h2><em>Modify a Contact</em></h2>
```

16. Begin your form. Assume that the method is POST and the action is a script called `do_modcontact.php`:

```
<FORM METHOD="POST" ACTION="do_modcontact.php">
```

17. Add a hidden field to hold the value of `$_POST[id]` so it will be passed along to the script:

```
<INPUT TYPE="hidden" name="id" value="<? echo "$_POST[id]"; ?>">
```

18. Begin an HTML table to assist in layout. Start a new table row, add two column headings, and then close that row:

```
<table cellspacing=3 cellpadding=5>
<tr>
<th>NAME & ADDRESS INFORMATION</th>
<th>OTHER CONTACT/PERSONAL INFORMATION</th>
</tr>
```

19. Create rows and cells to hold input fields for all the items in the record. Use the `value` attribute in each input field, and mingle HTML and PHP to echo the actual value:

```
<tr>
<td valign=top>
<P><STRONG>First Name:</STRONG><BR>
<INPUT TYPE="text" NAME="f_name" VALUE="<? echo "$f_name"; ?>"
SIZE=35 MAXLENGTH=75></P>
<P><STRONG>Last Name:</STRONG><BR>
<INPUT TYPE="text" NAME="l_name" VALUE="<? echo "$l_name"; ?>"
SIZE=35 MAXLENGTH=75></P>
```

```
<P><STRONG>Address Line 1:</STRONG><BR>
<INPUT TYPE="text" NAME="address1" VALUE="<? echo "$address1"; ?>"
SIZE=35 MAXLENGTH=100></P>
<P><STRONG>Address Line 2:</STRONG><BR>
<INPUT TYPE="text" NAME="address2" VALUE="<? echo "$address2"; ?>"
SIZE=35 MAXLENGTH=100></P>
<P><STRONG>Address Line 3:</STRONG><BR>
<INPUT TYPE="text" NAME="address3" VALUE="<? echo "$address3"; ?>"
SIZE=35 MAXLENGTH=100></P>
<P><STRONG>Zip/Postal Code:</STRONG><BR>
<INPUT TYPE="text" NAME="postcode" VALUE="<? echo "$postcode"; ?>"
SIZE=35 MAXLENGTH=25></P>
<P><STRONG>Country:</STRONG><BR>
<INPUT TYPE="text" NAME="country" VALUE="<? echo "$country"; ?>"
SIZE=35 MAXLENGTH=100></P>
</td>
<td valign=top>
<P><STRONG>Primary Telephone Number:</STRONG><BR>
<INPUT TYPE="text" NAME="prim_tel" VALUE="<? echo "$prim_tel"; ?>"
SIZE=35 MAXLENGTH=35></P>
<P><STRONG>Secondary Telephone Number:</STRONG><BR>
<INPUT TYPE="text" NAME="sec_tel" VALUE="<? echo "$sec_tel"; ?>"
SIZE=35 MAXLENGTH=35></P>
<P><STRONG>E-mail Address:</STRONG><BR>
<INPUT TYPE="text" NAME="email" VALUE="<? echo "$email"; ?>"
SIZE=35 MAXLENGTH=100></P>
<P><STRONG>Birthday (YYYY-MM-DD):</STRONG><BR>
<INPUT TYPE="text" NAME="birthday" VALUE="<? echo "$birthday"; ?>"
SIZE=10 MAXLENGTH=10></P>
</td>
</tr>
```

20. Start a new table row and table data cell that spans two columns. Inside, add a submit button as well as a link back to the main menu. Close the table data cell, the table row, and the table itself:

```
<tr>
<td align=center colspan=2><br>
<P><INPUT TYPE="SUBMIT" NAME="submit" VALUE="Update Contact
Record"></P>
<br>
<p><a href="contact_menu.php">Return to Main Menu</a></p>
</TD>
</TR>
</TABLE>
```

21. Close your form and add some more HTML so that the document is valid:

```
</FORM>
</BODY>
</HTML>
```

22. Save the file with the name `show_modcontact.php` and place this file in the document root of your Web server.

Your code should look something like this:

```php
<?
//check for required form variables
if (!$_POST[id]) {
    header( "Location: http://127.0.0.1/pick_modcontact.php");
    exit;
} else {
    //if form variables are present, start a session
    session_start();
}

//check for validity of user
if ($_SESSION[valid] != "yes") {
    header("Location: http://127.0.0.1/contact_menu.php");
    exit;
}

//set up table and database names
$db_name = "testDB";
$table_name = "my_contacts";

//connect to server and select database
$connection = @mysql_connect("localhost", "spike", "9sj7En4")
or die(mysql_error());
$db = @mysql_select_db($db_name, $connection) or
die(mysql_error());

//build and issue query
$sql = "SELECT f_name, l_name, address1, address2, address3,
postcode, country, prim_tel, sec_tel, email, birthday FROM
$table_name WHERE id = '$_POST[id]'";
$result = @mysql_query($sql,$connection) or die(mysql_error());

//get results for display
```

```
while ($row = mysql_fetch_array($result)) {
    $f_name = $row['f_name'];
    $l_name = $row['l_name'];
    $address1 = $row['address1'];
    $address2 = $row['address2'];
    $address3 = $row['address3'];
    $postcode = $row['postcode'];
    $country = $row['country'];
    $prim_tel = $row['prim_tel'];
    $sec_tel = $row['sec_tel'];
    $email = $row['email'];
    $birthday = $row['birthday'];
}
?>


<HTML>
<HEAD>
<TITLE>My Contact Management System: Modify a Contact</TITLE>
</HEAD>
<BODY>
<h1>My Contact Management System</h1>
<h2><em>Modify a Contact</em></h2>


<FORM METHOD="POST" ACTION="do_modcontact.php">
<INPUT TYPE="hidden" name="id" value="<? echo "$_POST[id]"; ?>">


<table cellspacing=3 cellpadding=5>
<tr>
<th>NAME & ADDRESS INFORMATION</th>
<th>OTHER CONTACT/PERSONAL INFORMATION</th>
</tr>
<tr>
<td valign=top>
<P><STRONG>First Name:</STRONG><BR>
<INPUT TYPE="text" NAME="f_name" VALUE="<? echo "$f_name"; ?>"
SIZE=35 MAXLENGTH=75></P>
<P><STRONG>Last Name:</STRONG><BR>
<INPUT TYPE="text" NAME="l_name" VALUE="<? echo "$l_name"; ?>"
SIZE=35 MAXLENGTH=75></P>
<P><STRONG>Address Line 1:</STRONG><BR>
<INPUT TYPE="text" NAME="address1" VALUE="<? echo "$address1"; ?>"
SIZE=35 MAXLENGTH=100></P>
```

```
<P><STRONG>Address Line 2:</STRONG><BR>
<INPUT TYPE="text" NAME="address2" VALUE="<? echo "$address2"; ?>"
SIZE=35 MAXLENGTH=100></P>
<P><STRONG>Address Line 3:</STRONG><BR>
<INPUT TYPE="text" NAME="address3" VALUE="<? echo "$address3"; ?>"
SIZE=35 MAXLENGTH=100></P>
<P><STRONG>Zip/Postal Code:</STRONG><BR>
<INPUT TYPE="text" NAME="postcode" VALUE="<? echo "$postcode"; ?>"
SIZE=35 MAXLENGTH=25></P>
<P><STRONG>Country:</STRONG><BR>
<INPUT TYPE="text" NAME="country" VALUE="<? echo "$country"; ?>"
SIZE=35 MAXLENGTH=100></P>
</td>


<td valign=top>
<P><STRONG>Primary Telephone Number:</STRONG><BR>
<INPUT TYPE="text" NAME="prim_tel" VALUE="<? echo "$prim_tel"; ?>"
SIZE=35 MAXLENGTH=35></P>
<P><STRONG>Secondary Telephone Number:</STRONG><BR>
<INPUT TYPE="text" NAME="sec_tel" VALUE="<? echo "$sec_tel"; ?>"
SIZE=35 MAXLENGTH=35></P>
<P><STRONG>E-mail Address:</STRONG><BR>
<INPUT TYPE="text" NAME="email" VALUE="<? echo "$email"; ?>"
SIZE=35 MAXLENGTH=100></P>
<P><STRONG>Birthday (YYYY-MM-DD):</STRONG><BR>
<INPUT TYPE="text" NAME="birthday" VALUE="<? echo "$birthday"; ?>"
SIZE=10 MAXLENGTH=10></P>
</td>
</tr>


<tr>
<td align=center colspan=2><br>
<P><INPUT TYPE="SUBMIT" NAME="submit" VALUE="Update Contact
Record"></P>
<br>
<p><a href="contact_menu.php">Return to Main Menu</a></p>
</TD>
</TR>
</TABLE>


</FORM>
</BODY>
</HTML>
```

In the next section, you'll create the script that takes the form input, creates a SQL statement, and updates the record in the database table.

Creating the Record-Modification Script

This script will update the record in the `my_contacts` table, using the value of `$_POST[id]` as the primary key (which it is!).

1. Open a new file in your text editor and start a PHP block:

```
<?
```

2. Start an `if…else` block that checks for values in `$_POST[f_name]` and `$_POST[l_name]`. If they don't have values, direct the user back to the selection form, and exit the script:

```
if ((!$_POST[f_name]) || (!$_POST[l_name])) {
    header( "Location: http://127.0.0.1/pick_modcontact.php");
    exit;
```

NOTE

You can have as many (or as few) required fields as you'd like.

---

3. If the required fields have values, start a session, or continue a session if one currently exists. Then close the block:

```
} else {
    session_start();
}
```

4. Start an `if…else` block that checks the value of `$_SESSION[valid]` and performs a particular action based on the result. If the value is not `yes`, the user didn't go through the proper authentication channels:

```
if ($_SESSION[valid] != "yes") {
```

5. Send the user back to the login form, and exit this script:

```
header("Location: http://127.0.0.1/contact_menu.php");
exit;
}
```

6. Create a variable to hold the name of the database on which the table resides:

```
$db_name = "testDB";
```

7. Create a variable to hold the name of the table you're populating with this script:

```
$table_name = "my_contacts";
```

8. Add the connection information as you have been:

```
$connection = @mysql_connect("localhost", "spike", "9sj7En4")
or die(mysql_error());
```

9. Select the database as you have learned:

```
$db = @mysql_select_db($db_name, $connection) or
die(mysql_error());
```

10. Create the SQL statement. This statement uses UPDATE to SET fields to specific values:

```
$sql = "UPDATE $table_name SET
    f_name = '$_POST[f_name]',
    l_name = '$_POST[l_name]',
    address1 = '$_POST[address1]',
    address2 = '$_POST[address2]',
    address3 = '$_POST[address3]',
    postcode = '$_POST[postcode]',
    country = '$_POST[country]',
    prim_tel = '$_POST[prim_tel]',
    sec_tel = '$_POST[sec_tel]',
    email = '$_POST[email]',
    birthday = '$_POST[birthday]'
    WHERE id = '$_POST[id]'";
```

11. Create a variable to hold the result of the `mysql_query()` function, as you have learned:

```
$result = @mysql_query($sql,$connection) or die(mysql_error());
```

12. Close your PHP block and add this HTML:

```
?>
<HTML>
<HEAD>
<TITLE>My Contact Management System: Contact Updated</TITLE>
```

```
</HEAD>
<BODY>
<h1>My Contact Management System</h1>
<h2><em>Modify a Contact - Contact Updated</em></h2>
```

13. Add a confirmation statement. Mingle HTML and PHP to include the value of the `$table_name` variable:

```
<P>The following information was successfully updated in <? echo
"$table_name"; ?></P>
```

14. Next you'll re-create the layout used in `show_modcontact.php`, only it won't contain form fields. Instead, you'll mingle HTML and PHP to show the values that were entered. Start a new table row, add two column headings, and then close that row:

```
<table cellspacing=3 cellpadding=5>
<tr>
<th>NAME & ADDRESS INFORMATION</th>
<th>OTHER CONTACT/PERSONAL INFORMATION</th>
</tr>
```

15. Start a new table row and table data cell, and then display a text label and value for each field:

```
<tr>
<td valign=top>
<P><STRONG>First Name:</STRONG><BR>
<? echo "$_POST[f_name]"; ?></P>
<P><STRONG>Last Name:</STRONG><BR>
<? echo "$_POST[l_name]"; ?></P>
<P><STRONG>Address Line 1:</STRONG><BR>
<? echo "$_POST[address1]"; ?></P>
<P><STRONG>Address Line 2:</STRONG><BR>
<? echo "$_POST[address2]"; ?></P>
<P><STRONG>Address Line 3:</STRONG><BR>
<? echo "$_POST[address3]"; ?></P>
<P><STRONG>Zip/Postal Code:</STRONG><BR>
<? echo "$_POST[postcode]"; ?></P>
<P><STRONG>Country:</STRONG><BR>
<? echo "$_POST[country]"; ?></P>
</td>
<td valign=top>
<P><STRONG>Primary Telephone Number:</STRONG><BR>
```

```
<? echo "$_POST[prim_tel]"; ?></P>
<P><STRONG>Secondary Telephone Number:</STRONG><BR>
<? echo "$_POST[sec_tel]"; ?></P>
<P><STRONG>E-mail Address:</STRONG><BR>
<? echo "$_POST[email]"; ?></P>
<P><STRONG>Birthday (YYYY-MM-DD):</STRONG><BR>
<? echo "$_POST[birthday]"; ?></P>
</td>
</tr>
```

16. Start a new table row and table data cell that spans two columns. Inside, add a link back to the main menu. Close the table data cell, the table row, and the table itself:

```
<tr>
<td align=center colspan=2><br>
<p><a href="contact_menu.php">Return to Main Menu</a></p>
</TD>
</TR>
</TABLE>
```

17. Add some more HTML so that the document is valid:

```
</BODY>
</HTML>
```

18. Save the file with the name do_modcontact.php and place this file in the document root of your Web server.

Your code should look something like this:

```
<?
//check for required form variables
if ((!$_POST[f_name]) || (!$_POST[l_name])) {
    header( "Location: http://127.0.0.1/pick_modcontact.php");
    exit;
} else {
    //if form variables are present, start a session
    session_start();
}

//check for validity of user
if ($_SESSION[valid] != "yes") {
    header("Location: http://127.0.0.1/contact_menu.php");
```

```
        exit;
    }

    //set up table and database names
    $db_name = "testDB";
    $table_name = "my_contacts";

    //connect to server and select database
    $connection = @mysql_connect("localhost", "spike", "9sj7En4")
    or die(mysql_error());
    $db = @mysql_select_db($db_name, $connection) or
    die(mysql_error());

    //build and issue query
    $sql = "UPDATE $table_name SET
        f_name = '$_POST[f_name]',
        l_name = '$_POST[l_name]',
        address1 = '$_POST[address1]',
        address2 = '$_POST[address2]',
        address3 = '$_POST[address3]',
        postcode = '$_POST[postcode]',
        country = '$_POST[country]',
        prim_tel = '$_POST[prim_tel]',
        sec_tel = '$_POST[sec_tel]',
        email = '$_POST[email]',
        birthday = '$_POST[birthday]'
        WHERE id = '$_POST[id]'";

    $result = @mysql_query($sql,$connection) or die(mysql_error());
    ?>
    <HTML>
    <HEAD>
    <TITLE>My Contact Management System: Contact Updated</TITLE>
    </HEAD>
    <BODY>
    <h1>My Contact Management System</h1>
    <h2><em>Modify a Contact - Contact Updated</em></h2>

    <P>The following information was successfully updated in <? echo
    "$table_name"; ?></P>

    <table cellspacing=3 cellpadding=5>
```

```html
<tr>
<th>NAME & ADDRESS INFORMATION</th>
<th>OTHER CONTACT/PERSONAL INFORMATION</th>
</tr>

<tr>
<td valign=top>
<P><STRONG>First Name:</STRONG><BR>
<? echo "$_POST[f_name]"; ?></P>
<P><STRONG>Last Name:</STRONG><BR>
<? echo "$_POST[l_name]"; ?></P>
<P><STRONG>Address Line 1:</STRONG><BR>
<? echo "$_POST[address1]"; ?></P>
<P><STRONG>Address Line 2:</STRONG><BR>
<? echo "$_POST[address2]"; ?></P>
<P><STRONG>Address Line 3:</STRONG><BR>
<? echo "$_POST[address3]"; ?></P>
<P><STRONG>Zip/Postal Code:</STRONG><BR>
<? echo "$_POST[postcode]"; ?></P>
<P><STRONG>Country:</STRONG><BR>
<? echo "$_POST[country]"; ?></P>
</td>
<td valign=top>
<P><STRONG>Primary Telephone Number:</STRONG><BR>
<? echo "$_POST[prim_tel]"; ?></P>
<P><STRONG>Secondary Telephone Number:</STRONG><BR>
<? echo "$_POST[sec_tel]"; ?></P>
<P><STRONG>E-mail Address:</STRONG><BR>
<? echo "$_POST[email]"; ?></P>

<P><STRONG>Birthday (YYYY-MM-DD):</STRONG><BR>
<? echo "$_POST[birthday]"; ?></P>
</td>
</tr>

<tr>
<td align=center colspan=2><br>
<p><a href="contact_menu.php">Return to Main Menu</a></p>
</TD>
</TR>
</TABLE>
```

```
</BODY>
</HTML>
```

Go on to the next step—modifying some of the contacts in your table.

Modifying Contacts

To start modifying contacts in the my_contacts table, open http://127.0.0.1/ contact_menu.php. If you've already logged in, you'll see your administrative menu. Otherwise, log in using the username (admin) and password (abc123).

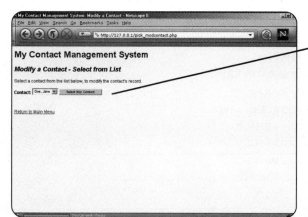

1. Select the Modify a Contact menu item.

You will see a drop-down menu of the contacts in the system, ordered by last name, as well as a submit button and a link back to the Main Menu.

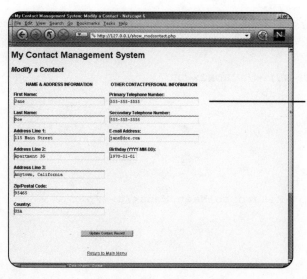

2. Select a contact from the list and click on the Select this Contact button. I selected a sample from my own list. It's a complete example, with a value in every field.

You will see the record modification form, with fields pre-populated with existing values.

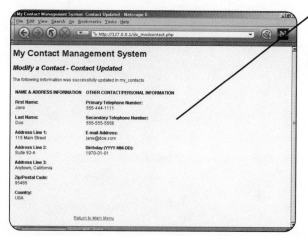

3. Change something in the record. In my sample, I changed Address 2 to "Suite 92-A" and the primary telephone number to "555-444-1111." Click on the Update Contact Record button. You should see a confirmation screen.

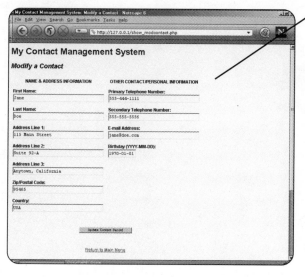

4. Return to the selection form and select your contact again to see that the value has really changed.

Modify the records of some of your own contacts. In the next chapter, you'll create the administrative scripts used to delete some records.

21

Deleting Contacts

There are plenty of times when I want to delete people from my address book, for one reason or another. You should be able to delete people from your online contact management system, too! In this chapter, you'll learn how to do the following:

- Create an administrative interface for deleting a record
- Create a script to delete the record from your table
- Require session-based authentication before the script can be viewed or the record can be deleted

Using the Record-Selection Form

The script that creates a selection form for record deletion is virtually identical to the script used to select a record for modification. This section will be very easy for you to skim through. Repetition makes for perfection!

1. Open a new file in your text editor and start a PHP block.

```
<?
```

2. Start a session, or continue a session if one currently exists:

```
session_start();
```

3. Start an if…else block that checks the value of $_SESSION[valid] and performs a particular action based on the result. If the value is not yes, the user didn't go through the proper authentication channels:

```
if ($_SESION[valid] != "yes") {
```

4. Send the user back to the login form, and exit this script:

```
header("Location: http://127.0.0.1/contact_menu.php");
exit;
}
```

5. Create a variable to hold the name of the database on which the table resides:

```
$db_name = "testDB";
```

6. Create a variable to hold the name of the table you're populating with this script:

```
$table_name = "my_contacts";
```

7. Add the connection information as you have been:

```
$connection = @mysql_connect("localhost", "spike", "9sj7En4")
or die(mysql_error());
```

8. Select the database as you have learned:

```
$db = @mysql_select_db($db_name, $connection) or
die(mysql_error());
```

9. Create the SQL statement. You want to select just the ID number, first name, and last name of each record in the table:

```
$sql = "SELECT id, f_name, l_name FROM $table_name ORDER BY l_name";
```

10. Create a variable to hold the result of the `mysql_query()` function, as you have learned:

```
$result = @mysql_query($sql,$connection) or die(mysql_error());
```

11. Check for results using the `mysql_num_rows()` function:

```
$num = @mysql_num_rows($result);
```

12. Check the value returned by the `mysql_num_rows()` function, and create a variable called `$display_block` to hold an error message if the number is less than 1 (in other words, if there are no rows returned, and therefore no records in the table).

```
if ($num < 1) {
    $display_block = "<P><em>Sorry! No results.</em></p>";
```

13. Continue the `if...else` block, so the script continues if the count of rows is one or more:

```
} else {
```

14. Start the `while` loop. The `while` loop will create an array called `$row` for each record in the result set (`$result`):

```
while ($row = mysql_fetch_array($result)) {
```

15. Get the individual elements of the record, and give them good names:

```
$id = $row['id'];
$f_name = $row['f_name'];
$l_name = $row['l_name'];
```

16. Create a variable called `$option_block`, which will contain the individual elements in the drop-down menu:

```
$option_block .= "<option value=\"$id\">$l_name, $f_name</option>";
```

17. Close the `while` loop:

```
}
```

18. Create a variable called `$display_block`, which will hold the form. While this same variable was used to hold an error message in Step 12, it will not be used at that point unless there is an error. If there is an error, the script will never get to this step, so you have no worries about over-writing variables and can begin your form. For the form, assume that the method is POST and the action is a script called show_delcontact.php:

```
$display_block = "
<FORM METHOD=\"POST\" ACTION=\"show_delcontact.php\">
```

19. Create a text label for the drop-down menu:

```
<P><strong>Contact:</strong>
```

20. Start the drop-down menu:

```
<select name=\"id\">
```

21. Place the $option_block string inside the <select> </select> tag pair. It should contain at least one <option> element:

```
$option_block
```

22. Finish the drop-down menu:

```
</select>
```

23. Add a submit button:

```
<INPUT TYPE=\"SUBMIT\" NAME=\"submit\" VALUE=\"Select this
Contact\"></P>
```

24. Close your form, the string, the if...else block and the PHP block:

```
</form>";
}
?>
```

25. Add this HTML:

```
<HTML>
<HEAD>
<TITLE>My Contact Management System: Delete a Contact</TITLE>
</HEAD>
<BODY>
<h1>My Contact Management System</h1>
<h2><em>Delete a Contact - Select from List</em></h2>
<P>Select a contact from the list below, to delete the contact's
record.</P>
```

26. Display the contents of $display_block:

```
<? echo "$display_block"; ?>
```

27. Add a link back to the main menu:

```
<br><p><a href="contact_menu.php">Return to Main Menu</a></p>
```

28. Add some more HTML so that the document is valid:

```
</BODY>
</HTML>
```

29. Save the file with the name pick_delcontact.php and place this file in the document root of your Web server.

Your code should look something like this:

```
<?
//start a session
session_start();

//check validity of user
if ($_SESSION[valid] != "yes") {
    header("Location: http://127.0.0.1/contact_menu.php");
    exit;
}

//set up table and database names
$db_name = "testDB";
$table_name = "my_contacts";

//connect to server and select database
$connection = @mysql_connect("localhost", "spike", "9sj7En4")
or die(mysql_error());
$db = @mysql_select_db($db_name, $connection) or
die(mysql_error());

//build and issue query
$sql = "SELECT id, f_name, l_name FROM $table_name ORDER BY
l_name";
$result = @mysql_query($sql,$connection) or die(mysql_error());

//check the number of results
```

```php
$num = @mysql_num_rows($result);

if ($num < 1) {
    //if there are no results, display message
    $display_block = "<P><em>Sorry! No results.</em></p>";
} else {
    //if results are found, loop through them
    //and make a form selection block
    while ($row = mysql_fetch_array($result)) {
        $id = $row['id'];
        $f_name = $row['f_name'];
        $l_name = $row['l_name'];
        $option_block .= "<option value=\"$id\">$l_name, $f_name</
option>";
    }

    //create the entire form block
    $display_block = "
<FORM METHOD=\"POST\" ACTION=\"show_delcontact.php\">
<P><strong>Contact:</strong>
<select name=\"id\">
$option_block
</select>
<INPUT TYPE=\"SUBMIT\" NAME=\"submit\" VALUE=\"Select this
Contact\"></P>
    </form>";
}
?>
<HTML>
<HEAD>
<TITLE>My Contact Management System: Delete a Contact</TITLE>
</HEAD>
<BODY>
<h1>My Contact Management System</h1>
<h2><em>Delete a Contact - Select from List</em></h2>
<P>Select a contact from the list below, to delete the contact's
record.</P>
<? echo "$display_block"; ?>
<br>
<p><a href="contact_menu.php">Return to Main Menu</a></p>
</BODY>
</HTML>
```

In the next section, you'll create a pre-deletion confirmation screen that shows all the current values of the selected record.

Creating the Record-Deletion Form

The record deletion form isn't a form in the usual sense of the word—you aren't typing anything into a form field. Instead, this screen will display the existing record in read-only format, and include hidden form fields and a submit button. By viewing the record before deleting it, you're certain to delete the correct record.

1. Open a new file in your text editor and start a PHP block:

```
<?
```

2. Start an if...else block that checks for a value for $_POST[id], the one variable sent from the record-selection form. If a value doesn't exist, direct the user back to the selection form, and exit the script:

```
if (!$_POST[id]) {
    header( "Location: http://127.0.0.1/pick_delcontact.php");
    exit;
```

3. If the required field has a value, start a session, or continue a session if one currently exists. Then close the block.

```
} else {
    session_start();
}
```

4. Start an if...else block that checks the value of $_SESSION[valid] and performs a particular action based on the result. If the value is not yes, the user didn't go through the proper authentication channels:

```
if ($_SESSION[valid] != "yes") {
```

5. Send the user back to the login form, and exit this script:

```
header("Location: http://127.0.0.1/contact_menu.php");
exit;
}
```

6. Create a variable to hold the name of the database on which the table resides:

```
$db_name = "testDB";
```

7. Create a variable to hold the name of the table you're populating with this script:

```
$table_name = "my_contacts";
```

8. Add the connection information as you have been:

```
$connection = @mysql_connect("localhost", "spike", "9sj7En4")
or die(mysql_error());
```

9. Select the database as you have learned:

```
$db = @mysql_select_db($db_name, $connection) or
die(mysql_error());
```

10. Create the SQL statement. You want to select all the fields in the database except `id`, for the record with an ID equal to the value of $_POST[id]:

```
$sql = "SELECT f_name, l_name, address1, address2, address3,
postcode, country, prim_tel, sec_tel, email, birthday FROM
$table_name WHERE id = '$_POST[id]'";
```

11. Create a variable to hold the result of the `mysql_query()` function, as you have learned:

```
$result = @mysql_query($sql,$connection) or die(mysql_error());
```

12. Start the `while` loop. The `while` loop will create an array called $row for each record in the result set ($result):

```
while ($row = mysql_fetch_array($result)) {
```

13. Get the individual elements of the record, and give them good names:

```
$f_name = $row['f_name'];
$l_name = $row['l_name'];
$address1 = $row['address1'];
$address2 = $row['address2'];
$address3 = $row['address3'];
$postcode = $row['postcode'];
$country = $row['country'];
$prim_tel = $row['prim_tel'];
$sec_tel = $row['sec_tel'];
$email = $row['email'];
$birthday = $row['birthday'];
```

14. Close the `while` loop, then your PHP block:

```
}
?>
```

15. Type this HTML to start building the record-confirmation screen:

```
<HTML>
<HEAD>
<TITLE>My Contact Management System: Delete a Contact</TITLE>
</HEAD>
<BODY>
<h1>My Contact Management System</h1>
<h2><em>Delete a Contact</em></h2>
```

16. Begin your form. Assume that the method is POST and the action is a script called do_delcontact.php:

```
<FORM METHOD="POST" ACTION="do_delcontact.php">
```

17. Add a hidden field to hold the value of $_POST[id]:

```
<INPUT TYPE="hidden" name="id" value="<? echo "$_POST[id]"; ?>">
```

18. Add two more hidden fields to hold the value of $f_name and $1_name. You'll use these fields for display purposes in the final confirmation screen, after the deletion has occurred:

```
<INPUT TYPE="hidden" name="f_name" value="<? echo "$f_name"; ?>">
<INPUT TYPE="hidden" name="l_name" value="<? echo "$1_name"; ?>">
```

19. Next, you'll re-create the layout used in the record-addition and modification forms, mingling HTML and PHP to show the values for the selected record. Start a new table row, add two column headings, and then close that row:

```
<table cellspacing=3 cellpadding=5>
<tr>
<th>NAME & ADDRESS INFORMATION</th>
<th>OTHER CONTACT/PERSONAL INFORMATION</th>
</tr>
```

20. Start a new table row and table data cell, and then display a text label and value for the fields in the record:

```
<tr>
<td valign=top>
<P><STRONG>First Name:</STRONG><BR>
<? echo "$f_name"; ?></P>
<P><STRONG>Last Name:</STRONG><BR>
<? echo "$1_name"; ?></P>
<P><STRONG>Address Line 1:</STRONG><BR>
```

```
<? echo "$address1"; ?></P>
<P><STRONG>Address Line 2:</STRONG><BR>
<? echo "$address2"; ?></P>
<P><STRONG>Address Line 3:</STRONG><BR>
<? echo "$address3"; ?></P>
<P><STRONG>Zip/Postal Code:</STRONG><BR>
<? echo "$postcode"; ?></P>
<P><STRONG>Country:</STRONG><BR>
<? echo "$country"; ?></P>
</td>
<td valign=top>
<P><STRONG>Primary Telephone Number:</STRONG><BR>
<? echo "$prim_tel"; ?></P>
<P><STRONG>Secondary Telephone Number:</STRONG><BR>
<? echo "$sec_tel"; ?></P>
<P><STRONG>E-mail Address:</STRONG><BR>
<? echo "$email"; ?></P>
<P><STRONG>Birthday (YYYY-MM-DD):</STRONG><BR>
<? echo "$birthday"; ?></P>
</td>
</tr>
```

21. Start a new table row and table data cell that spans two columns. Inside, add a submit button and a link back to the main menu. Close the table data cell, the table row, and the table itself:

```
<tr>
<td align=center colspan=2><br>
<P><INPUT TYPE="SUBMIT" NAME="submit" VALUE="Delete this
Contact"></P>
<p><a href="contact_menu.php">Return to Main Menu</a></p>
</TD>
</TR>
</TABLE>
```

22. Close the form and add some more HTML so that the document is valid:

```
</FORM>
</BODY>
</HTML>
```

23. Save the file with the name show_delcontact.php and place this file in the document root of your Web server.

Your code should look something like this:

```
<?
//check for required form variables
if (!$_POST[id]) {
    header( "Location: http://127.0.0.1/pick_delcontact.php");
    exit;
} else {
    //if form variables are present, start a session
    session_start();
}

//check for validity of user
if ($_SESSION[valid] != "yes") {
    header("Location: http://127.0.0.1/contact_menu.php");
    exit;
}

//set up table and database names
$db_name = "testDB";
$table_name = "my_contacts";

//connect to server and select database
$connection = @mysql_connect("localhost", "spike", "9sj7En4")
or die(mysql_error());
$db = @mysql_select_db($db_name, $connection) or
die(mysql_error());

//build and issue query
$sql = "SELECT f_name, l_name, address1, address2, address3,
postcode, country, prim_tel, sec_tel, email, birthday FROM
$table_name WHERE id = '$_POST[id]'";
$result = @mysql_query($sql,$connection) or die(mysql_error());

//get results for display
while ($row = mysql_fetch_array($result)) {
    $f_name = $row['f_name'];
    $l_name = $row['l_name'];
    $address1 = $row['address1'];
    $address2 = $row['address2'];
    $address3 = $row['address3'];
    $postcode = $row['postcode'];
```

```
        $country = $row['country'];
        $prim_tel = $row['prim_tel'];
        $sec_tel = $row['sec_tel'];
        $email = $row['email'];
        $birthday = $row['birthday'];
    }
?>


<HTML>
<HEAD>
<TITLE>My Contact Management System: Delete a Contact</TITLE>
</HEAD>
<BODY>
<h1>My Contact Management System</h1>
<h2><em>Delete a Contact</em></h2>

<FORM METHOD="POST" ACTION="do_delcontact.php">
<INPUT TYPE="hidden" name="id" value="<? echo "$_POST[id]"; ?>">
<INPUT TYPE="hidden" name="f_name" value="<? echo "$f_name"; ?>">
<INPUT TYPE="hidden" name="l_name" value="<? echo "$l_name"; ?>">

<table cellspacing=3 cellpadding=5>
<tr>
<th>NAME & ADDRESS INFORMATION</th>
<th>OTHER CONTACT/PERSONAL INFORMATION</th>
</tr>
<tr>
<td valign=top>
<P><STRONG>First Name:</STRONG><BR>
<? echo "$f_name"; ?></P>
<P><STRONG>Last Name:</STRONG><BR>
<? echo "$l_name"; ?></P>
<P><STRONG>Address Line 1:</STRONG><BR>
<? echo "$address1"; ?></P>
<P><STRONG>Address Line 2:</STRONG><BR>
<? echo "$address2"; ?></P>
<P><STRONG>Address Line 3:</STRONG><BR>
<? echo "$address3"; ?></P>
<P><STRONG>Zip/Postal Code:</STRONG><BR>
<? echo "$postcode"; ?></P>
```

```
<P><STRONG>Country:</STRONG><BR>
<? echo "$country"; ?></P>
</td>
<td valign=top>
<P><STRONG>Primary Telephone Number:</STRONG><BR>
<? echo "$prim_tel"; ?></P>
<P><STRONG>Secondary Telephone Number:</STRONG><BR>
<? echo "$sec_tel"; ?></P>
<P><STRONG>E-mail Address:</STRONG><BR>
<? echo "$email"; ?></P>
<P><STRONG>Birthday (YYYY-MM-DD):</STRONG><BR>
<? echo "$birthday"; ?></P>
</td>
</tr>

<tr>
<td align=center colspan=2><br>
<P><INPUT TYPE="SUBMIT" NAME="submit" VALUE="Delete this
Contact"></P>
<p><a href="contact_menu.php">Return to Main Menu</a></p>
</TD>
</TR>
</TABLE>

</FORM>
</BODY>
</HTML>
```

In the next section, you'll create the script that takes the value of $_POST[id] (currently held in a hidden form field) and deletes the corresponding record from the database table.

Creating the Record-Deletion Script

This script will delete the record in the my_contacts table, using the value of $_POST[id] as the primary key.

1. Open a new file in your text editor and start a PHP block:

```
<?
```

2. Start an if…else block that checks for a value for $_POST[id]. If no value is present, direct the user back to the selection form, and exit the script:

```
if (!$_POST[id]) {
    header( "Location: http://127.0.0.1/pick_delcontact.php");
    exit;
```

3. If the required field has a value, start a session, or continue a session if one currently exists. Then close the block.

```
} else {
    session_start();
}
```

4. Start an if…else block that checks the value of $_SESSION[valid] and performs a particular action based on the result. If the value is not yes, the user didn't go through the proper authentication channels:

```
if ($_SESSION[valid] != "yes") {
```

5. Send the user back to the login form, and exit this script:

```
header("Location: http://127.0.0.1/contact_menu.php");
exit;
}
```

6. Create a variable to hold the name of the database on which the table resides:

```
$db_name = "testDB";
```

7. Create a variable to hold the name of the table you're populating with this script:

```
$table_name = "my_contacts";
```

8. Add the connection information as you have been:

```
$connection = @mysql_connect("localhost", "spike", "9sj7En4")
or die(mysql_error());
```

9. Select the database as you have learned:

```
$db = @mysql_select_db($db_name, $connection) or
die(mysql_error());
```

10. Create the SQL statement to delete the record:

```
$sql = "DELETE FROM $table_name WHERE id = '$_POST[id]'";
```

11. Create a variable to hold the result of the `mysql_query()` function, as you have learned:

```
$result = @mysql_query($sql,$connection) or die(mysql_error());
```

12. Close your PHP block and add this HTML:

```
?>
<HTML>
<HEAD>
<TITLE>My Contact Management System: Contact Deleted</TITLE>
</HEAD>
<BODY>
<h1>My Contact Management System</h1>
<h2><em>Delete a Contact - Contact Deleted</em></h2>
```

13. Add a confirmation statement. Mingle HTML and PHP to include the values of the `$_POST[f_name]`, `$_POST[l_name]`, and `$table_name` variables:

```
<P><? echo "$_POST[f_name] $_POST[l_name]"; ?> has been deleted
from <? echo "$table_name"; ?></p>
```

14. Add a link back to the main menu, and then add some more HTML so that the document is valid:

```
<br><p><a href="contact_menu.php">Return to Main Menu</a></p>
</BODY>
</HTML>
```

15. Save the file with the name `do_delcontact.php` and place this file in the document root of your Web server.

Your code should look something like this:

```
<?
//check for required form variables
if ((!$_POST[f_name]) || (!$_POST[l_name])) {
    header( "Location: http://127.0.0.1/pick_delcontact.php");
    exit;
} else {
    //if form variables are present, start a session
    session_start();
}

//check for validity of user
```

```php
if ($_SESSION[valid] != "yes") {
   header("Location: http://127.0.0.1/contact_menu.php");
   exit;
}

//set up table and database names
$db_name = "testDB";
$table_name = "my_contacts";

//connect to server and select database
$connection = @mysql_connect("localhost", "spike", "9sj7En4")
or die(mysql_error());
$db = @mysql_select_db($db_name, $connection) or
die(mysql_error());

//build and issue query
$sql = "DELETE FROM $table_name WHERE id = '$_POST[id]'";

$result = @mysql_query($sql,$connection) or die(mysql_error());
?>
<HTML>
<HEAD>
<TITLE>My Contact Management System: Contact Deleted</TITLE>
</HEAD>
<BODY>
<h2><em>Delete a Contact - Contact Deleted</em></h2>
<P><? echo "$_POST[f_name] $_POST[l_name]"; ?> has been deleted
from <? echo "$table_name"; ?></p>
<br><p><a href="contact_menu.php">Return to Main Menu</a></p>
</BODY>
</HTML>
```

Go on to the next step and delete some of the contacts in your database table.

Deleting Contacts

To start deleting contacts from the my_contacts table, open http://127.0.0.1/ contact_menu.php. If you've already logged in, you'll see your administrative menu. Otherwise, log in using the username (admin) and password (abc123).

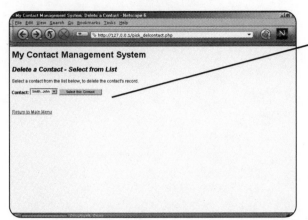

1. Select the Delete a Contact menu item.

You will see a drop-down menu of the contacts in the system, as well as a submit button and a link back to the Main Menu.

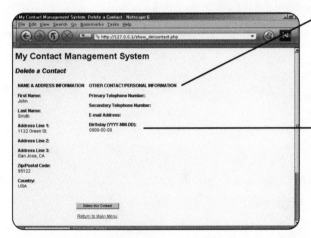

2. Select a contact from the list and click on the Select this Contact button. I selected a sample from my own list.

NOTE

The birthday in the displayed record shows 0000-00-00 because no date was entered in the original record. MySQL uses a default date for date fields.

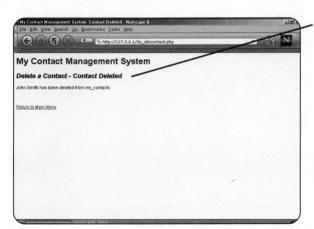

3. Click on the Delete this Contact button. You should see a confirmation screen.

Return to the selection form and select your contact again to see that the record no longer exists in the drop-down menu.

Delete a record or two, and then move on to the next chapter, where you'll create the read-only contact information screens.

22

Working with Contacts

You have all this information in a table, and I haven't shown you how to create any scripts for selecting and displaying read-only data. It's time to remedy that! In this chapter, you'll learn how to do the following:

- Count and display the number of contacts in your system
- Display the current date
- Check for birthdays in the current month and display special text
- Display read-only contact details
- Require session-based authentication before the script can be viewed or the record deleted

Modifying Your Administration Menu

The next few sections show some modifications you can make to the original `contact_menu.php` to display elements such as the current date, the number of contacts in the database, and other pieces of information that make your system more customized.

Showing the Number of Contacts

The following modifications will modify the `contact_menu.php` script so that it displays the current number of contacts in the `my_contacts` table.

1. Open `contact_menu.php` in your text editor.

2. Find this block of code, highlight it, and cut it out of the file (prepare to paste):

```
//build form block
$form_block = "
<h1>Login</h1>
<form method=POST action=\"$_SERVER[PHP_SELF]\">
$msg
<P><strong>username:</strong><br>
<input type=\"text\" name=\"username\" size=15 maxlength=25></P>
<P><strong>password:</strong><br>
<input type=\"password\" name=\"password\" size=15 maxlength=25>
</P>
<input type=\"hidden\" name=\"op\" value=\"ds\">
<P><input type=\"submit\" name=\"submit\" value=\"login\"></P>
</FORM>";
```

3. Find the `if…else` block that looks like the following:

```
if ($show_form == "yes") {
    $display_block = $form_block;
} else if ($show_menu == "yes") {
    $display_block = $menu_block;
}
```

4. Replace the following line with the section you cut in step 2:

```
$display_block = $form_block;
```

The if...else block should now look like this:

```
if ($show_form == "yes") {
    $form_block = "
    <h1>Login</h1>
    <form method=POST action=\"$_SERVER[PHP_SELF]\">
    $msg
    <P><strong>username:</strong><br>
    <input type=\"text\" name=\"username\" size=15 maxlength=25>
</P>
    <P><strong>password:</strong><br>
    <input type=\"password\" name=\"password\" size=15
maxlength=25></P>
    <input type=\"hidden\" name=\"op\" value=\"ds\">
    <P><input type=\"submit\" name=\"submit\" value=\"login\"></P>
    </FORM>";
} else if ($show_menu == "yes") {
    $display_block = $menu_block;
}
```

5. Change the name of the variable from `$form_block` to `$display_block`.

6. The if...else block should look like this:

```
if ($show_form == "yes") {
    //build form block
    $display_block = "
    <h1>Login</h1>
    <form method=POST action=\"$_SERVER[PHP_SELF]\">
    $msg
    <P><strong>username:</strong><br>
    <input type=\"text\" name=\"username\" size=15 maxlength=25>
</P>
    <P><strong>password:</strong><br>
    <input type=\"password\" name=\"password\" size=15
maxlength=25></P>
    <input type=\"hidden\" name=\"op\" value=\"ds\">
    <P><input type=\"submit\" name=\"submit\" value=\"login\"></P>
    </FORM>";
} else if ($show_menu == "yes") {
    $display_block = $menu_block;
}
```

7. Find the following block of code, highlight it, and cut it out of the file (prepare to paste):

```
$menu_block = "
<h1>My Contact Management System</h1>
<P><strong>Administration</strong>
<ul>
<li><a href=\"show_addcontact.php\">Add a Contact</a>
<li><a href=\"pick_modcontact.php\">Modify a Contact</a>
<li><a href=\"pick_delcontact.php\">Delete a Contact</a>
</ul>
<P><strong>View Records</strong>
<ul>
<li><a href=\"show_contactsbyname.php\">Show Contacts, Ordered by
Name</a>
</ul>";
```

8. Find the if...else block that contains the following:

```
} else if ($show_menu == "yes") {
    $display_block = $menu_block;
}
```

9. Replace the following line with the section you cut in step 7:

```
$display_block = $menu_block;
```

The if...else block should now look like this:

```
if ($show_form == "yes") {
    $display_block = "
    <h1>Login</h1>
    <form method=POST action=\"$_SERVER[PHP_SELF]\">
    $msg
    <P><strong>username:</strong><br>
    <input type=\"text\" name=\"username\" size=15 maxlength=25></P>
    <P><strong>password:</strong><br>
    <input type=\"password\" name=\"password\" size=15
maxlength=25></P>
    <input type=\"hidden\" name=\"op\" value=\"ds\">
    <P><input type=\"submit\" name=\"submit\" value=\"login\"></P>
    </FORM>";
} else if ($show_menu == "yes") {
    $menu_block = "
```

```
    <h1>My Contact Administration System</h1>
    <P><strong>Administration</strong>
    <ul>
    <li><a href=\"show_addcontact.php\">Add a Contact</a>
    <li><a href=\"pick_modcontact.php\">Modify a Contact</a>
    <li><a href=\"pick_delcontact.php\">Delete a Contact</a>
    </ul>
    <P><strong>View Records</strong>
    <ul>
    <li><a href=\"show_contactsbyname.php\">Show Contacts, Ordered
by Name</a>
    </ul>";
}
```

10. Change the name of the variable from $menu_block to $display_block.

11. The complete if...else block should look like this:

```
if ($show_form == "yes") {
    $display_block = "
    <h1>Login</h1>
    <form method=POST action=\"$_SERVER[PHP_SELF]\">
    $msg
    <P><strong>username:</strong><br>
    <input type=\"text\" name=\"username\" size=15 maxlength=25></P>
    <P><strong>password:</strong><br>
    <input type=\"password\" name=\"password\" size=15
maxlength=25></P>
    <input type=\"hidden\" name=\"op\" value=\"ds\">
    <P><input type=\"submit\" name=\"submit\" value=\"login\"></P>
    </FORM>";
} else if ($show_menu == "yes") {
    $display_block = "
    <h1>My Contact Administration System</h1>
    <P><strong>Administration</strong>
    <ul>
    <li><a href=\"show_addcontact.php\">Add a Contact</a>
    <li><a href=\"pick_modcontact.php\">Modify a Contact</a>
    <li><a href=\"pick_delcontact.php\">Delete a Contact</a>
    </ul>
    <P><strong>View Records</strong>
    <ul>
```

```
    <li><a href=\"show_contactsbyname.php\">Show Contacts, Ordered
by Name</a>
    </ul>";
}
```

12. Save your changes before going any further.

None of those changes modified the display in any way. They simply organized your code a little bit better in preparation for the next changes. These next changes will all take place within the second part of the if...else block you just modified.

1. Find this line, because the rest of the changes go right after it:

```
} else if ($show_menu == "yes") {
```

2. Create a variable to hold the name of the database on which the table resides:

```
$db_name = "testDB";
```

3. Create a variable to hold the name of the table you're populating with this script:

```
$table_name = "my_contacts";
```

4. Add the connection information as you have been:

```
$connection = @mysql_connect("localhost", "spike", "9sj7En4")
or die(mysql_error());
```

5. Select the database as you have learned:

```
$db = @mysql_select_db($db_name, $connection) or
die(mysql_error());
```

6. Create a SQL statement that counts the number of entries in the id field:

```
$sql = "SELECT count(id) FROM $table_name";
```

7. Create a variable to hold the result of the mysql_query() function, as you have learned:

```
$result = @mysql_query($sql,$connection) or die(mysql_error());
```

8. Create a variable to hold the specific value within the result:

```
$count = @mysql_result($result,0,"count(id)") or
die(mysql_error());
```

NOTE

If you're working with a one-field result, the `mysql_result()` function is simpler than fetching an entire row. This function requires the result of a valid query, a row (starting at 0), and the field name.

9. The next modification is primarily aesthetic. Take the string within `$display_block` and replace it with the following HTML, creating a two-column table for menu options:

```
$display_block = "
<h1>My Contact Management System</h1>
<table cellspacing=3 cellpadding=3>
<tr>
<td valign=top>
<P><strong>Administration</strong>
<ul>
<li><a href=\"show_addcontact.php\">Add a Contact</a>
<li><a href=\"pick_modcontact.php\">Modify a Contact</a>
<li><a href=\"pick_delcontact.php\">Delete a Contact</a>
</ul>
<P><strong>View Records</strong>
<ul>
<li><a href=\"show_contactsbyname.php\">Show Contacts, Ordered by
Name</a>
</ul>
</td>
<td valign=top>
<P><strong>Miscellaneous</strong></P>
</td>
</tr>
</table>";
```

10. In the new `$display_block` string, find the section for `Miscellaneous`. Start a bullet list, and then print a list item with a text label and a bold representation of the value of `$count`. After that list item, close the list itself:

```
<ul>
<li>Contacts in system: <strong>$count</strong>
</ul>
```

11. Save your changes.

Your new code should look like this:

```php
<?
//start a session
session_start();

//check if user is coming from a form
if ($_POST[op] == "ds") {
    //check username and password
    if (($_POST[username] != "admin") || ($_POST[password] !=
"abc123")) {
        //handle bad login
        $msg = "<P><font color=\"#FF0000\"><strong>Bad Login - Try
Again</strong></font></P>";
        $show_form = "yes";
    } else {
        //handle good login
        $valid = "yes";
        $_SESSION[valid] = $valid;
        $show_menu = "yes";
    }
} else {
    //determine what to show
    if ($_SESSION[valid] == "yes") {
        $show_menu = "yes";
    } else {
        $show_form = "yes";
    }
}
//assign the block to show to the $display_block variable
if ($show_form == "yes") {
    //build form block
    $display_block = "
    <h1>Login</h1>
    <form method=POST action=\"$_SERVER[PHP_SELF]\">
    $msg
    <P><strong>username:</strong><br>
    <input type=\"text\" name=\"username\" size=15 maxlength=25></P>
    <P><strong>password:</strong><br>
    <input type=\"password\" name=\"password\" size=15
```

```
maxlength=25></P>
    <input type=\"hidden\" name=\"op\" value=\"ds\">
    <P><input type=\"submit\" name=\"submit\" value=\"login\"></P>
    </FORM>";
} else if ($show_menu == "yes") {
    //set up table and database names
    $db_name = "testDB";
    $table_name = "my_contacts";

    //connect to server and select database
    $connection = @mysql_connect("localhost", "spike", "9sj7En4")
or die(mysql_error());
    $db = @mysql_select_db($db_name, $connection) or
die(mysql_error());

    //build and issue query
    $sql = "SELECT count(id) FROM $table_name";
    $result = @mysql_query($sql,$connection) or die(mysql_error());
    $count = @mysql_result($result,0,"count(id)") or
die(mysql_error());

    //build menu block
    $display_block = "
    <h1>My Contact Management System</h1>
    <table cellspacing=3 cellpadding=3>
    <tr>
    <td valign=top>
    <P><strong>Administration</strong>
    <ul>
    <li><a href=\"show_addcontact.php\">Add a Contact</a>
    <li><a href=\"pick_modcontact.php\">Modify a Contact</a>
    <li><a href=\"pick_delcontact.php\">Delete a Contact</a>
    </ul>
    <P><strong>View Records</strong>
    <ul>
    <li><a href=\"show_contactsbyname.php\">Show Contacts, Ordered
by Name</a>
    </ul>
    </td>
    <td valign=top>
    <P><strong>Miscellaneous</strong></P>
    <ul>
```

```
    <li>Contacts in system: <strong>$count</strong>
    </ul>
    </td>
    </tr>
    </table>";
}
?>
<HTML>
<HEAD>
<TITLE>My Contact Management System</TITLE>
</HEAD>
<BODY>
<? echo "$display_block"; ?>
</BODY>
</HTML>
```

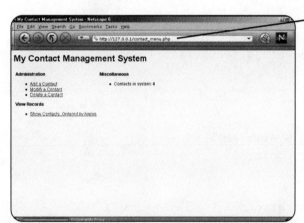

Open `http://127.0.0.1/ contact_menu.php`. If you've already logged in, you'll see your administrative menu. Otherwise, log in using the username (`admin`) and password (`abc123`). You should now see a new layout for the menu, as well as the number of contacts in the table, in the appropriate places.

In the next section, you'll display the current date on your menu.

Displaying Today's Date

Compared to the previous section, the changes needed to display the current date are a snap! The `date()` function is highly customizable once you know all the options.

NOTE

You can find a list of `date()` function options in Appendix B, "Basic PHP Language Reference."

---

1. Open `contact_menu.php` in your text editor.

2. Find this line because the rest of the changes go in this block:

```
} else if ($show_menu == "yes") {
```

3. After the line that assigns a value to the $count variable, add this line to create a variable called $today, containing a formatted date string:

```
$today = date("l, F jS, Y");
```

The date format options are interpreted as in Table 22.1.

Table 22.1 Date Formatting Example

Format Option	Description
l,	Long name of day (literal comma)
F	Long name of month
j	Day of month (2-digit)
S	Ordinal suffix
Y	Year (4-digit)

4. Find this line in the $display_block string:

```
<h1>My Contact Management System</h1>
```

5. After it, add the following to print the date string:

```
<p><em>Today is $today</em></p>
```

6. Save your file.

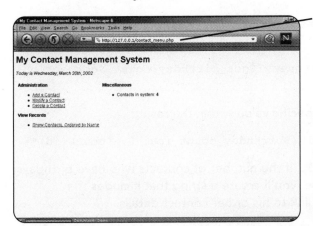

Open http://127.0.0.1/contact_menu.php. If you've already logged in, you'll see your administrative menu. Otherwise, log in using the username (admin) and password (abc123). You should now see a line of text that says "Today is [your date here]."

In the next section, you'll do some neat SQL to find the number of contacts whose birthdays occur during the current month, and you'll print their names in a list. This is helpful for people like me, who can't remember their mother's birthday, let alone anyone else's!

Showing the Birthdays in the Current Month

One of the fields in your database is a field for the person's birthday. It's not required, but if you take the time to enter someone's birthday, chances are good that you actually want to remember it. This next section will print the number of contacts who have birthdays in the current month, as well as the person's name and birthday and a link to his or her contact details. Nifty!

1. Open `contact_menu.php` in your text editor.

2. Find this line because the rest of the changes go in this block:

```
} else if ($show_menu == "yes") {
```

3. Now find the line that assigns a value to the `$today` variable because you'll start typing things after this line:

```
$today = date("l, F jS Y");
```

4. Create a SQL statement that gets the number of people who have birthdays in the current month:

```
$get_birthday_count = "SELECT count(id) FROM $table_name WHERE
MONTH(birthday) = MONTH(NOW())";
```

NOTE

`MONTH()` and `NOW()` are MySQL functions used to get the month out of a date string (in this case, the value of the birthday field) and the current date, respectively. You can learn more about MySQL functions in Appendix D, "Basic MySQL Reference."

---

5. Create a variable to hold the result of the `mysql_query()` function, as you have learned:

```
$birthday_count_res = @mysql_query($get_birthday_count,$connection)
or die(mysql_error());
```

6. Create a variable to hold the specific value within the result:

```
$birthday_count = mysql_result($birthday_count_res, 0, "count(id)");
```

Next, you'll have more fun with SQL. If the number of contacts who have birthdays in the current month is one or more, you'll create a string that includes the person's name and birthday and a link to his or her contact details.

1. Find the line in `contact_menu.php` that assigns a value to the `$birthday_count` variable, and after it create an `if` statement that will be executed if the value is true. In this case, it's looking for a positive value for `$birthday_count`:

```
if ($birthday_count > 0) {
```

2. You'll create a bullet list within a `while` block in a moment. Start the bullet list outside the `while` block:

```
$bd_string = "<ul>";
```

3. Create a SQL statement that selects the ID, first name, last name, month of the birthday, and day of the birthday and that orders the result set by birthday:

```
$get_contacts_bd = "SELECT id, f_name, l_name, MONTH(birthday) as
month, DAYOFMONTH(birthday) as date FROM $table_name WHERE
MONTH(birthday) = MONTH(NOW())ORDER BY birthday";
```

NOTE

You can select fields or parts of fields and assign a new name to them using as [new name] within your SQL statement. In the previous statement, you're extracting the month of a birthday and giving it a name of month, and you're extracting the day of a birthday and giving it a name of date.

---

4. Create a variable to hold the result of the `mysql_query()` function, as you have learned:

```
$contacts_bd_res = @mysql_query($get_contacts_bd, $connection)
or die(mysql_error());
```

5. Start the `while` loop. The `while` loop will create an array called `$contacts_bd` for each record in the result set (`$contacts_bd_res`):

```
while ($contacts_bd = mysql_fetch_array($contacts_bd_res)) {
```

6. Get the individual elements of the record, and give them good names:

```
$contact_id = $contacts_bd['id'];
$contact_fname = $contacts_bd['f_name'];
$contact_lname = $contacts_bd['l_name'];
$contact_bd_month = $contacts_bd['month'];
$contact_bd_date = $contacts_bd['date'];
```

7. Append a list item to `$bd_string` that contains the person's name and birthday. Create a link to a script called `show_contact.php`, which you'll create in the next section:

```
$bd_string .= "<li>
<a href=\"show_contact.php?id=$contact_id\">$contact_fname
$contact_lname</a> ($contact_bd_month"."-"."$contact_bd_date)";
```

8. Close the `while` loop, then the bullet list, then the `if` statement:

```
}
$bd_string .= "</ul>";
}
```

9. Inside `$display_block`, within the bullet list under the `Miscellaneous` heading, and under a "Birthdays this month" list item, add the following:

```
$bd_string
```

10. Save your file. The final `contact_menu.php` script should look like this:

```
<?
//start a session
session_start();

//check if user is coming from a form
if ($_POST[op] == "ds") {

    //check username and password
    if (($_POST[username] != "admin") || ($_POST[password] !=
"abc123")) {
        //handle bad login
        $msg = "<P><font color=\"#FF0000\"><strong>Bad Login - Try
Again</strong></font></P>";
        $show_form = "yes";
    } else {
        //handle good login
        $valid = "yes";
        $_SESSION[valid] = $valid;
        $show_menu = "yes";
    }
} else {
    //determine what to show
    if ($_SESSION[valid] == "yes") {
        $show_menu = "yes";
```

```php
    } else {
        $show_form = "yes";
    }
}

//assign the block to show to the $display_block variable
if ($show_form == "yes") {
    //build form block
    $display_block = "
    <h1>Login</h1>
    <form method=POST action=\"$_SERVER[PHP_SELF]\">
    $msg
    <P><strong>username:</strong><br>
    <input type=\"text\" name=\"username\" size=15 maxlength=25>
</P>
    <P><strong>password:</strong><br>
    <input type=\"password\" name=\"password\" size=15
maxlength=25></P>
    <input type=\"hidden\" name=\"op\" value=\"ds\">
    <P><input type=\"submit\" name=\"submit\" value=\"login\"></P>
    </FORM>";
} else if ($show_menu == "yes") {
    //set up table and database names
    $db_name = "testDB";
    $table_name = "my_contacts";

    //connect to server and select database
    $connection = @mysql_connect("localhost", "spike", "9sj7En4")
or die(mysql_error());
    $db = @mysql_select_db($db_name, $connection) or
die(mysql_error());

    //build and issue query
    $sql = "SELECT count(id) FROM $table_name";
    $result = @mysql_query($sql,$connection) or die(mysql_error());
    $count = @mysql_result($result,0,"count(id)") or
die(mysql_error());

    //get current date
    $today = date("l, F jS, Y");

    //get birthday count
```

```php
    $get_birthday_count = "SELECT count(id) FROM $table_name WHERE
MONTH(birthday) = MONTH(NOW())";
    $birthday_count_res = @mysql_query($get_birthday_count,
$connection) or die(mysql_error());
    $birthday_count = mysql_result($birthday_count_res, 0,
"count(id)");

    //create a list, based on a postive result
    if ($birthday_count > 0) {
        $bd_string = "<ul>";
        $get_contacts_bd = "SELECT id, f_name, l_name,
MONTH(birthday) as month, DAYOFMONTH(birthday) as date FROM
$table_name WHERE MONTH(birthday) = MONTH(NOW())ORDER BY
birthday";
        $contacts_bd_res = @mysql_query($get_contacts_bd,
$connection) or die(mysql_error());

        while ($contacts_bd = mysql_fetch_array($contacts_bd_res))
{
            $contact_id = $contacts_bd['id'];
            $contact_fname = $contacts_bd['f_name'];
            $contact_lname = $contacts_bd['l_name'];
            $contact_bd_month = $contacts_bd['month'];
            $contact_bd_date = $contacts_bd['date'];

            $bd_string .= "<li>
<a href=\"show_contact.php?id=$contact_id\">$contact_fname
$contact_lname</a> ($contact_bd_month"."-"."$contact_bd_date)";
        }

        $bd_string .= "</ul>";
    }

    //build menu block
    $display_block = "
    <h1>My Contact Management System</h1>
    <p><em>Today is $today</em></p>
    <table cellspacing=3 cellpadding=3>
    <tr>
    <td valign=top>
    <P><strong>Administration</strong>
    <ul>
    <li><a href=\"show_addcontact.php\">Add a Contact</a>
```

```
            <li><a href=\"pick_modcontact.php\">Modify a Contact</a>
            <li><a href=\"pick_delcontact.php\">Delete a Contact</a>
            </ul>
            <P><strong>View Records</strong>
            <ul>
            <li><a href=\"show_contactsbyname.php\">Show Contacts, Ordered
        by Name</a>
            </ul>
            </td>
            <td valign=top>
            <P><strong>Miscellaneous</strong></P>
            <ul>
            <li>Contacts in system: <strong>$count</strong>
            <li>Birthdays this month: <strong>$birthday_count</strong>
            $bd_string
            </ul>
            </td>
            </tr>
            </table>";
        }
        ?>
        <HTML>
        <HEAD>
        <TITLE>My Contact Management System</TITLE>
        </HEAD>
        <BODY>
        <? echo "$display_block"; ?>
        </BODY>
        </HTML>
```

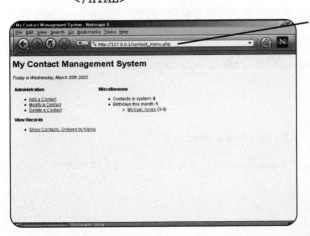

Open http://127.0.0.1/
contact_menu.php. If you've already
logged in, you'll see your administrative
menu. Otherwise, log in using the username
(admin) and password (abc123). If you have
any contacts in your database table whose
birthdays are in the current month, you
should see their names and birthdays listed.

In the next section, you'll create the contact
details script to display all the contact
information you've been putting in the
my_contacts table.

Selecting Data from the my_contacts Table

Now that all the difficult scripting is out of the way, it's time to do some simple SQL selects to display the data in the my_contacts table. You'll start by listing the contacts, and then you'll show the contact details.

Displaying the Record List

The goal of this script is to display a bullet list of the contacts in your database table, complete with a link to the show_contact.php script.

1. Open a new file in your text editor and start a PHP block:

```
<?
```

2. Start a session, or continue a session if one currently exists:

```
session_start();
```

3. Start an if…else block that checks the value of $_SESSION[valid] and performs a particular action based on the result. If the value is not yes, the user didn't go through the proper authentication channels:

```
if ($_SESSION[valid] != "yes") {
```

4. Send the user back to the login form, and exit this script:

```
header("Location: http://127.0.0.1/contact_menu.php");
exit;
}
```

5. Create a variable to hold the name of the database on which the table resides:

```
$db_name = "testDB";
```

6. Create a variable to hold the name of the table you're populating with this script:

```
$table_name = "my_contacts";
```

7. Add the connection information as you have been:

```
$connection = @mysql_connect("localhost", "spike", "9sj7En4")
or die(mysql_error());
```

8. Select the database as you have learned:

```
$db = @mysql_select_db($db_name, $connection) or
die(mysql_error());
```

9. Create the SQL statement. You want to select just the ID number, first name, and last name of each record in the table:

```
$sql = "SELECT id, f_name, l_name FROM $table_name ORDER BY l_name";
```

10. Create a variable to hold the result of the mysql_query() function, as you have learned:

```
$result = @mysql_query($sql,$connection) or die(mysql_error());
```

11. You'll create a bullet list within a while block in a moment. Start the bullet list outside the while block:

```
$contact_list = "<ul>";
```

12. Start the while loop. The while loop will create an array called $row for each record in the result set ($result):

```
while ($row = mysql_fetch_array($result)) {
```

13. Get the individual elements of the record, and give them good names:

```
$id = $row['id'];
$f_name = $row['f_name'];
$l_name = $row['l_name'];
```

14. Append a list item to $contact_list that contains the person's name within a link to a script called show_contact.php:

```
$contact_list .= "<li><a href=\"show_contact.php?id=$id\">$l_name,
$f_name</a>";
```

15. Close the while loop, the bullet list, and the PHP block:

```
}
$contact_list .= "</ul>";
?>
```

16. Add this HTML:

```
<HTML>
<HEAD>
<TITLE>My Contact Management System: Contacts Listed by Name</TITLE>
</HEAD>
```

```
<BODY>
<h1>My Contact Management System</h1>
<P>Select a contact from the list below, to view the contact's
record.</P>
```

17. Display the contents of `$contact_list`:

```
<? echo "$contact_list"; ?>
```

18. Add a link back to the main menu:

```
<br><p><a href="contact_menu.php">Return to Main Menu</a></p>
```

19. Add some more HTML so that the document is valid:

```
</BODY>
</HTML>
```

20. Save the file with the name `show_contactsbyname.php` and place this file in the document root of your Web server.

Your code should look something like this:

```
<?
//start a session
session_start();

//check for validity of user
if ($_SESSION[valid] != "yes") {
    header("Location: http://127.0.0.1/contact_menu.php");
    exit;
}

//set up table and database names
$db_name = "testDB";
$table_name = "my_contacts";

//connect to server and select database
$connection = @mysql_connect("localhost", "spike", "9sj7En4")
or die(mysql_error());
$db = @mysql_select_db($db_name, $connection) or
die(mysql_error());

//build and issue query
```

```php
$sql = "SELECT id, f_name, l_name FROM $table_name ORDER BY l_name";
$result = @mysql_query($sql,$connection) or die(mysql_error());

//create list block of results
$contact_list = "<ul>";
while ($row = mysql_fetch_array($result)) {
    $id = $row['id'];
    $f_name = $row['f_name'];
    $l_name = $row['l_name'];
    $contact_list .= "<li><a
href=\"show_contact.php?id=$id\">$l_name, $f_name</a>";
}
$contact_list .= "</ul>";
?>
<HTML>
<HEAD>
<TITLE>My Contact Management System: Contacts Listed by Name
</TITLE>
</HEAD>
<BODY>
<h1>My Contact Management System</h1>
<P>Select a contact from the list below, to view the contact's
record.</P>
<? echo "$contact_list"; ?>
<br><p><a href="contact_menu.php">Return to Main Menu</a></p>
</BODY>
</HTML>
```

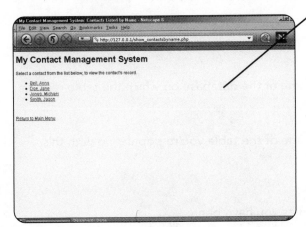

Open http://127.0.0.1/
contact_menu.php. If you've already
logged in, you'll see your administrative
menu. Otherwise, log in using the username
(admin) and password (abc123). Select the
Show Contacts, Ordered by Name link.

In the next section, you'll create the contact
display page, show_contact.php.

Displaying Read-Only Records

It's the moment of truth: displaying your contacts!

1. Open a new file in your text editor and start a PHP block:

```
<?
```

2. Start an if...else block that checks for a value for $_GET[id], the one variable sent in the link's query string. If a value doesn't exist, direct the user back to the menu, and exit the script:

```
if (!$_GET[id]) {
    header( "Location: http://127.0.0.1/contact_menu.php");
    exit;
```

3. If the required field has a value, start a session or continue a session if one currently exists, and then close the block:

```
} else {
    session_start();
}
```

4. Start an if...else block that checks the value of $_SESSION[valid] and performs a particular action based on the result. If the value is not yes, the user didn't go through the proper authentication channels:

```
if ($_SESSION[valid] != "yes") {
```

5. Send the user back to the login form, and exit this script:

```
header("Location: http://127.0.0.1/contact_menu.php");
exit;
}
```

6. Create a variable to hold the name of the database on which the table resides:

```
$db_name = "testDB";
```

7. Create a variable to hold the name of the table you're populating with this script:

```
$table_name = "my_contacts";
```

8. Add the connection information as you have been:

```
$connection = @mysql_connect("localhost", "spike", "9sj7En4")
or die(mysql_error());
```

9. Select the database as you have learned:

```
$db = @mysql_select_db($db_name, $connection) or die(mysql_error());
```

10. Perform some validation on the value of $_GET[id]. You want to make sure that the number really exists in the system before you run SQL queries using a bad key!

```
$chk_id = "SELECT id FROM $table_name WHERE id = '$_GET[id]'";
```

11. Create a variable to hold the result of the mysql_query() function, as you have learned:

```
$chk_id_res = @mysql_query($chk_id,$connection) or
die(mysql_error());
```

12. Create a variable to count the number of rows within the result. There should be one row:

```
$chk_id_num = mysql_num_rows($chk_id_res);
```

13. Start an if...else block to deal with the results of the validation. The first section checks the row count. You want there to be one, and only one, row:

```
if ($chk_id_num != 1) {
```

14. If the row count is anything other than 1, the id was invalid. Redirect the user to the menu, and exit the script:

```
header("Location: http://127.0.0.1/contact_menu.php");
exit;
```

15. Continue the if...else statement, now preparing to act on a valid result:

```
} else {
```

16. Create the SQL statement. You want to select all the fields in the database except id for the record that has an ID equal to the value of $_GET[id]:

```
$sql = "SELECT f_name, l_name, address1, address2, address3,
postcode, country, prim_tel, sec_tel, email, birthday FROM
$table_name WHERE id = '$_GET[id]'";
```

17. Create a variable to hold the result of the mysql_query() function, as you have learned:

```
$result = @mysql_query($sql,$connection) or die(mysql_error());
```

18. Start the while loop. The while loop will create an array called $row for each record in the result set ($result):

```
while ($row = mysql_fetch_array($result)) {
```

19. Get the individual elements of the record, and give them good names:

```
$f_name = $row['f_name'];
$l_name = $row['l_name'];
$address1 = $row['address1'];
$address2 = $row['address2'];
$address3 = $row['address3'];
$postcode = $row['postcode'];
$country = $row['country'];
$prim_tel = $row['prim_tel'];
$sec_tel = $row['sec_tel'];
$email = $row['email'];
$birthday = $row['birthday'];
```

20. Close the `while` loop, the `if...else` loop, and the PHP block:

```
    }
}
?>
```

21. Type this HTML to start building the record details screen:

```
<HTML>
<HEAD>
<TITLE>My Contact Management System: Read-Only Contact Details</
TITLE>
</HEAD>
<BODY>
<h1>My Contact Management System</h1>
```

22. Mingle HTML and PHP to show a nice title with the contact's full name:

```
<h2>Contact Details for <? echo "$f_name $l_name"; ?></h2>
```

23. Start a paragraph with a text label:

```
<P><strong>Name & Address:</strong><br>
```

24. Display all the individual elements for name and address:

```
<? echo "$f_name $l_name"; ?><br>
<? echo "$address1"; ?><br>
<? echo "$address2"; ?><br>
<? echo "$address3"; ?><br>
<? echo "$postcode"; ?><br>
<? echo "$country"; ?></P>
```

25. Start a paragraph, then print text labels and results for the telephone and e-mail fields:

```
<P><strong>Tel 1:</strong> <? echo "$prim_tel"; ?><br>
<strong>Tel 2:</strong> <? echo "$sec_tel"; ?><br>
<strong>E-Mail:</strong> <? echo "<a
href=\"mailto:$email\">$email</a>"; ?></P>
```

26. Start a paragraph, then print a text label and result for the birthday:

```
<P><strong>Birthday:</strong> <? echo "$birthday"; ?></P>
```

27. Add a link back to the main menu, and then add some more HTML so that the document is valid:

```
<p><a href="contact_menu.php">Return to Main Menu</a></p>
</BODY>
</HTML>
```

28. Save the file with the name show_contact.php and place this file in the document root of your Web server.

Your code should look something like this:

```
<?
//check for required query string variables
if (!$_GET[id]) {
    header( "Location: http://127.0.0.1/contact_menu.php");
    exit;
} else {
    //if form variables are present, start a session
    session_start();
}

//check for validity of user
if ($_SESSION[valid] != "yes") {
    header("Location: http://127.0.0.1/contact_menu.php");
    exit;
}

//set up table and database names
$db_name = "testDB";
$table_name = "my_contacts";

//connect to server and select database
```

```php
$connection = @mysql_connect("localhost", "spike", "9sj7En4")
or die(mysql_error());
$db = @mysql_select_db($db_name, $connection) or
die(mysql_error());

//build and issue query
$chk_id = "SELECT id FROM $table_name WHERE id = '$_GET[id]'";
$chk_id_res = @mysql_query($chk_id,$connection) or
die(mysql_error());
$chk_id_num = mysql_num_rows($chk_id_res);

//check for valid results
if ($chk_id_num != 1) {
    //if not valid, redirect to menu
    header("Location: http://127.0.0.1/contact_menu.php");
    exit;
} else {
    //if valid, get information
    $sql = "SELECT f_name, l_name, address1, address2, address3,
postcode, country, prim_tel, sec_tel, email, birthday FROM
$table_name WHERE id = '$_GET[id]'";
    $result = @mysql_query($sql,$connection) or die(mysql_error());

//get results for display
    while ($row = mysql_fetch_array($result)) {
        $f_name = $row['f_name'];
        $l_name = $row['l_name'];
        $address1 = $row['address1'];
        $address2 = $row['address2'];
        $address3 = $row['address3'];
        $postcode = $row['postcode'];
        $country = $row['country'];
        $prim_tel = $row['prim_tel'];
        $sec_tel = $row['sec_tel'];
        $email = $row['email'];
        $birthday = $row['birthday'];
    }
}
?>
<HTML>
<HEAD>
```

```
<TITLE>My Contact Management System: Read-Only Contact Details
</TITLE>
</HEAD>
<BODY>
<h1>My Contact Management System</h1>
<h2>Contact Details for <? echo "$f_name $l_name"; ?></h2>
<P><strong>Name & Address:</strong><br>
<? echo "$f_name $l_name"; ?><br>
<? echo "$address1"; ?><br>
<? echo "$address2"; ?><br>
<? echo "$address3"; ?><br>
<? echo "$postcode"; ?><br>
<? echo "$country"; ?></P>
<P><strong>Tel 1:</strong> <? echo "$prim_tel"; ?><br>
<strong>Tel 2:</strong> <? echo "$sec_tel"; ?><br>
<strong>E-Mail:</strong> <? echo "<a
href=\"mailto:$email\">$email</a>"; ?></P>
<P><strong>Birthday:</strong> <? echo "$birthday"; ?></P>
<p><a href="contact_menu.php">Return to Main Menu</a></p>
</BODY>
</HTML>
```

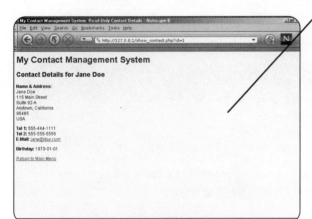

Open `http://127.0.0.1/contact_menu.php`. If you've already logged in, you'll see your administrative menu. Otherwise, log in using the username (`admin`) and password (`abc123`). Select the Show Contacts, Ordered by Name link, and then select one of your contacts from the list.

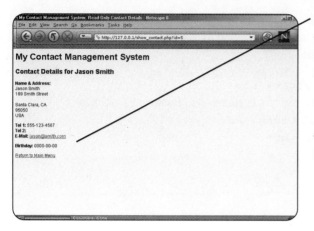

Looks good! This is a contact in my database table that's complete. But here's what happens when the contact isn't complete, and no birthday has been entered.

Pretty ugly! Make some modifications to show_contact.php to take into account the fact that only two fields (first name and last name) are required.

1. Open show_contact.php.

2. Scroll down to the Name & Address section:

3. Delete this section:

```
<? echo "$address1"; ?><br>
<? echo "$address2"; ?><br>
<? echo "$address3"; ?><br>
<? echo "$postcode"; ?><br>
<? echo "$country"; ?></P>
<P><strong>Tel 1:</strong> <? echo "$prim_tel"; ?><br>
<strong>Tel 2:</strong> <? echo "$sec_tel"; ?><br>
<strong>E-Mail:</strong> <? echo "<a
href=\"mailto:$email\">$email</a>"; ?></P>
<P><strong>Birthday:</strong> <? echo "$birthday"; ?></P>
```

4. Type the following series of if statements, which look for a value of the specific variable and print the line only if a value is present:

```
<?
    if ($address1 != "") {
        echo "$address1 <br>";
    }
    if ($address2 != "") {
        echo "$address2 <br>";
    }
    if ($address3 != "") {
        echo "$address3 <br>";
```

```
        }
    if ($postcode != "") {
        echo "$postcode <br>";
    }
    if ($country != "") {
        echo "$country <br>";
    }
?>
</P>
<P>
<?
    if ($prim_tel != "") {
        echo "<strong>Tel 1:</strong> $prim_tel <br>";
    }
    if ($sec_tel != "") {
        echo "<strong>Tel 2:</strong> $sec_tel <br>";
    }
    if ($email != "") {
        echo "<strong>E-Mail:</strong> <a
href=\"mailto:$email\">$email</a> <br>";
    }
?>
</P>
<?
    if ($birthday != "0000-00-00") {
        echo "<P><strong>Birthday:</strong> $birthday </P>";
    }
?>
```

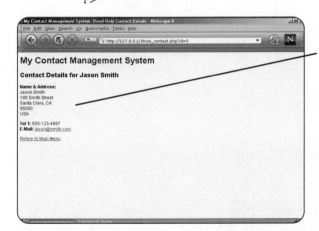

5. Save this file.

Now when I view an incomplete record, I don't see all that white space.

So there you have it—a complete online contact management system utilizing sessions and user authentication. There are plenty of areas for modification and additional validation checks, so take some time and play with these scripts until you are comfortable with the concepts. These simple concepts will help you to understand and build larger applications.

### PART VII

Additional Administration Scripts

23

Managing a Simple Mailing List

Eventually, your Web site will have users, and someday you might even want to send a newsletter to them. You can create a very simple subscription and publication mechanism using PHP and MySQL. In this chapter, you'll learn how to do the following:

- Create a subscribe/unsubscribe script
- Create a front end to sending a newsletter
- Create a script that mails your newsletter to all recipients in your database

A Brief Word about Mailing List Software

Several very good mailing list applications are available to send mail to large numbers of e-mail addresses. The type of system you'll build in this chapter should be used for only small lists of less than a few hundred e-mail addresses.

The system described in this chapter was born from my own laziness one day when I didn't want to download and install any third-party software. I just made some very simple files that performed a task.

That's the beauty of PHP: it's such a simple language that sometimes it's easier to write a few scripts than to download or install something. However, when your mailing list grows large enough, please move to a more robust mailing list application that's a bit easier on your outgoing mail server, and also on you, the administrator.

Developing a Subscription Mechanism

Before you can start sending mail to a mailing list, you need to build up that subscriber base. A simple subscribe/unsubscribe script will take care of that! All this script does is add or delete records in a MySQL database table, called `subscribers`, which you'll create in the next section.

Creating the subscribers Table

My subscribers table has three fields, as shown in Table 23.1. You can have as many or as few fields as you'd like.

Table 23.1   Fields for Subscribers

Field Name	Description
id	A primary key that holds the subscriber's auto-incrementing ID number
email_addr	Holds the subscriber's e-mail address
date_added	The date the user subscribed

Next, you'll actually create this table using the table-creation scripts you're familiar with at this point!

1. Open your Web browser and type **http://127.0.0.1/show_createtable.html**

2. In the Table Name field, type **subscribers**.

3. In the Number of Fields field, type **3**.

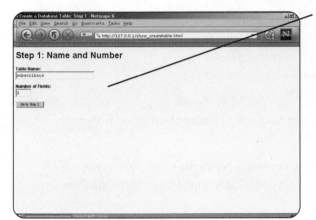

Before you submit the form, it should look like this.

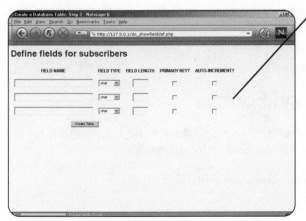

4. Click on the Go to Step 2 button. You should see the form in the figure.

There are three rows, corresponding to the three fields you want to create in the subscribers table. Populate the fields in these next steps:

1. In the first row, type **id** for Field Name, select int from the Field Type drop-down menu, check the box for Primary Key, and check the box for Auto-Increment.

2. In the second row, type **email_addr** for Field Name, select varchar from the Field Type drop-down menu, and specify a Field Length of **100**.

3. In the third row, type **date_added** for Field Name and select date from the Field Type drop-down menu.

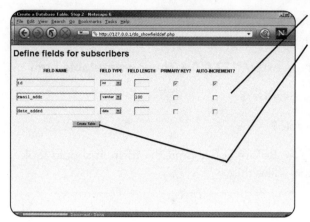

The completed form should look like the figure.

4. Click on the Create Table button to create the `subscribers` table.

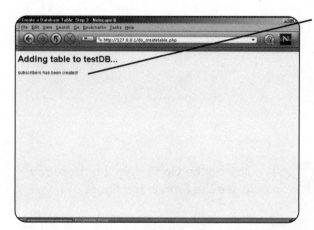

You will see a confirmation of the table creation.

In the next section, you will create the subscribe/unsubscribe form mechanism.

Creating the Subscription Form

Like the all-in-one mail form in Chapter 8, "Sending E-Mail," the subscription form will be used for subscribing, unsubscribing, and error checking.

1. Open a new file in your text editor and start a PHP block:

```
<?
```

2. Create a variable to hold the name of the database on which the table resides:

```
$db_name = "testDB";
```

3. Create a variable to hold the name of the table you're populating with this script:

```
$table_name = "subscribers";
```

4. Create a variable to hold the current date in MySQL date format:

```
$add_date = date("Y-m-d");
```

Next, you'll check for a variable you haven't yet created. When you create the actual HTML form, you'll add a hidden field called op with a value of ds. The $_POST[op] variable will be present only if the form has been submitted.

5. Start an if...else block, and first check if the value of $_POST[op] is ds:

```
if ($_POST[op] != "ds") {
```

6. If the value of $_POST[op] is not ds, the user hasn't seen the form. If the user hasn't seen the form, you need to show it. Create a variable called $text_block, which will hold the entire form. Start with the form action, and assume that the method is POST and the action is $_SERVER[PHP_SELF]:

```
$text_block = "
<form method=POST action=\"$_SERVER[PHP_SELF]\">
```

7. Add the hidden field:

```
<input type=hidden name=op value=ds>
```

8. Create an input field for the user's e-mail address with a text label:

```
<p><strong>Your E-Mail Address:</strong><br>
<input type=text name=\"email_addr\" size=25 maxlength=100></p>
```

9. Create a set of radio buttons so that the user can select an action of subscribe or unsubscribe. The default should be the subscribe radio button:

```
<p><strong>Action:</strong><br>
<input type=radio name=\"action\" value=\"sub\" checked> subscribe
<input type=radio name=\"action\" value=\"unsub\"> unsubscribe</p>
```

10. Add a submit button, then close the form and string:

```
<p><input type=submit name=\"submit\" value=\"Submit Form\"></p>
</form>";
```

11. Continue the if...else block to check for a value of ds for $_POST[op] as well as a value of sub for the $_POST[action] variable. This means that the user is attempting to subscribe:

```
} else if (($_POST[op] == "ds") && ($_POST[action] == "sub")) {
```

12. But what if someone clicks on the button and doesn't enter an e-mail address? Add an `if` block that checks for a value in `$_POST[email_addr]`. If a value is not found, redirect the user to the original form:

```
if ($_POST[email_addr] == "") {
    header("Location: http://127.0.0.1/manage.php");
    exit;
}
```

13. You'll need to check that the user isn't already subscribed, so open a database connection as you have learned:

```
$connection = @mysql_connect("localhost", "spike", "9sj7En4")
or die(mysql_error());
```

14. Select the database as you have learned:

```
$db = @mysql_select_db($db_name, $connection) or die(mysql_error());
```

15. Create a SQL statement that looks for records matching the user's e-mail address:

```
$check = "select email_addr from $table_name where email_addr =
'$_POST[email_addr]'";
```

16. Create a variable to hold the result of the `mysql_query()` function, as you have learned:

```
$check_result = @mysql_query($check,$connection) or
die(mysql_error());
```

17. Create a variable to count the number of rows in the result set:

```
$check_num = mysql_num_rows($check_result);
```

18. Create an inner `if...else` block that performs an action based on the value of `$check_num`. If `$check_num` is less than 1, no entries in the `subscribers` table have the user's e-mail address, so it's safe to insert one:

```
if ($check_num < 1) {
```

19. Create a SQL statement to insert the e-mail address and current date (leave a blank entry for the auto-incrementing `id`):

```
$sql = "insert into $table_name values('', '$_POST[email_addr]',
'$add_date')";
```

20. Execute the query, as you have learned:

```
$result = @mysql_query($sql,$connection) or die(mysql_error());
```

21. Create a message string so that the user knows the result:

```
$text_block = "<P>Thanks for signing up!</P>";
```

22. Finish the if...else block by creating a message string that tells the user she has already signed up. Then close the inner if...else block:

```
} else {
    $text_block = "<P>You're already subscribed!</P>";
}
```

23. Continue the outer if...else block to check for a value of ds for $_POST[op] as well as a value of unsub for the $_POST[action] variable. This means that the user is attempting to unsubscribe.

```
} else if (($_POST[op] == "ds") && ($_POST[action] == "unsub")) {
```

24. Again, add the validation that checks for a value in $_POST[email]_addr. If a value is not found, redirect the user to the original form:

```
if ($_POST[email_addr] == "") {
    header("Location: http://127.0.0.1/manage.php");
    exit;
}
```

25. You'll need to check that the user is in fact subscribed, so open a database connection and select the database:

```
$connection = @mysql_connect("localhost", "spike", "9sj7En4")
or die(mysql_error());
$db = @mysql_select_db($db_name, $connection) or
die(mysql_error());
```

26. Create a SQL statement that looks for records matching the user's e-mail address. Also select the id field because you'll use it to unsubscribe if you find a match:

```
$check = "select id, email_addr from $table_name where email_addr
= '$_POST[email_addr]'";
```

27. Execute the query:

```
$check_result = @mysql_query($check, $connection) or
die(mysql_error());
```

28. Create a variable to count the number of rows in the result set:

```
$check_num = mysql_num_rows($check_result);
```

29. Create an inner `if...else` block that performs an action based on the value of `$check_num`. If `$check_num` is less than 1, no entries in the `subscribers` table have the user's e-mail address, so you can't unsubscribe the user.

```
if ($check_num < 1) {
```

30. Create a message string so that the user knows the result:

```
$text_block = "<P>Couldn't find your e-mail on the list!</P>
<P>You haven't been unsubscribed, because the e-mail you entered
is not in the database.</P>";
```

31. Continue the inner `if...else` block:

```
} else {
```

32. Create a variable to hold the specific value of `id` from the previous result set:

```
$id = @mysql_result($check_result, 0, "id");
```

33. Create a SQL statement that deletes the user's e-mail address from the `subscribers` table:

```
$sql = "delete from $table_name where id = '$_POST[id]'";
```

34. Execute the query:

```
$result = @mysql_query($sql,$connection) or die(mysql_error());
```

35. Create a message string so that the user knows the result:

```
$text_block = "<P>You're unsubscribed!</p>";
```

36. Close the inner `if...else` block, the outer `if...else` block, and the PHP block:

```
    }
}
?>
```

37. Add the following HTML:

```
<HTML>
<HEAD>
<TITLE>Subscribe/Unsubscribe</TITLE>
</HEAD>
<BODY>
<h1>Subscribe/Unsubscribe</h1>
```

38. Display the contents of $text_block:

```php
<?php echo "$text_block"; ?>
```

39. Add some more HTML so that the document is valid:

```
</BODY>
</HTML>
```

40. Save the file with the name manage.php and place this file in the document root of your Web server.

Your entire code should look something like this:

```php
<?
//set up table and database names
$db_name = "testDB";
$table_name = "subscribers";

//get current date
$add_date = date("Y-m-d");

//determine if they need to see the form or not
if ($_POST[op] != "ds") {
    //create form block
    $text_block = "
    <form method=POST action=\"$_SERVER[PHP_SELF]\">
    <input type=hidden name=op value=ds>
    <p><strong>Your E-Mail Address:</strong><br>
    <input type=text name=\"email_addr\" size=25 maxlength=100></p>
    <p><strong>Action:</strong><br>
    <input type=radio name=\"action\" value=\"sub\" checked> subscribe
    <input type=radio name=\"action\" value=\"unsub\"> unsubscribe</p>
    <p><input type=submit name=\"submit\" value=\"Submit Form\"></p>
    </form>";
} else if (($_POST[op] == "ds") && ($_POST[action] == "sub")) {
    //trying to subscribe; validate email address
    if ($_POST[email_addr] == "") {
        header("Location: http://127.0.0.1/manage.php");
        exit;
    }

//connect to server and select database
```

```php
    $connection = @mysql_connect("localhost", "spike", "9sj7En4")
or die(mysql_error());
    $db = @mysql_select_db($db_name, $connection) or
die(mysql_error());

    //check that email is not already in list
    $check = "select email_addr from $table_name where email_addr =
'$_POST[email_addr]'";
    $check_result = @mysql_query($check,$connection) or
die(mysql_error());
    $check_num = mysql_num_rows($check_result);

    //get number of results and do action
    if ($check_num < 1) {
        //add record
        $sql = "insert into $table_name values('',
'$_POST[email_addr]', '$add_date')";
        $result = @mysql_query($sql,$connection) or
die(mysql_error());
        $text_block = "<P>Thanks for signing up!</P>";
    } else {
        //print failure message
        $text_block = "<P>You're already subscribed!</P>";
    }

} else if (($_POST[op] == "ds") && ($_POST[action] == "unsub")) {
    //trying to unsubscribe; validate email address
    if ($_POST[email_addr] == "") {
        header("Location: http://127.0.0.1/manage.php");
        exit;
    }

//connect to server and select database
    $connection = @mysql_connect("localhost", "spike", "9sj7En4")
or die(mysql_error());
    $db = @mysql_select_db($db_name, $connection) or
die(mysql_error());

    //check that email is in list
    $check = "select id, email_addr from $table_name where
email_addr = '$_POST[email_addr]'";
```

```
    $check_result = @mysql_query($check, $connection) or
die(mysql_error());
    $check_num = mysql_num_rows($check_result);

    //get number of results and do action
    if ($check_num < 1) {
        //print failure message
        $text_block = "<P>Couldn't find your e-mail on the list!
</P>
        <P>You haven't been unsubscribed, because the e-mail you
entered is not in the database.</P>";
    } else {
        //unsubscribe the address
        $id = @mysql_result($check_result, 0, "id");
        $sql = "delete from $table_name where id = '$id'";
        $result = @mysql_query($sql,$connection) or
die(mysql_error());
        $text_block = "<P>You're unsubscribed!</p>";
    }
}
?>
<HTML>
<HEAD>
<TITLE>Subscribe/Unsubscribe</TITLE>
</HEAD>
<BODY>
<h1>Subscribe/Unsubscribe</h1>
<?php echo "$text_block"; ?>
</BODY>
</HTML>
```

In the next section, you'll subscribe and unsubscribe sample users and see how all the address validation works out.

Testing the Subscription Form

Now that you've made it through all those steps in creating the subscription form, it's time to test it!

1. Open your Web browser and type **http://127.0.0.1/manage.php**

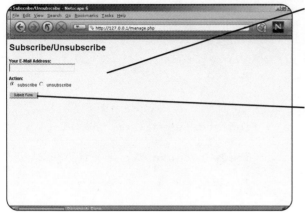

You will see a form containing a text field for the person's e-mail address, two radio buttons for either subscribing or unsubscribing, and a button that says Submit Form.

2. Type your e-mail address in the Your E-Mail Address field, and select the subscribe radio button, then submit the form.

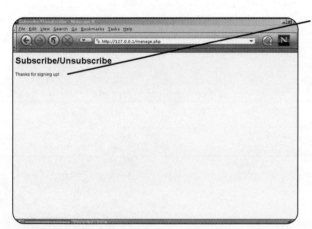

You will see a confirmation that your subscription was successful.

3. Return to the form using your Web browser's Back button, and type the same e-mail address in the Your E-Mail Address field.

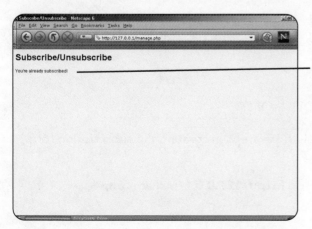

4. Select the subscribe radio button (again), then submit the form.

You will see a message indicating that you've already subscribed.

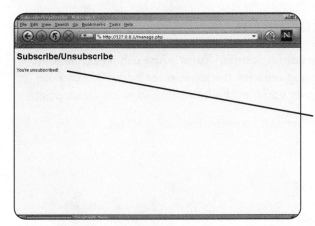

5. Return to the form using your Web browser's Back button, and type the same e-mail address in the Your E-Mail Address field. This time, select the unsubscribe radio button and submit the form.

You will see a confirmation that you have unsubscribed.

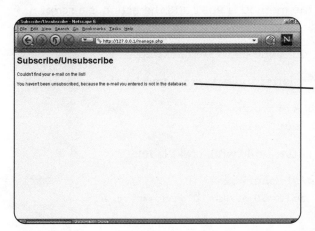

6. Return to the form using your Web browser's Back button, and attempt to unsubscribe the same e-mail address.

You will see a confirmation that your e-mail address wasn't in the database, so you haven't been unsubscribed.

Continue adding a few of your own e-mail addresses because in the next section you'll create the form and script to send a newsletter to a list of people, and it would be great to have a real list of people.

Developing the Mailing Mechanism

Now that you have the subscribe/unsubscribe mechanism in place, you can create a very basic form interface to a mailing script. This mailing mechanism will take the contents of your form and send it to every address in your subscribers table.

Creating the Newsletter Form

I wasn't kidding when I said you'd create a "simple" form. I just use a text field for the subject of the newsletter and a text area for the newsletter body. You can use as many form fields as you like, as long as you modify the form and script appropriately.

1. Open a new file in your text editor and type the following HTML:

```
<HTML>
<HEAD>
<TITLE>Send a Newsletter</TITLE>
</HEAD>
<BODY>
<h1>Send a Newsletter</h1>
```

2. Begin your form. Assume that the method is POST and the action is a script called do_send_newsletter.php:

```
<FORM METHOD="POST" ACTION="do_send_newsletter.php">
```

3. Create an input field for the newsletter subject with a text label:

```
<P><strong>Give it a subject:</strong><br>
<input type="text" name="subject" size=30></p>
```

4. Create a text area for the newsletter body with a text label:

```
<P><strong>Newsletter body:</strong><br>
<textarea name="newsletter" cols=50 rows=10 wrap=virtual>
</textarea>
```

5. Add a submit button:

```
<p><input type="submit" name="submit" value="Send Newsletter"></p>
```

6. Close your form and add some more HTML so that the document is valid:

```
</FORM>
</BODY>
</HTML>
```

7. Save the file with the name send_newsletter.html and place this file in the document root of your Web server.

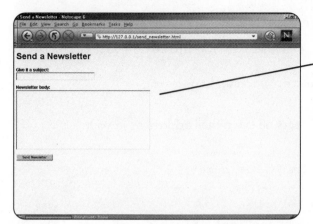

8. Open your Web browser and type **http://127.0.0.1/send_newsletter.html**

You will see a form containing a text field for the newsletter subject, a text area for the message, and a button that says Send Newsletter.

In the next section, you'll create the back-end script. That script will expect two variables: $_POST[subject] and $_POST[newsletter].

Creating the Script to Mail Your Newsletter

According to the form action in send_newsletter.html, you need a script called do_send_newsletter.php. The goal of this script is to accept the text in $_POST[subject] and $_POST[newsletter], and then send it off in the form of an e-mail to everyone listed in your subscribers table.

1. Open a new file in your text editor and begin a PHP block:

```
<?
```

2. Start an if...else block and check that a value has been entered for $_POST[subject] and $_POST[newsletter]. If either variable is empty, direct the user back to the form:

```
if (($_POST[subject] =="") || ($_POST[newsletter] == "")) {
    header("Location: http://127.0.0.1/send_newsletter.html");
    exit;
```

3. Continue the if...else block:

```
} else {
```

4. Create a variable to hold the name of the database on which the table resides:

```
$db_name = "testDB";
```

5. Create a variable to hold the name of the table you need to access:

```
$table_name = "subscribers";
```

6. Connect to the database server and select the database, as you have learned:

```
$connection = @mysql_connect("localhost", "spike", "9sj7En4")
or die(mysql_error());
$db = @mysql_select_db($db_name, $connection) or
die(mysql_error());
```

7. Create a SQL statement that selects all the e-mail addresses in your `subscribers` table:

```
$sql = "select email_addr from $table_name";
```

8. Execute the query:

```
$result = @mysql_query($sql,$connection) or die(mysql_error());
```

9. Create a variable to hold a `From` mailheader.

```
$headers = "From: Your Mailing List <you@yourdomain.com>\n";
```

10. Start the `while` loop. The `while` loop will send an e-mail message to each record in the table, and then print a confirmation that the mail was sent:

```
while ($row = mysql_fetch_array($result)) {
```

11. Get the e-mail address for the record:

```
$email_addr = $row['email_addr'];
```

12. Format the call to the `mail()` function. Use the `stripslashes()` function on the value of the `$_POST[subject]` and `$_POST[newsletter]` variables. This will remove any slashes automatically entered in your text by PHP to escape special characters:

```
mail("$email_addr", stripslashes($_POST[subject]),
stripslashes($_POST[newsletter]), $headers);
```

13. Print a confirmation:

```
echo "newsletter sent to: $email_addr<br>";
```

14. Close the `while` loop, if...else block, and PHP block:

```
    }
}
?>
```

15. Save the file with the name `do_send_newsletter.php` and place this file in the document root of your Web server.

Your code should look something like this:

```
<?
//check for required fields
if (($_POST[subject] =="") || ($_POST[newsletter] == "")) {
    header("Location: http://127.0.0.1/send_newsletter.html");
    exit;
} else {
    //set up table and database names
    $db_name = "testDB";
    $table_name = "subscribers";

//connect to server and select database
    $connection = @mysql_connect("localhost", "spike", "9sj7En4")
or die(mysql_error());
    $db = @mysql_select_db($db_name, $connection) or
die(mysql_error());

    //build and issue query
    $sql = "select email_addr from $table_name";
    $result = @mysql_query($sql,$connection) or die(mysql_error());

    //create a From: mailheaders
    $headers = "From: Your Mailing List <you@yourdomain.com>\n";

//loop through results and send mail
    while ($row = mysql_fetch_array($result)) {
        $email_addr = $row['email_addr'];
        mail("$email_addr", stripslashes($_POST[subject]),
stripslashes($_POST[newsletter]), $headers);
        echo "newsletter sent to: $email_addr<br>";
    }
}
?>
```

In the next section, you'll create and send a sample newsletter to your subscribers.

Testing Your Mailing List Mechanism

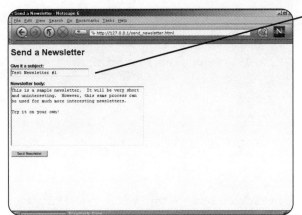

1. With your Web browser already open to the form for sending the newsletter, type a subject in the Subject field and a chunk of text in the text area to represent the newsletter.

NOTE

The figures show sample text that I typed and e-mail addresses on my sample subscriber list. Your results will differ, although the sequence of events remains the same.

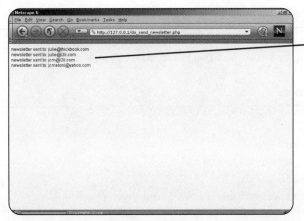

2. Submit the form.

You will see a confirmation of the e-mail addresses to which your newsletter was sent.

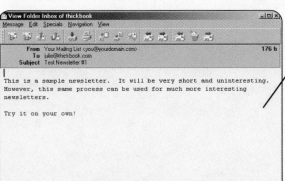

3. Check your e-mail if your address is in the subscribers table.

You should have a nicely-formatted newsletter in your mailbox!

Troubleshooting Your Mailing List Mechanism

If you receive an error such as "Warning: Can't connect," you must make sure you modified the value of SMTP in your `php.ini` file. This topic is covered in Chapter 8, "Sending E-Mail," and is a simple fix.

Another common problem when using this type of mailing list mechanism is that the script will eventually time out if your list is long enough. This is one of the reasons not to use this type of mechanism for sending newsletters to large lists of recipients. Because all this script does is execute the `mail()` function numerous times, it does not take into account the queuing factors in real mailing list software, which are designed to ease the burden on your outgoing mail server.

To get around a problem with the script timing out, you can reset the timer within the execution of the script. Essentially, by inserting the following line within your `while` loop, you are setting the timer at 0 before each call to the `mail()` function:

```
set_time_limit(0);
```

Your `while` loop would now look like this:

```
while ($row = mysql_fetch_array($result)) {
    set_time_limit(0);
    $email_addr = $row['email_addr'];
    mail("$email_addr", stripslashes($_POST[$subject]),
stripslashes($_POST[newsletter]), $headers);
    echo "newsletter sent to: $email_addr<br>";
    }
```

Remember, this does not ease the burden on your outgoing mail server, it just allows the script to continue to run when it might have timed out before.

24

Creating Custom Logs and Reports

If you're building a Web site for public use, chances are good that you'll want to know which part of your site is most popular, least popular, what types of Web browsers are used, and so on. Although Apache keeps a generic log file of accesses and errors, you can create a few code snippets to store specific information in your MySQL database. In this chapter, you'll learn how to do the following:

- Create a simple access-counting mechanism with MySQL
- Display the access counts on a page and in a report
- Track form submissions
- Create a synopsis report of the form submissions

A Note about Apache Log Files

The Apache Web server automatically logs specific information regarding user accesses and errors. These log files are found in the logs directory. A file called `access.log` handles the accesses, and the `error.log` file handles errors.

The default display for the access log looks something like the following (this was taken from my own access log):

```
127.0.0.1 [22/Mar/2002:05:27:10] "GET /show_createtable.html HTTP/
1.1" 304 -
127.0.0.1 [22/Mar/2002:05:27:46] "POST /do_showfielddef.php HTTP/
1.1" 200 2402
127.0.0.1 [22/Mar/2002:05:28:49] "POST /do_createtable.php HTTP/
1.1" 200 185
127.0.0.1 [22/Mar/2002:05:43:33] "GET /manage.php HTTP/1.1" 200
562
```

This looks rather cryptic, I know. You can set the format in your `httpd.conf` file like so:

```
LogFormat "%h %l %u %t \"%r\" %s %b"
```

In this case, the format maps to the descriptions listed in Table 24.1.

Table 24.1   Apache Log File Settings

Symbol	Description
%h	Remote host name of the machine making the request, or IP if `HostnameLookup = off`
%l	Remote log name (usually empty)
%u	URL path requested by the user
%t	Time of access
"%r"	First line of request, inside quotation marks
%s	Status of the request
%b	Number of bytes sent, excluding headers

NOTE

You can also log elements such as the user agent (Web browser) within the Apache access log.

Although many log analysis packages are available to purchase or download, the all-encompassing Apache access log might be overkill for simple tasks. This chapter shows you some methods of tracking specific accesses and actions, which has more relevance to you than "all access, all information, all the time."

Simple Access Counting with MySQL

If you want to capture access information for specific subsections of your Web site, or even just the main page, you can create a simple database table and accompanying PHP code snippet to do just that.

Using the now-familiar process of table creation, first you'll create a simple database table to hold all your access records.

Creating the Database Table

In this example, you will log four elements: page name, page description, user agent, and date accessed. First, create the database table.

1. Open your Web browser and type **http://127.0.0.1/show_createtable.html**

2. In the Table Name field, type **page_track**.

3. In the Number of Fields field, type **4**.

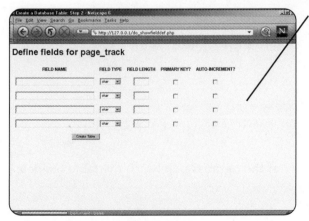

4. Click on the Go to Step 2 button. You should see the form shown in the figure.

There are four rows, corresponding to the four fields you want to create in the `page_track` table. Populate the fields in these next steps:

1. In the first row, type **page_name** for the Field Name, select `varchar` from the Field Type drop-down menu, and specify a Field Length of **50**.

2. In the second row, type **page_desc** for the Field Name and select `text` from the Field Type drop-down menu.

3. In the third row, type **user_agent** for the Field Name and select text from the Field Type drop-down menu.

4. In the fourth row, type **date_added** for the Field Name and select date from the Field Type drop-down menu.

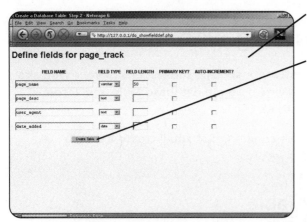

The completed form should look like the figure.

5. Click on the Create Table button to create the page_track table.

In the next section, you'll create a code snippet that writes tracking information to the page_track table.

Creating the Code Snippet

"Code snippet" is a highly technical term that means "a little bit of code." I'm kidding about the "highly technical" part, but a code snippet is usually something that doesn't qualify as a long script. Rather, it just serves a simple purpose. In this case, your code snippet will write some basic information to the page_track table and then merrily finish displaying some rather boring HTML.

1. Open a new file in your text editor and start a PHP block:

```
<?
```

2. Create four variables, corresponding to the four fields in the page_track table, and give them some values:

```
$page_name = "sample 1";
$page_desc = "This is a sample page of no use.";
$user_agent = getenv("HTTP_USER_AGENT");
$date_added = date("Y-m-d");
```

3. Create a variable to hold the name of the database on which the table resides:

```
$db_name = "testDB";
```

4. Create a variable to hold the name of the table you're populating with this script:

```
$table_name = "page_track";
```

5. Add the connection information as you have been:

```
$connection = @mysql_connect("localhost", "spike", "9sj7En4")
or die(mysql_error());
```

6. Select the database as you have learned:

```
$db = @mysql_select_db($db_name, $connection) or
die(mysql_error());
```

7. Create a SQL statement that inserts the four values into the four fields in the page_track table:

```
$sql = "insert into $table_name values ('$page_name',
'$page_desc', '$user_agent', '$date_added')";
```

8. Execute the query, then close the PHP block:

```
$result = @mysql_query($sql,$connection) or die(mysql_error());
?>
```

You've just created the code snippet, which should look something like this:

```
<?
//setup static variables
$page_name = "sample 1";
$page_desc = "This is a sample page of no use.";
$user_agent = getenv("HTTP_USER_AGENT");
$date_added = date("Y-m-d");

//set up table and database names
$db_name = "testDB";
$table_name = "page_track";

//connect to server and select database
$connection = @mysql_connect("localhost", "spike", "9sj7En4")
or die(mysql_error());
$db = @mysql_select_db($db_name, $connection) or
die(mysql_error());

//build and issue query
$sql = "insert into $table_name values ('$page_name',
'$page_desc', '$user_agent', '$date_added')";
$result = @mysql_query($sql,$connection) or die(mysql_error());
?>
```

9. Now create a useless bit of HTML, directly after the code snippet:

```
<HTML>
<HEAD>
<TITLE>Sample Page #1</TITLE>
</HEAD>
<BODY>
<h1>Useless Sample Page #1</h1>
<P>This sample page serves no real purpose!</p>
</BODY>
</HTML>
```

10. Save the file with the name `sample_page1.php` and place this file in the document root of your Web server. To make things a little more interesting in your reports, make another one of these sample files so that you've got something more to count than just this one file. Copy `sample_page1.php` to `sample_page2.php`, and change the first two variables in `sample_page2.php` to the following:

```
$page_name = "sample 2";
$page_desc = "Another useless sample page.";
```

11. Replace the HTML block in `sample_page2.php` with this:

```
<HTML>
<HEAD>
<TITLE>Sample Page #2</TITLE>
</HEAD>
<BODY>
<h1>Useless Sample Page #2</h1>
<P>I can't believe how useless this page is!</p>
</BODY>
</HTML>
```

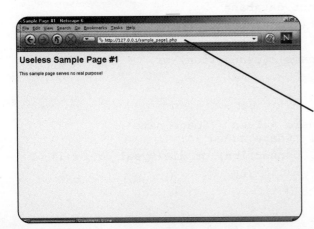

Now save this file and place it in the document root of your Web server as well.

Next, you'll access these pages a few times to get the internal counting going.

1. Open your Web browser and type **http://127.0.0.1/sample_page1.php**

You will see the HTML page, with a heading and some text.

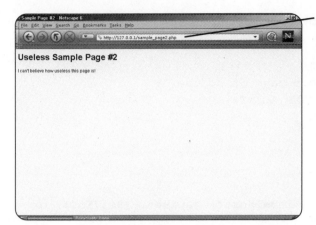

2. Open your Web browser and type **http://127.0.0.1/sample_page2.php**

You will see the HTML page with a heading and some text.

Keep reloading these pages a few times, and then move on to the next section, where the count will be displayed.

Displaying the Count

Displaying the count on each of these pages is a snap. You just need to add three lines to your code snippet and one line inside your HTML block.

1. Open `sample_page1.php` in your text editor.

2. Directly before the end of the PHP block, create a SQL statement that gets the number of accesses for this particular page:

```
$count_sql = "select count(page_name) from $table_name where
page_name = '$page_name'";
```

NOTE

Place the counting code after the insertion code to be sure that you're counting the current access as well!

---

3. Execute the query:

```
$count_res = @mysql_query($count_sql,$connection) or
die(mysql_error());
```

4. Create a variable to hold the specific count within the context of the current result set:

```
$count = @mysql_result($count_res, 0, "count(page_name)");
```

5. In your HTML block, mingle HTML with PHP to print the value of $count:

```
<P>Accesses: <? echo "$count"; ?></p>
```

Your new `sample_page1.php` script should look like this:

```
<?
$page_name = "sample 1";
$page_desc = "This is a sample page of no use.";
$user_agent = getenv("HTTP_USER_AGENT");
$date_added = date("Y-m-d");

$db_name = "testDB";
$table_name = "page_track";

$connection = @mysql_connect("localhost", "spike", "9sj7En4") or
die(mysql_error());
$db = @mysql_select_db($db_name, $connection) or
die(mysql_error());

$sql = "insert into $table_name values ('$page_name',
'$page_desc', '$user_agent', '$date_added')";
$result = @mysql_query($sql,$connection) or die(mysql_error());

$count_sql = "select count(page_name) from $table_name where
page_name = '$page_name'";
$count_res = @mysql_query($count_sql,$connection) or
die(mysql_error());
$count = @mysql_result($count_res, 0, "count(page_name)");
?>
<HTML>
<HEAD>
<TITLE>Sample Page #1</TITLE>
</HEAD>
<BODY>
<h1>Useless Sample Page #1</h1>
<P>This sample page serves no real purpose!</p>
<P>Accesses: <? echo "$count"; ?></p>
</BODY>
</HTML>
```

Make the same changes to `sample_page2.php`, and make sure you save both files.

Next, you'll access these pages and see the count display on the page.

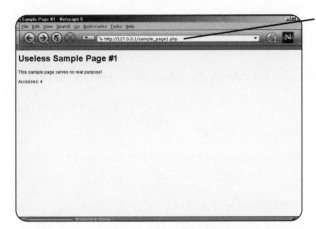

1. Open your Web browser and type
http://127.0.0.1/sample_page1.php

You will see the HTML page, with a heading and some text, followed by the access count you've reached. In this example, I've accessed this sample page four times.

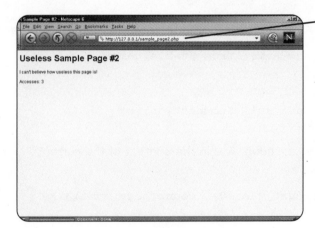

2. Open your Web browser and type
http://127.0.0.1/sample_page2.php

You will see the HTML page, with a heading and some text, followed by the access count you've reached. In this example, I've accessed this sample page three times.

In the next section, you'll create an access report page, which you can use to check the status of the pages you're tracking in the `page_track` table.

Creating Your Personal Access Report

You have all this great data in your `page_track` table, so now it's time to create a simple page that counts it all up for you. There's no need to weed through cryptic Apache access logs or install additional software packages to display statistics for you when it's this simple!

Start by creating a simple count of the total hits to your tracked pages (all-inclusive).

1. Open a new file in your text editor and start a PHP block:

```
<?
```

2. Create a variable to hold the name of the database on which the table resides:

```
$db_name = "testDB";
```

3. Create a variable to hold the name of the table you're populating with this script:

```
$table_name = "page_track";
```

4. Add the connection information as you have been:

```
$connection = @mysql_connect("localhost", "spike", "9sj7En4")
or die(mysql_error());
```

5. Select the database as you have learned:

```
$db = @mysql_select_db($db_name, $connection) or
die(mysql_error());
```

6. Create a SQL statement that counts all the entries in the `page_track` table:

```
$count_sql = "select count(page_name) from $table_name";
```

7. Execute the query:

```
$count_res = @mysql_query($count_sql, $connection) or
die(mysql_error());
```

8. Create a variable to hold the specific count within the context of the current result set, then close the PHP block:

```
$all_count = @mysql_result($count_res, 0, "count(page_name)");
?>
```

9. Add this HTML:

```
<HTML>
<HEAD>
<TITLE>My Access Report</TITLE>
</HEAD>
<BODY>
<h1>My Access Report</h1>
```

10. Mingle HTML and PHP to print the name of the table as well as the number of accesses tracked in the table:

```
<P><strong>Total Accesses Tracked in <? echo "$table_name"; ?>:</
strong> <? echo "$all_count"; ?></p>
```

11. Add some more HTML so that the document is valid:

```
</BODY>
</HTML>
```

12. Save the file with the name access_report.php and place this file in the document root of your Web server.

Your code should look something like this:

```
<?
//set up table and database names
$db_name = "testDB";
$table_name = "page_track";

//connect to server and select database
$connection = @mysql_connect("localhost", "spike", "9sj7En4")
or die(mysql_error());
$db = @mysql_select_db($db_name, $connection) or
die(mysql_error());

//issue query and select results
$count_sql = "select count(page_name) from $table_name";
$count_res = @mysql_query($count_sql, $connection) or
die(mysql_error());
$all_count = @mysql_result($count_res, 0, "count(page_name)");
?>
<HTML>
<HEAD>
<TITLE>My Access Report</TITLE>
</HEAD>
<BODY>
<h1>My Access Report</h1>
<P><strong>Total Accesses Tracked in <? echo "$table_name"; ?>:</
strong> <? echo "$all_count"; ?></p>
</BODY>
</HTML>
```

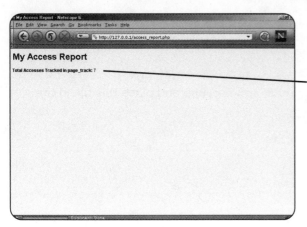

13. Next, test it! Open your Web browser and type **http://127.0.0.1/ access_report.php**.

You will see the HTML page with a heading and some text, followed by the access count you've reached for all pages. In this example, I've accessed the two sample pages a total of seven times.

Displaying the User Agents

In this section, you'll make some minor additions to the `access_report.php` script to display and count the different Web browsers used by those accessing your pages.

1. Open `access_report.php` in your text editor.

2. Before the closing PHP tag, create a SQL statement that finds all distinct entries in the `user_agent` field of the `page_track` table, counts these entries, and returns the results in descending order:

```
$user_agent_sql = "select distinct user_agent, count(user_agent) as
count from $table_name group by user_agent order by count desc";
```

3. Execute the query:

```
$user_agent_res = @mysql_query($user_agent_sql, $connection) or
die(mysql_error());
```

4. You'll create a bullet list within a `while` block in a moment. Start the bullet list outside the `while` block:

```
$user_agent_block = "<ul>";
```

5. Start the `while` loop. The `while` loop will create an array called `$row_ua` for each record in the result set (`$user_agent_res`):

```
while ($row_ua = mysql_fetch_array($user_agent_res)) {
```

6. Get the individual elements of the record, and give them good names:

```
$user_agent = $row_ua['user_agent'];
$user_agent_count = $row_ua['count'];
```

7. Add to `$user_agent_block` by creating one bullet item and additional bullet list. The bullet item will show the name of the user agent. Then, the second bullet list will show the number of accesses by that particular user agent. After adding to `$user_agent_block`, close the `while` loop:

```
$user_agent_block .= "
<li>$user_agent
<ul>
<li><em>accesses per browser: $user_agent_count</em>
</ul>";
}
```

8. Close the bullet list you created in `$user_agent_block`:

```
$user_agent_block .= "</ul>";
```

9. In the HTML section, add the following, then save the file:

```
<P><strong>Web Browsers Used:</strong>
<? echo "$user_agent_block"; ?>
```

Your new code should look something like this:

```
<?
//set up table and database names
$db_name = "testDB";
$table_name = "page_track";

//connect to server and select database
$connection = @mysql_connect("localhost", "spike", "9sj7En4")
or die(mysql_error());
$db = @mysql_select_db($db_name, $connection) or
die(mysql_error());

//issue query and select results for counts
$count_sql = "select count(page_name) from $table_name";
$count_res = @mysql_query($count_sql, $connection) or
die(mysql_error());
$all_count = @mysql_result($count_res, 0, "count(page_name)");

//issue query and select results for user agents
```

```php
$user_agent_sql = "select distinct user_agent, count(user_agent) as
count from $table_name group by user_agent order by count desc";
$user_agent_res = @mysql_query($user_agent_sql, $connection) or
die(mysql_error());


//start user agent display block
$user_agent_block = "<ul>";

//loop through results
while ($row_ua = mysql_fetch_array($user_agent_res)) {
    $user_agent = $row_ua['user_agent'];
    $user_agent_count = $row_ua['count'];
    $user_agent_block .= "
    <li>$user_agent
    <ul>
    <li><em>accesses per browser: $user_agent_count</em>
    </ul>";
}
//finish up the user agent block
$user_agent_block .= "</ul>";
?>
<HTML>
<HEAD>
<TITLE>My Access Report</TITLE>
</HEAD>
<BODY>
<h1>My Access Report</h1>
<P><strong>Total Accesses Tracked in <? echo "$table_name"; ?>:
</strong> <? echo "$all_count"; ?></p>

<P><strong>Web Browsers Used:</strong>
<? echo "$user_agent_block"; ?>

</BODY>
</HTML>
```

Let's see what user agents have been accessing your pages. Open your Web browser and type **http://127.0.0.1/access_report.php**.

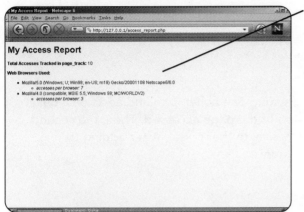

You will see the HTML page, with a heading and some text, followed by the access count you've reached for all pages. You will also see a list of user agents and the total accesses for each type. In this example, I've accessed the two sample pages a total of 10 times, with two different Web browsers.

In the next section, you'll make the final modifications to the `access_report.php` script, displaying the individual page breakdowns.

Displaying Specific Page Breakdowns

In this section, you'll make some minor additions to the `access_report.php` script to provide a breakdown of the specific pages that you're tracking in the `page_track` table.

1. Open `access_report.php` in your text editor.

2. Before the closing PHP tag, create a SQL statement that finds all distinct entries in the `page_name` field of the `page_track` table, counts these entries, and returns the results in descending order:

```
$page_name_sql = "select distinct page_name, page_desc,
count(page_name) as count from $table_name group by page_name
order by count desc";
```

3. Execute the query:

```
$page_name_res = @mysql_query($page_name_sql, $connection) or
die(mysql_error());
```

4. You'll create a bullet list within a `while` block in a moment. Start the bullet list outside the `while` block:

```
$page_name_block = "<ul>";
```

5. Start the `while` loop. The `while` loop will create an array called `$row_pn` for each record in the result set (`$page_name_res`):

```
while ($row_pn = mysql_fetch_array($page_name_res)) {
```

6. Get the individual elements of the record, and give them good names:

```
$page_name = $row_pn['page_name'];
$page_desc = $row_pn['page_desc'];
$page_count = $row_pn['count'];
```

7. Add to $page_name_block by creating one bullet item and additional bullet list. The bullet item will show the name of the page accessed. Then, the second bullet list will show the number of accesses to that page. After adding to $page_name_block, close the while loop:

```
$page_name_block .= "
<li>$page_name (\"$page_desc\")
    <ul>
    <li><em>accesses per page: $page_count</em>
    </ul>";
}
```

8. Close the bullet list you created in $page_name_block:

```
$page_name_block .= "</ul>";
```

9. In the HTML section, add the following, then save the file:

```
<P><strong>Individual Pages:</strong>
<? echo "$page_name_block"; ?>
```

Your new code should look something like this:

```
<?
//set up table and database names
$db_name = "testDB";
$table_name = "page_track";

//connect to server and select database
$connection = @mysql_connect("localhost", "spike", "9sj7En4")
or die(mysql_error());
$db = @mysql_select_db($db_name, $connection) or
die(mysql_error());

//issue query and select results for counts
$count_sql = "select count(page_name) from $table_name";
$count_res = @mysql_query($count_sql, $connection) or
die(mysql_error());
```

```
$all_count = @mysql_result($count_res, 0, "count(page_name)");

//issue query and select results for user agents
$user_agent_sql = "select distinct user_agent, count(user_agent) as
count from $table_name group by user_agent order by count desc";
$user_agent_res = @mysql_query($user_agent_sql, $connection) or
die(mysql_error());

//start user agent display block
$user_agent_block = "<ul>";

//loop through results
while ($row_ua = mysql_fetch_array($user_agent_res)) {
    $user_agent = $row_ua['user_agent'];
    $user_agent_count = $row_ua['count'];
    $user_agent_block .= "
    <li>$user_agent
    <ul>
    <li><em>accesses per browser: $user_agent_count</em>
    </ul>";
}
//finish up the user agent block
$user_agent_block .= "</ul>";

//issue query and select results for pages
$page_name_sql = "select distinct page_name, page_desc,
count(page_name) as count from $table_name group by page_name
order by count desc";
$page_name_res = @mysql_query($page_name_sql, $connection) or
die(mysql_error());

//start page name display block
$page_name_block = "<ul>";

//loop through results
while ($row_pn = mysql_fetch_array($page_name_res)) {
    $page_name = $row_pn['page_name'];
    $page_desc = $row_pn['page_desc'];
    $page_count = $row_pn['count'];
    $page_name_block .= "
    <li>$page_name (\"$page_desc\")
    <ul>
```

```
        <li><em>accesses per page: $page_count</em>
        </ul>";
}
//finish up the page name block
$page_name_block .= "</ul>";
?>
<HTML>
<HEAD>
<TITLE>My Access Report</TITLE>
</HEAD>
<BODY>
<h1>My Access Report</h1>
<P><strong>Total Accesses Tracked in <? echo "$table_name"; ?>:
</strong> <? echo "$all_count"; ?></p>

<P><strong>Web Browsers Used:</strong>
<? echo "$user_agent_block"; ?>

<P><strong>Individual Pages:</strong>
<? echo "$page_name_block"; ?>

</BODY>
</HTML>
```

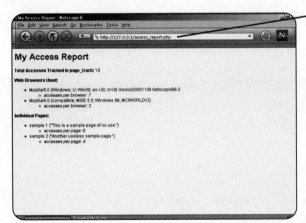

It's time to check the final results. Open your Web browser and type **http://127.0.0.1/access_report.php**.

You will see the HTML page with a heading and some text, followed by the access count you've reached for all pages. You will also see a list of user agents and the total accesses for each type. Finally, you'll see a list of all pages accessed, as well as the short description and individual access count for each.

That's a lot easier than wading through Apache access logs, but I wouldn't recommend completely replacing your access logs with a database-driven system. That's a bit too much database-connection overhead, even if MySQL is particularly nice on your system. Instead, target your page tracking to something particularly important to you.

PART VIII

Appendixes

A

Additional Configuration Options

The installation instructions at the beginning of this book detailed a simple configuration of PHP. If you feel like venturing out on your own by adding additional extensions (on Windows) or recompiling PHP (on Linux), this appendix gives you a brief rundown of some of your options. PHP can be as powerful or as streamlined as you want it to be, but a general rule of thumb is only to add functionality that you really need. For example, if you have no plans for connecting to an Oracle database, you do not need to enable support for the Oracle functions. But PHP is extendable, meaning you do have the ability to add functionality whenever you want—like if your company decides to buy an Oracle license!

Windows Extensions

Basic functionality is already built into the PHP 4.2.1 binary distribution for Windows, including

- Regular expression support

- Dynamic library support

- Internal Sendmail support

- Perl-compatible regular expression support

- ODBC support

- Session support

- XML support

- MySQL support

- and much more!

To get additional functionality, you must use additional extensions (.dll files), over 40 of which are included with the distribution. Some of the more popular extensions are listed in Table A.1.

To turn an extension "on," you must modify your php.ini file.

1. Open php.ini in a text editor and find the following lines:

```
; Directory in which the loadable extensions (modules) reside.
extension_dir = ./
```

2. Change the second line so that it points to the directory containing your extensions, such as

```
extension_dir = /php/extensions
```

3. Next, find a section that starts like this:

```
;Windows Extensions
```

4. For each extension you want to use, take away the semicolon before the name if the file is in the list. If the file is not in the list, add it:

```
extension=[your_extension_name].dll
```

Table A.1   Windows Extensions

File Name	Description
php_cpdf.dll	Enables ClibPDF functions
php_curl.dll	Enables CURL-related functions
php_cybercash.dll	Enables Cybercash payment gateway functions
php_domxml.dll	Enables DOM XML functions
php_dotnet.dll	Enables .NET functions
php_gd.dll	Enables GD library image functions
php_ifx.dll	Enables Informix functions
php_java.dll	Java extension
php_ldap.dll	Enables LDAP functions
php_mhash.dll	Enables mhash functions
php_ming.dll	Enables Ming-related Macromedia Flash functions
php_msql.dll	Enables mSQL functions
php_mssql.dll	Enables Microsoft SQLServer functions
php_oci8.dll	Enables Oracle 8 functions
php_oracle.dll	Enables Oracle functions (for Oracle 7)
php_pgsql.dll	Enables PostgreSQL functions
php_sablot.dll	Enables XSLT functions
php_sybase_ct.dll	Enables Sybase functions

5. After changing anything in the php.ini file, restart the Web server and then check the output of phpinfo() to verify your changes.

For more information on the Windows configuration options in PHP, please see the PHP manual's section on installation and configuration.

Linux Configuration Options

Here is the configuration line used in Chapter 3, "Installing PHP," to build PHP:

```
./configure --with-mysql=/usr/local/mysql/
--with-apxs=/usr/local/apache_1.3.26/bin/apxs
```

This line tells PHP to include support for MySQL and to build as a dynamic module. Many other configuration options are available to you, many of which you'll never use (I know I don't). Table A.2 lists them in case you want to fiddle with your installation. Remember, since PHP is an Apache dynamic module, you don't have to recompile Apache when making changes to PHP!

For more information on Linux/UNIX configuration options in PHP, please see the PHP manual's section on installation and configuration.

Table A.2 Configuration Options

Option	Description
`--with-informix[=DIR]`	Includes Informix support. `DIR` is the Informix installation directory.
`--with-msql[=DIR]`	Includes mSQL support. `DIR` is the mSQL installation directory.
`--with-oci8[=DIR]`	Includes Oracle-oci8 support. Default `DIR` is `ORACLE_HOME`.
`--with-oracle[=DIR]`	Includes Oracle-oci7 support. Default `DIR` is `ORACLE_HOME`.
`--with-ibm-db2[=DIR]`	Includes IBM DB2 support. `DIR` is the DB2 installation directory.
`--with-iodbc[=DIR]`	Includes iODBC support. `DIR` is the iODBC installation directory.
`--with-unixODBC[=DIR]`	Includes unixODBC support. `DIR` is the unixODBC installation directory.
`--with-pgsql[=DIR]`	Includes PostgreSQL support. `DIR` is the PostgreSQL installation directory.
`--with-sybase[=DIR]`	Includes Sybase-DB support. `DIR` is the Sybase home directory.
`--with-gd[=DIR]`	Includes GD support. `DIR` is GD's installation directory.
`--with-openssl[=DIR]`	Includes OpenSSL support (requires OpenSSL >= 0.9.5). `DIR` is the OpenSSL installation directory.
`--with-zlib[=DIR]`	Includes zlib support (requires zlib >= 1.0.9). `DIR` is the zlib install directory.
`--enable-bcmath`	Enables bc style precision math functions.

Table A.2   Configuration Options (continued)

Option	Description
`--with-curl[=DIR]`	Includes CURL support. `DIR` is the CURL installation directory.
`--with-cybercash[=DIR]`	Includes CyberCash support. `DIR` is the CyberCash MCK installation directory.
`--enable-ftp`	Enables FTP support
`--with-java[=DIR]`	Includes Java support. `DIR` is the installation directory for the JDK.
`--with-ldap[=DIR]`	Includes LDAP support. `DIR` is the LDAP installation directory.
`--with-mcal[=DIR]`	Includes MCAL support. `DIR` is the MCAL installation directory.
`--with-mcrypt[=DIR]`	Includes mcrypt support. `DIR` is the mcrypt installation directory.
`--with-mhash[=DIR]`	Includes mhash support. `DIR` is the mhash installation directory.
`--with-pfpro[=DIR]`	Includes Verisign PayFlow Pro support. `DIR` is the PayFlow Pro Installation directory.
`--disable-posix`	Disables POSIX-like functions
`--enable-trans-sid`	Enables transparent session id propagation
`--with-config-file-path=PATH`	Sets the path in which to look for `php.ini`, defaults to `PREFIX/lib`.
`--enable-safe-mode`	Enables safe mode by default
`--enable-magic-quotes`	Enables magic quotes by default

B

Basic PHP Language Reference

This appendix is nowhere near as comprehensive as the PHP manual (found at http://www.php.net/manual/), which contains descriptions of every PHP function that exists, plus user-submitted comments and code samples. Instead, this appendix serves as a basic, or "essential" reference—it contains the elements of PHP that (in my opinion) you can't live without. The PHP development team and all of the documentation contributors have done a wonderful job with the entire PHP manual, and there's no need to reinvent the wheel. However, since this appendix touches on only a small percentage of all there is to know about PHP, check the PHP manual before asking a question on one of the PHP mailing lists.

NOTE

In all of these examples, when something like "string" or "int" appears in a function, it is a placeholder for your own string or integer.

PHP Start and End Tags

To combine PHP code with HTML, the PHP code must be *escaped*, or set apart, from the HTML. The PHP engine will consider anything within the tag pairs shown in Table B.1 as PHP code.

Table B.1 Basic PHP Start and End Tags

Opening Tag	Closing Tag
`<?php`	`?>`
`<?`	`?>`
`<script language="php">`	`</script>`

Variables

You create variables to represent data. For instance, the following variable holds a value for sales tax:

```
$sales_tax = 0.0875;
```

This variable holds a SQL statement:

```
$sql = "SELECT * FROM MY_TABLE";
```

You can refer to the value of other variables when determining the value of a new variable:

```
$tax_total = $sales_tax * $sub_total;
```

The following are true of variable names:

- They begin with a dollar sign ($).

- They cannot begin with a numeric character.

- They can contain numbers and the underscore character (_).

- They are case-sensitive.

Here are some common variable types:

- floats

- integers

- strings

These types are determined by PHP, based on the context in which they appear.

Floats

Each of the following variables is a float, or floating-point number. Floats are also known as "numbers with decimal points."

```
$a = 1.552;
$b = 0.964;
$sales_tax = 0.875;
```

Integers

Integers are positive or negative whole numbers, zero, or "numbers without decimal points." Each of the following variables is an integer:

```
$a = 15;
$b = -521;
```

Strings

A series of characters grouped within double quotation marks is considered a string:

```
$a = "I am a string.";
$b = "<P>This book is <strong>cool</strong>!";
```

You can also reference other variables within your string, which will be replaced when your script is executed. For example:

```
$num = 57; // an integer
$my_string = "I read this book $num times!"; // a string
```

When you run the script, `$my_string` will become "I read this book 57 times!"

Variables from HTML Forms

Depending on the method of your HTML form (GET or POST), the variables will be part of the `$_POST` or `$_GET` superglobal associative array. The name of the input field will become the name of the variable. For example, when a form is sent using the POST method, the following input field produces the variable `$_POST[first_name]`:

```
<input type="text" name="first_name" size="20">
```

If the method of this form were GET, this variable would be `$_GET[first_name]`.

Variables from Cookies

Like variables from forms, variables from cookies are kept in a superglobal associative array called `$_COOKIE`. If you set a cookie called `user` with a value of `Joe Smith`, like so

```
SetCookie ("user", "Joe Smith", time()+3600);
```

a variable called `user` is placed in `$_COOKIE`, with a value of `Joe Smith`. You then refer to `$_COOKIE[user]` to get that value.

Environment Variables

When a Web browser makes a request of a Web server, it sends along with the request a list of extra variables called *environment* variables. They can be very useful for displaying dynamic content or authorizing users.

By default, environment variables are available to PHP scripts as `$VAR_NAME`. However, to be absolutely sure that you're reading the correct value, you can use the `getenv()` function to assign a value to a variable of your choice. The following are some common environment variables.

REMOTE_ADDR gets the IP address of the machine making the request. For example:

```
$remote_address = getenv("REMOTE_ADDR");
echo "Your IP address is $remote_address.";
```

HTTP_USER_AGENT gets the browser type, browser version, language encoding, and platform. For example:

```
$browser_type = getenv("HTTP_USER_AGENT");
echo "You are using $browser_type.";
```

For a list of HTTP environment variables and their descriptions, visit http://hoohoo.ncsa.uiuc.edu/cgi/env.html.

Arrays

Simply put, arrays are sets of variables that are contained as a group. In the following example, $fave_colors is an array that contains strings representing array elements. In this case, the array elements (0 to 3) are names of colors.

```
$fave_colors[0] = "red";
$fave_colors[1] = "blue";
$fave_colors[2] = "black";
$fave_colors[3] = "white";
```

Array elements are counted with 0 as the first position in the numerical index.

Operators

An operator is a symbol that represents a specific action. For example, the + arithmetic operator adds two values, and the = assignment operator assigns a value to a variable.

Arithmetic Operators

Arithmetic operators bear a striking resemblance to simple math, as shown in Table B.2.

Table B.2 Arithmetic Operators

Operator	Example	Action
+	$b = $a + 3;	Adds values together
-	$b = $a - 3;	Subtracts values
*	$b = $a * 3;	Multiplies values
/	$b = $a / 3;	Divides values
%	$b = $a % 3;	Returns the modulus, or remainder

Assignment Operators

The = is the basic assignment operator:

```
$a = 124; // the value of $a is 124
```

Other assignment operators are shown in Table B.3.

Table B.3 Assignment Operators

Operator	Example	Action
+=	$a += 3;	Changes the value of a variable to the current value plus the value on the right side
-=	$a -= 3;	Changes the value of the variable to the current value minus the value on the right side
.=	$a .= "string";	Concatenates (adds on to) the value on the right side with the current value

Comparison Operators

It should come as no surprise that comparison operators compare two values. A value of true or false is returned by the comparison. The comparison operators are shown in Table B.4.

Table B.4 Comparison Operators

Operator	Definition
==	Equal to
!=	Not equal to
>	Greater than
<	Less than
>=	Greater than or equal to
<=	Less than or equal to

Increment/Decrement Operators

The increment/decrement operators do just what their name implies: add or subtract from a variable (see Table B.5).

Table B.5 Increment/Decrement Operators

Operator	Usage	Definition
++$a	Pre-increment	Increments by 1 and returns $a
$a++	Post-increment	Returns $a and then increments $a by 1
--$a	Pre-decrement	Decrements by 1 and returns $a
$a--	Post-decrement	Returns $a and then decrements $a by 1

Logical Operators

Logical operators allow your script to determine the status of conditions and, in the context of your if...else or while statements, execute certain code based on which conditions are true and which are false (see Table B.6).

Table B.6 **Logical Operators**

Operator	Example	Result
!	!$a	TRUE if $a is not true
&&	$a && $b	TRUE if both $a and $b are true
||	$a || $b	TRUE if either $a or $b is true

Control Structures

Programs are essentially a series of statements. Control structures, as their name implies, control how those statements are executed. Control structures are usually built around a series of conditions, such as, "If the sky is blue, go outside and play." In this example, the condition is "If the sky is blue" and the statement is "go outside and play."

Control structures utilize curly braces ({}) to separate the groups of statements from the remainder of the program. Examples of common control structures follow; memorizing these will make your life much easier.

if...else if...else

The if...else if...else construct executes a statement based on the value of the expression being tested. In the following sample if statement, the expression being tested is "$a is equal to 10."

```
if ($a == "10") {
    // execute some code
}
```

After $a is evaluated, if it is found to have a value of 10 (that is, if the condition is true), the code inside the curly braces will execute. If $a is found to be something other than 10 (if the condition is false), the code will be ignored, and the program will continue.

To offer an alternative series of statements, should $a not have a value of 10, add an else statement to the structure to execute a section of code when the condition is false:

```
if ($a == "10") {
    echo "a equals 10";
} else {
    echo "a does not equal 10";
}
```

The else if (or one word: elseif) statement can be added to the structure to evaluate an alternative expression before heading to the final else statement. For example, the following structure first evaluates whether $a is equal to 10. If that condition is false, the else if statement is evaluated. If it is found to be true, the code within its curly braces executes. Otherwise, the program continues to the final else statement:

```
if ($a == "10") {
    echo "a equals 10";
} else if ($b == "8") {
    echo "b equals 8";
} else {
    echo "a does not equal 10 and b does not equal 8.";
}
```

You can use if statements alone or as part of an if...else or if...else if...else statement. Whichever you choose, you will find this structure to be an invaluable element in your programs!

while

Unlike the if...else if...else structure, in which each expression is evaluated once and an action is performed based on its value of true or false, the while statement continues to loop until an expression is false. In other words, the while loop continues while the expression is true.

For example, in the following while loop, the value of $a is printed on the screen and is incremented by 1 as long as the value of $a is less than or equal to 3:

```
$a = 0 // set a starting point
while ($a <= "3") {
    echo "a equals $a<br>";
    $a++;
}
```

for

Like `while` loops, `for` loops evaluate the set of conditional expressions at the beginning of each loop. Here is the syntax of the `for` loop:

```
for (expr1; expr2; expr3) {
    // code to execute
}
```

At the beginning of each loop, the first expression is evaluated, followed by the second expression. If the second expression is true, the loop continues by executing the code and then evaluating the third expression. If the second expression is false, the loop does not continue, and the third expression is never evaluated.

Take the counting example used in the `while` loop, and rewrite it using a `for` loop:

```
for ($a = 0; $a <= "3"; $a++) {
    echo "a equals $a<br>";
}
```

Built-In Functions

All of the following functions are part of the numerous functions that make up the PHP language. These really are just a small number of the PHP functions; they are the ones I use on a regular basis. Depending on the types of things you'll be doing with PHP, you may or may not need more functions, but please visit the PHP manual at http://www.php.net/manual/ and familiarize yourself with what is available.

Array Functions

Numerous PHP functions are available for use with arrays. Only a few are noted here—those that I find absolutely essential, and those that form a foundation of knowledge for working with arrays.

array()

The `array()` function allows you to manually assign values to an array. Here is the syntax of the `array()` function:

```
$array_name = array("val1", "val2", "val3", ...);
```

array_push()

The `array_push()` function allows you to add one or more elements to the end of an existing array. Its syntax is

```
array_push($array_name, "element 1", "element 2", ...);
```

array_pop()

The `array_pop()` function allows you to take (pop) off the last element of an existing array. Its syntax is

```
array_pop($array_name);
```

array_unshift()

The `array_unshift()` function allows you to add elements to the beginning of an existing array. Its syntax is

```
array_unshift($array_name, "element 1", "element 2", ...);
```

array_shift()

The `array_shift()` function allows you to take (pop) off the first element of an existing array. Its syntax is

```
array_shift($array_name);
```

array_merge()

The `array_merge()` function allows you to combine two or more existing arrays. Its syntax is

```
array_merge($array1, $array2, ...);
```

array_keys()

The `array_keys()` function returns an array of all the key names in an existing array. Its syntax is

```
array_keys($array_name);
```

array_values()

The `array_values()` function returns an array of all the values in an existing array. Its syntax is

```
array_values($array_name);
```

count()

The `count()` function counts the number of elements in a variable. It's usually used to count the number of elements in an array because any variable that is not an array has only one element—itself.

In the following example, $a is assigned a value equal to the number of elements in the $colors array:

```
$a = count($colors);
```

If $colors contains the values blue, black, red, and green, $a will be assigned a value of 4.

each() and list()

The `each()` and `list()` functions usually appear together, in the context of stepping through an array and returning its keys and values. Here is the syntax for these functions:

```
each(arrayname);
list(val1, val2, val3, ...);
```

For example, when you submit an HTML form via the GET method, each key/value pair is placed in the global variable $_GET. If your form input fields are named first_name and last_name and the user enters values of Joe and Smith, the key/value pairs are first_name/Joe and last_name/Smith. In the $_GET array, these variables are represented as the following:

```
$_GET["first_name"] // value is "Joe"
$_GET["last_name"] // value is "Smith"
```

You can use the `each()` and `list()` functions to step through the array in this fashion, printing the key and value for each element in the array:

```
while (list($key, $val) = each($_GET)) {
  echo "$key has a value of $val<br>";
}
```

reset()

The `reset()` function rewinds the pointer to the beginning of the array. Its syntax is

```
reset($array_name);
```

shuffle()

The `shuffle()` function randomizes the elements of a given array. Its syntax is

```
shuffle($array_name);
```

sizeof()

The `sizeof()` function counts the number of elements in an array. In the following example, $a is assigned a value equal to the number of elements in the `$colors` array:

```
$a = sizeof($colors);
```

If `$colors` contains the values `blue`, `black`, `red`, and `green`, $a is assigned a value of 4.

Database Connectivity Functions for MySQL

Numerous PHP functions exist for connecting to and querying a MySQL server. Following are some basic functions and their syntax. See the PHP manual at http://www.php.net/manual/ for a complete listing of MySQL functions—there are plenty!

mysql_connect()

This function opens a connection to MySQL. It requires a server name, username, and password.

```
$connection = mysql_connect("servername","username","password");
```

mysql_create_db()

This function creates a database on the MySQL server. It requires a valid established connection.

```
mysql_create_db("myDB");
```

mysql_drop_db()

This function drops a database on the MySQL server. It requires a valid established connection.

```
mysql_drop_db("myDB");
```

mysql_select_db()

This function selects a database on the MySQL server for use by subsequent queries. It requires a valid established connection.

```
$db = mysql_select_db("myDB", $connection);
```

mysql_query()

This function issues the SQL statement. It requires an open connection to the database.

```
$sql_result = mysql_query("SELECT * FROM SOMETABLE",$connection);
```

mysql_error()

This function returns a meaningful error message when something goes wrong with your connection or query. It's usually used in the context of the `die()` function, like this:

```
$sql_result = mysql_query("SELECT * FROM SOMETABLE",$connection)
or die(mysql_error());
```

mysql_fetch_array()

This function automatically places the SQL statement result row into an array.

```
$row = mysql_fetch_array($sql_result);
```

mysql_num_rows()

This function returns the number of rows in a result set.

```
$num = mysql_num_rows($sql_result);
```

Date and Time Functions

The basic PHP date and time functions let you easily format timestamps for use in database queries and calendar functions, as well as for simply printing the date on an order form receipt.

date()

The `date()` function returns the current server timestamp, formatted according to a given set of parameters. Its syntax is

```
date(format, [timestamp]);
```

If the timestamp parameter is not provided, the current timestamp is assumed. Table B.7 shows the available formats.

checkdate()

The `checkdate()` function validates a given date. Successful validation means that the year is between 0 and 32767, the month is between 1 and 12, and the proper number of days are in each month (leap years are accounted for). Its syntax is

```
checkdate(month, day, year);
```

mktime()

The `mktime()` function returns the UNIX timestamp as a long integer (in the format of seconds since the Epoch, or January 1, 1970) for a given date. Thus the primary use of `mktime()` is to format dates in preparation for mathematical functions and date validation. Its syntax is

```
mktime(hour, minute, second, month, day, year);
```

time() and microtime()

The `time()` function returns the current system time, measured in seconds since the Epoch. The syntax of `time()` is simply

```
time();
```

You could get a result such as 958950466.

Using `microtime()` adds a count of microseconds, so instead of just receiving a result like 958950466, you would get a result like 0.93121600 958950466, at the exact moment you asked for the time since the Epoch (this includes both seconds and microseconds).

Table B.7 date() Function Formats

Character	Meaning
a	Prints "am" or "pm"
A	Prints "AM" or "PM"
h	Hour in 12-hour format (01 to 12)
H	Hour in 24-hour format (00 to 23)
g	Hour in 12-hour format without a leading zero (1 to 12)
G	Hour in 24-hour format without a leading zero (0 to 23)
i	Minutes (00 to 59)
s	Seconds (00 to 59)
Z	Time zone offset in seconds (-43200 to 43200)
U	Seconds since the Epoch (January 1, 1970 00:00:00 GMT)
d	Day of the month in two digits (01 to 31)
j	Day of the month in two digits without a leading zero (1 to 31)
D	Day of the week in text (Mon to Sun)
l	Day of the week in long text (Monday to Sunday)
w	Day of the week in numeric, Sunday to Saturday (0 to 6)
F	Month in long text (January to December)
m	Month in two digits (01 to 12)
n	Month in two digits without a leading zero (1 to 12)
M	Month in three-letter text (Jan to Dec)
Y	Year in four digits (2000)
y	Year in two digits (00)
z	Day of the year (0 to 365)
t	Number of days in the given month (28 to 31)
S	English ordinal suffix (th, nd, st)

File System Functions

The built-in file system functions can be very powerful tools—or weapons, if used incorrectly. Be very careful when using file system functions, especially if you have PHP configured to run as root or some other system-wide user. For example, using a PHP script to issue an `rm -R` command while at the root level of your directory structure would be a very bad thing.

chmod(), chgrp(), and chown()

Like the shell commands of the same name, the `chmod()`, `chgrp()`, and `chown()` functions modify the permissions, group, and owner of a directory or file. Here is the syntax of these functions:

```
chmod("filename", mode);
chgrp("filename", newgroup);
chown("filename", newowner);
```

In order to change permissions, groups, and owners, the PHP user must be the owner of the file, or the permissions must already be set to allow such changes by that user.

copy()

The `copy()` function works much like the `cp` shell command: It needs a file name and a destination in order to copy a file. The syntax of `copy()` is

```
copy("source filename", "destination");
```

The PHP user must have permission to write into the destination directory, or the `copy()` function will fail.

fopen()

The `fopen()` function opens a specified file or URL for reading and/or writing. The syntax of `fopen()` is

```
fopen("filename", "mode")
```

To open a URL, use `http://` or `ftp://` at the beginning of the file name string. You can open URLs only for reading, not writing.

If the file name begins with anything else, the file is opened from the file system and a file pointer to the opened file is returned. Otherwise, the file is assumed to reside on the local file system.

The specified mode determines whether the file is opened for reading, writing, or both. Table B.8 lists the valid modes.

Table B.8   fopen() Function Modes

Mode	Description
r	Read-only. The file pointer is at the beginning of the file.
r+	Reading and writing. The file pointer is at the beginning of the file.
w	Write-only. The file pointer is at the beginning of the file, and the file is truncated to zero length. If the file does not exist, attempt to create it.
w+	Reading and writing. The file pointer is at the beginning of the file, and the file is truncated to zero length. If the file does not exist, attempt to create it.
a	Write-only. The file pointer is at the end of the file (it appends content to the file). If the file does not exist, attempt to create it.
a+	Reading and writing. The file pointer is at the end of the file (it appends content to the file). If the file does not exist, attempt to create it.

fread()

Use the `fread()` function to read a specified number of bytes from an open file pointer. Its syntax is

```
fread(filepointer, length);
```

fputs()

The `fputs()` function writes to an open file pointer. Its syntax is

```
fputs(filepointer, content, [length]);
```

The file pointer must be open in order to write to the file. The length parameter is optional. If it isn't specified, all specified content is written to the file.

fclose()

Use the `fclose()` function to close an open file pointer. Its syntax is

```
fclose(filepointer);
```

mkdir()

Like the `mkdir` shell command, the `mkdir()` function creates a new directory on the file system. Its syntax is

```
mkdir("pathname", mode);
```

The PHP user must have write permission in the specified directory.

rename()

As its name suggests, the `rename()` function attempts to give a new name to an existing file. Its syntax is

```
rename("oldname", "newname");
```

The PHP user must have permission to modify the file.

rmdir()

Like the `rmdir` shell command, the `rmdir()` function removes a directory from the file system. Its syntax is

```
rmdir("pathname");
```

The PHP user must have write permission in the specified directory.

symlink()

The `symlink()` function creates a symbolic link from an existing file or directory on the file system to a specified link name. Its syntax is

```
symlink("targetname", "linkname");
```

The PHP user must have write permission in the specified directory.

unlink()

The `unlink()` function deletes a file from the file system. Its syntax is

```
unlink("filename");
```

The PHP user must have write permission for this file.

HTTP Functions

The built-in functions for sending specific HTTP headers and cookie data are crucial aspects of developing large Web-based applications in PHP. Luckily, the syntax for these functions is quite easy to understand and implement.

header()

The `header()` function outputs an HTTP header string, such as a location redirection. This output must occur before any other data is sent to the browser, including HTML tags.

NOTE

This information bears repeating: do not attempt to send information of any sort to the browser before sending a `header()`. You can perform any sort of database manipulations or other calculations before the `header()`, but you cannot print anything to the screen—not even a new line character.

For example, to use the `header()` function to redirect a user to a new location, use this code:

```
header("Location: http://www.newlocation.com");
exit;
```

TIP

Follow a `header()` statement with the `exit` command. This ensures that the code does not continue to execute.

---

setcookie()

The `setcookie()` function sends a cookie to the user. Cookies must be sent before any other header information is sent to the Web browser. The syntax for `setcookie()` is

```
setcookie("name", "value", "expire", "path", "domain", "secure");
```

For example, you would use the following code to send a cookie called `username` with a value of `joe` that is valid for one hour within all directories on the testcompany.com domain:

```
setcookie("username","joe", time()+3600, "/", ".testcompany.com");
```

Mail Function

The PHP mail function makes the interface between your HTML forms and your server's outgoing mail program a snap!

If your server has access to sendmail or an external SMTP server, the `mail()` function sends mail to a specified recipient. Its syntax is

```
mail("recipient", "subject", "message", "mail headers");
```

For example, the following code sends mail to julie@thickbook.com, with a subject of "I'm sending mail!" and a message body saying "PHP is cool!" The `From` line is part of the additional mail headers.

```
mail("julie@thickbook.com", "I'm sending mail!", "PHP is cool!",
"From: youremail@yourdomain.com\n");
```

Mathematical Functions

Since I have very little aptitude for mathematics, I find PHP's built-in mathematical functions to be of the utmost importance! In addition to all the functions, the value of pi (3.14159265358979323846) is already defined as a constant in PHP (`M_PI`).

ceil()

The `ceil()` function rounds a fraction up to the next higher integer. Its syntax is

```
ceil(number);
```

decbin() and bindec()

The `decbin()` and `bindec()` functions convert decimal numbers to binary numbers and binary numbers to decimal numbers, respectively. The syntax of these functions is

```
decbin(number);
bindec(number);
```

dechex() and hexdec()

The `dechex()` and `hexdec()` functions convert decimal numbers to hexadecimal numbers and hexadecimal numbers to decimal numbers, respectively. The syntax of these functions is

```
dechex(number);
hexdec(number);
```

decoct() and octdec()

The `decoct()` and `octdec()` functions convert decimal numbers to octal numbers and octal numbers to decimal numbers, respectively. The syntax of these functions is

```
decoct(number);
octdec(number);
```

floor()

The `floor()` function rounds a fraction down to the next lower integer. Its syntax is

```
floor(number);
```

number_format()

The `number_format()` function returns the formatted version of a specified number. Its syntax is

```
number_format("number", "decimals", "dec_point", "thousands_sep");
```

For example, to return a formatted version of the number 12156688 with two decimal places and a comma separating each group of thousands, use

```
echo number_format("12156688","2",".",",");
```

The result is 12,156,688.00.

If only a number is provided, the default formatting does not use a decimal point and puts a comma between every group of thousands.

pow()

The `pow()` function returns the value of a given number raised to the power of a given exponent. Its syntax is

```
pow(number, exponent);
```

rand()

The `rand()` function generates a random value from a specific range of numbers. Its syntax is

```
rand(min, max);
```

round()

The `round()` function rounds a fraction to the next higher or next lower integer. Its syntax is

```
round(number);
```

sqrt()

The `sqrt()` function returns the square root of a given number. Its syntax is

```
sqrt(number);
```

srand()

The `srand()` function provides the random number generator with a set of possible values. Its syntax is

```
srand(seed);
```

A common practice is to seed the random number generator by using a number of microseconds:

```
srand((double)microtime()*1000000);
```

Miscellaneous Functions

The die() and exit functions provide useful control over the execution of your script, offering an "escape route" for programming errors. Other functions have found their way into this "miscellaneous" category.

die()

The die() function outputs a given message and terminates the script when a returned value is false. Its syntax is

```
die("message");
```

For example, you would use the following code to print a message and stop the execution of your script upon failure to connect to your database:

```
$connection = mysql_connect("servername", "username", "password")
or die ("Can't connect to database.");
```

exit

The exit statement terminates the execution of the current script at the point where the exit statement is made.

sleep() and usleep()

The sleep() and usleep() functions put a pause, or a delay, at a given point in the execution of your PHP code. The syntax of these functions is

```
sleep(seconds);
usleep(microseconds);
```

The only difference between sleep() and usleep() is that the given wait period for sleep() is in seconds, and the wait period for usleep() is in microseconds.

uniqid()

The uniqid() function generates a unique identifier with a prefix if you want one. Its syntax is

```
uniqid("prefix");
```

That's boring, though. Suppose you want a unique ID with a prefix of `phpuser`. You would use

```
$id = uniqid("phpuser");
echo "$id";
```

and you would get something like `phpuser38b320a6b5482`.

But if you use something really cool like

```
$id = md5(uniqid(rand()));
echo "$id";
```

you would get an ID like `999d8971461bedfc7caadcab33e65866`.

Program Execution Functions

You can use PHP's built-in program execution functions to use programs residing on your system, such as encryption programs, third-party image manipulation programs, and so forth. For all program execution functions, the PHP user must have permission to execute the given program.

exec()

The `exec()` function executes an external program. Its syntax is

```
exec(command, [array], [return_var]);
```

If an array is specified, the output of the `exec()` function will append to the array. If `return_var` is specified, it will be assigned a value of the program's return status.

For example, you would use the following code to perform a "ping" of a server five times and print the output:

```
$command = "ping -c5 www.thickbook.com";
exec($command, $result, $rval);
for ($i = 0; $i < sizeof($result); $i++) {
echo "$result[$i]<br>";
}
```

passthru()

Like the exec() function, the passthru() function executes an external program. The difference between the two is that passthru() returns the raw output of the action. The syntax of passthru() is

```
passthru(command, return_var);
```

If return_var is specified, it will be assigned a value of the program's return status.

system()

The system() function executes an external program and displays output as the command is being executed. Its syntax is

```
system(command, [return_var]);
```

If return_var is specified, it will be assigned a value of the program's return status.

For example, you would use the following code to perform a "ping" of a server five times and print the raw output:

```
$command = "ping -c5 www.thickbook.com";
system($command);
```

Regular Expression Functions

ereg_replace() and eregi_replace()

The ereg_replace() and eregi_replace() functions replace instances of a pattern within a string and return the new string. The ereg_replace() function performs a case-sensitive match, and eregi_replace() performs a case-insensitive match. Here is the syntax for both functions:

```
ereg_replace(pattern, replacement, string);
eregi_replace(pattern, replacement, string);
```

For example, you would use the following code to replace "ASP" with "PHP" in the string "I really love programming in ASP!"

```
$old_string = "I really love programming in ASP!";
$new_string = ereg_replace("ASP", "PHP", $old_string);
echo "$new_string";
```

If "ASP" is mixed case, such as "aSp", use the `eregi_replace()` function:

```
$old_string = "I really love programming in aSp!";
$new_string = eregi_replace("ASP", "PHP", $old_string);
echo "$new_string";
```

split()

The `split()` function splits a string into an array using a certain separator (comma, colon, semicolon, and so on). Its syntax is

```
split(pattern, string, [limit]);
```

If a limit is specified, the `split()` function stops at the named position—for example, at the tenth value in a comma-delimited list.

Session-Handling Functions

Session handling is a way of holding on to data as a user navigates your Web site. Data can be variables or entire objects. These simple functions are just a few of the session-related functions in PHP; see the PHP manual at http://www.php.net/manual/ for more.

session_start()

The `session_start()` function starts a session if one has not already been started, or it resumes a session if the session ID is present for the user. This function takes no arguments and is called simply by placing the following at the beginning of your code:

```
session_start();
```

session_destroy()

The `session_destroy()` function effectively destroys all the variables and values registered for the current session. This function takes no arguments and is called simply by placing the following in your code:

```
session_destroy();
```

String Functions

This section only scratches the surface of PHP's built-in string manipulation functions, but if you understand these common functions, your programming life will be quite a bit easier!

addslashes() and stripslashes()

The addslashes() and stripslashes() functions are very important when inserting and retrieving data from a database. Often, text inserted into a database will contain special characters (single quotes, double quotes, backslashes, NULL) that must be "escaped" before being inserted. The addslashes() function does just that, using this syntax:

```
addslashes(string);
```

Similarly, the stripslashes() function returns a string with the slashes taken away, using this syntax:

```
stripslashes(string);
```

chop(), ltrim(), and trim()

All three of these functions remove errant white space from a string. The chop() function removes white space from the end of a string, and ltrim() removes white space from the beginning of a string. The trim() function removes both leading and trailing white space from a string. Here is the syntax of these functions:

```
chop(string);
ltrim(string);
trim(string);
```

echo()

The echo() function returns output. The syntax of echo() is

```
echo (parameter1, parameter 2, ...)
```

For example:

```
echo "I'm using PHP!";                   // output is: I'm using PHP!
echo 2+6; // output is: 8
```

The parentheses are not required when using echo.

explode() and implode()

The `explode()` function splits a string using a given separator and returns the values in an array. The syntax of `explode()` is

```
explode("separator", "string");
```

For example, the following code takes a string called `$color_list`, containing a comma-separated list of colors, and places each color into an array called `$my_colors`:

```
$color_list = "blue,black,red,green,yellow,orange";
$mycolors = explode(",", $color_list);
```

Conversely, the `implode()` function takes an array and makes it into a string, using a given separator. The syntax of `implode()` is

```
implode("separator", "string");
```

For example, the following code takes an array called `$color_list` and then creates a string called `$mycolors`, containing the values of the `$color_list` array, separated by commas:

```
$mycolors = implode(",", $color_list);
```

htmlspecialchars() and htmlentities()

The `htmlspecialchars()` and `htmlentities()` functions convert special characters and HTML entities within strings into their acceptable entity representations. The `htmlspecialchars()` function converts only the less-than sign (< becomes <), greater-than sign (> becomes >), double quotes ("" becomes "), and the ampersand (& becomes &).

The `htmlentities()` function converts the characters in the ISO-8859-1 character set to the proper HTML entity. Here is the syntax of these functions:

```
htmlspecialchars(string);
htmlentities(string);
```

nl2br()

The `nl2br()` function replaces all ASCII new lines with the HTML line break (<BR>). The syntax of the `nl2br()` function is

```
nl2br(string);
```

sprintf()

The `sprintf()` function returns a string that has been formatted according to a set of directives, as listed in Table B.9. The syntax of `sprintf()` is

```
sprintf(directives, string);
```

Table B.9 sprintf() Function Formatting Directives

Directive	Result
%	Adds a percent sign
b	Considers the string an integer and formats it as a binary number
c	Considers the string an integer and formats it with that ASCII value
d	Considers the string an integer and formats it as a decimal number
f	Considers the string a double and formats it as a floating-point number
o	Considers the string an integer and formats it as an octal number
s	Considers and formats the string as a string
x	Considers the string an integer and formats it as a hexadecimal number (lowercase letters)
X	Considers the string an integer and formats it as a hexadecimal number (uppercase letters)

For example, to turn the number 5 into $5.00 (five dollars), use:

```
$newnumber = sprintf("%0.02f", 5);
```

strlen()

The `strlen()` function returns the length of a given string. Its syntax is

```
strlen(string);
```

strtolower()

The `strtolower()` function returns a given string with all alphabetic characters in lowercase. Its syntax is

```
strtolower(str);
```

strtoupper()

The `strtoupper()` function returns a given string with all alphabetic characters in uppercase. Its syntax is

```
strtoupper (str);
```

substr()

The `substr()` function returns a portion of a string, given a starting position and optional ultimate length. Its syntax is

```
substr(string, start, [length]);
```

If the start position is a positive number, the starting position is counted from the beginning of the string. If the start position is negative, the starting position is counted from the end of the string.

Similarly, if the optional length parameter is used and is a positive number, the length is counted from the beginning of the string. If the length parameter is used and is a negative number, the length is counted from the end of the string.

For example:

```
$new_string = substr("PHP is great!", 1);    // returns "HP is
great!"
$new_string = substr("PHP is great!", 0, 7); // returns "PHP is "
$new_string = substr("PHP is great!", -1);   // returns "!"
$new_string = substr("PHP is great!", -6, 5);    // returns
"great"
```

ucfirst()

The `ucfirst()` function changes the first alphabetic character in a string to an uppercase character. Its syntax is

```
ucfirst(string);
```

ucwords()

The `ucwords()` function changes the first letter of each word in a string to uppercase. Its syntax is

```
ucwords(string);
```

Variable Functions

The two basic variable functions, `isset()` and `unset()`, help you manage your variables within the scope of an application.

The `isset()` function determines whether a variable exists. The `unset()` function explicitly destroys the named variable. Here is the syntax of each:

```
isset(var);
unset(var);
```

The `isset()` function returns true if the variable exists and false if it does not.

C

Writing Your Own Functions

As you become more comfortable with writing code, you may realize that many times you will write the same bits of code over and over again. A prime example of this would be the database connection code used throughout this book. How many times did you think to yourself, "This is really repetitive!" Quite often, I'm sure. This is where writing your own functions comes in to play.

When you program in PHP, you will use predefined functions to achieve certain results. For example, the `mail()` function is a predefined function that sends mail. The `mysql_connect()` function is a predefined function that connects to a MySQL database. The code that makes up these functions is built into the PHP scripting engine, so you never see it. However, you can write your own functions and use them in your scripts, even storing your own functions in external files for use only when you need them.

The Structure of Functions

Functions have a very specific structure, as you can see in the following code, where `[function name]` and `[arguments]` should be replaced with your own function name and any arguments you may want to use.

```
function [function_name] ([arguments]) {
    // code
}
```

When you create a function, you precede the name of the function with the literal word `function`. After that and the name of your function comes the list of arguments inside a set of parentheses. The arguments—which are optional, as you don't have to pass any arguments to a function if you don't want to—are separated by commas, and hold values that your function needs in order to complete its task or tasks.

After the arguments, you open a set of curly braces, type in all of your code and finally close the set of braces. For example, the function below (called `multiplier`) takes an argument called `$num`, and multiplies the value by 5.

```
function multiplier ($num) {
    $answer = $num * 5;
}
```

Say you have already determined that `$num` equals 8, and that's what you're passing to the `multiplier` function. Using your own math skills, you know that `$answer` will equal 40. To get that number back to your script, outside of the function, you must return the value.

Returning Values from Functions

The basic method for returning values from your functions is to use the `return` statement. Usually, this statement comes at the end of the function, like so:

```
function multiplier ($num) {
    $answer = $num * 5;
    return $answer;
}
```

NOTE

A `return` statement can be anywhere in a function, but when used it will end the execution of the function. This means the code that is executed is the line of your script from which the `return` statement was called.

When you use a `return` statement, you can then call the function in your code like so:

```
echo multiplier(5);
```

This usage would result in the following on your screen:

```
40
```

Since you are passing 8 as the `$num` argument to the `multiplier()` function, `$answer` becomes 40. Since `$answer` is being returned as the result of the function's actions, and you are using `echo` following by the function call, you're telling PHP to print the result of the code within the function. In this case, that result is the number 40.

NOTE

You can also use the `return` statement to get multiple values, but only if they are part of an array or an object.

Using a `return` statement to pass results from your functions to your main script is a simple and safe method, and one of the most common. If you do not use a `return` statement, you must declare as global any variables you wish to pass back to your main script. For example:

```
function multiplier($num) {
    global $answer;
    $answer = $num * 5;
}
```

In this case, you call the `multiplier()` function and then use the name of the variable in the `echo` statement, since it's not returned directly from your function. For example, using the modified function, the following code will print the number 40 to your screen:

```
multiplier(5);
echo $answer;
```

If you had not declared $answer as a global variable, the result would have been a blank screen.

NOTE

Use some thought to determine which variables you really want to become globally available to your scripts. Each time you declare something as global, you must employ additional programming constraints in order to maintain the integrity of the data. In other words, you have to be careful and watch what you do. If you have declared a variable as global, but use a variable of the same name in another part of your script, you will overwrite one or the other. A good rule of thumb is to keep a handle on your global variables and keep them local to the procedures that are directly using them.

Using Functions in Your Code

So far, you've learned the basic structure of a user-defined function, but not how it fits within your own scripts. In the case of the `multiplier()` function, it does seem awfully time-consuming to create a script like the following, just to print a number on the screen:

```
<?
function multiplier($num) {
    $answer = $num * 5;
    return $answer;
}
echo multiplier(5);
?>
```

Instead, imagine a function called `db_connect()`, which contains your database connection and selection code:

```
function db_connect();
    $connection = @mysql_connect("localhost", "spike", "9sj7En4")
    or die(mysql_error());
    $db = @mysql_select_db($db_name, $connection)
    or die(mysql_error());
}
```

Instead of typing those two lines over and over in every script, imagine simply typing:

```
db_connect();
```

If your host name, username, password, or database name change, you only have to change this information in one place—the db_connect() function code. Now the only trick is where to put this function. Obviously, if you are creating a function in order to reuse the code within it, you don't want the function to be part of the script. Instead, you place the function in a file of its own (or a file containing other functions) and use include() or require() to pull the information into your script as appropriate.

Using include() and require()

The include() and require() functions do essentially the same thing: when called, the code in the included file becomes part of the script calling it. From that point forward, anything in the included file can be used in the script calling it.

The difference between include() and require() pops up when the file to be included cannot be opened. This could occur because of incorrect permissions, or perhaps the file isn't in the location specified. When a failure occurs using include() you get a warning, but the code continues to execute as best it can, which is to say not very well if it needs a function that's in some other file! When require() cannot find or open the file, you will get a fatal error and PHP will stop processing the code all together.

Included files look just like any other PHP files, starting with an opening PHP tag and ending with a closing PHP tag. For example, suppose you have a file called myfunctions.php, containing the following code:

```
<?
/* The multiplier() function multiplies a number by 5 and returns
it */
function multiplier($num) {
    $answer = $num * 5;
    return $answer;
}

/* The db_connect() function connects to my database. */
function db_connect() {
    $connection = @mysql_connect("localhost", "spike", "9sj7En4")
    or die(mysql_error());
```

```
        $db = @mysql_select_db($db_name, $connection)
        or die(mysql_error());
}
?>
```

Then, in your actual PHP script, which needs to connect to a database, you would have the following:

```
<?
//include the file that has the function you need
include("/path/to/myfunctions.php");

//call a function
db_connect();

//now you can do things like issue queries and get results
?>
```

Obviously, this is a very simple example of using included files as function libraries, but you probably can already see the benefits! Anywhere you have repetitive code, think about using your own function to replace it. You can have multiple files full of function libraries named appropriately for their tasks. You can easily optimize your code when you go through the exercise of determining where functions can be used. Try it out yourself—there is plenty of repetitive code used in this book, which you can quickly turn into your own tightly-wound application!

D

Basic MySQL Reference

This appendix is a very brief glance at the Structured Query Language (SQL) and some basic functions you can use with MySQL to make development a lot easier. See the MySQL manual at http://www.mysql.com/ for a comprehensive list of MySQL functions and language elements, or for a good introduction to using MySQL, pick up my book *Teach Yourself MySQL in 24 Hours*.

> **NOTE**
>
> Throughout this appendix, anything inside brackets should be considered placeholder text. For example, you would replace `[yourDBName]` in the command with your actual database name.

Create or Drop a Database

Starting with something simple, you can use the `CREATE` command to create a new database. The syntax is

```
CREATE DATABASE IF NOT EXISTS [yourDBName];
```

When you create a database with this command, you're really just creating a directory to hold the files that make up the tables in the database.

To delete an entire database from the system, use the `DROP` command:

```
DROP DATABASE IF EXISTS [yourDBName];
```

Be extremely careful when using the `DROP` command, because once you drop the database, all of the tables are dropped as well!

Create or Drop a Table

You can also use the `CREATE` command to create a table within the current database. The syntax is

```
CREATE TABLE [yourTableName] ([fieldName1] [type], [fieldName2]
[type], ...) [options]
```

To delete a table from the current database, use the `DROP` command:

```
DROP TABLE [yourTableName];
```

Be extremely careful when using the `DROP` command, because once you drop the tables, they're gone!

Altering a Table

The ALTER command gives you the opportunity to modify elements of a particular table, such as renaming columns, changing the type of a column, adding columns, deleting columns, and so on. Following are some common uses:

- To add a column to a table, use this:

  ALTER TABLE [yourTableName] ADD [newColumn] [fieldDefinition];

- To delete a column from a table, use this:

  ALTER TABLE [yourTableName] DROP [columnName];

- To change a column from one type to another, use this:

  ALTER TABLE [yourTableName] CHANGE [columnName]
  [newfieldDefinition];

- To make a unique column in your table, use this:

  ALTER TABLE [yourTableName] ADD UNIQUE [columnName]
  ([columnName]);

- To index a column in your table, use this:

  ALTER TABLE [yourTableName] ADD INDEX [columnName]
  ([columnName]);

Using the ALTER command alleviates the need to delete an entire table and re-create it just because you spelled a field name incorrectly or made other minor mistakes.

Insert, Update, or Replace within a Table

The INSERT and REPLACE commands populate your tables one record at a time. The syntax of INSERT is

INSERT INTO [yourTableName] ([fieldName1], [fieldName2], ...)
VALUES ('[value of fieldName1]', '[value of fieldName2]'...);

When inserting records, be sure to separate your strings with single quotes or double quotes. If you use single quotes around your strings and the data you are adding contains apostrophes, avoid errors by escaping the apostrophe (\') within the INSERT statement. Similarly, if you use double quotes around your strings and you want to include double quotes as part of the data, escape them (\") within your INSERT statement.

The REPLACE command has the same syntax and requirements as the INSERT command. The only difference is that you use REPLACE to overwrite a record in a table, based on a unique value:

```
REPLACE INTO [yourTableName] ([fieldName1], [fieldName2], ...)
VALUES ('[value of fieldName1]', '[value of fieldName2]'...);
```

The UPDATE command modifies parts of a record without replacing the entire record. To update an entire column in a table with the same new value, use this:

```
UPDATE [yourTableName] SET [fieldName] = '[new value]';
```

If you want to update only specific rows, use a WHERE clause:

```
UPDATE [yourTableName] SET [fieldName] = '[new value]' WHERE [some
expression];
```

UPDATE can be a very powerful SQL command. For example, you can perform string functions and mathematical functions on existing records and use the UPDATE command to modify their values.

Deleting from a Table

Like the DROP command, using DELETE without paying attention to what you're doing can have horrible consequences in a production environment. Once you drop a table or delete a record, it's gone forever. Don't be afraid; just be careful. To delete all the contents of a table, use the following:

```
DELETE FROM [yourTableName];
```

If you want to delete only specific rows, use a WHERE clause:

```
DELETE FROM [yourTableName] WHERE [some expression];
```

If you're going to start deleting records, be sure you have a backup, just in case something goes wrong. Everyone screws up once.

Selecting from a Table

When creating database-driven Web sites, the SELECT command will likely be the most often-used command in your arsenal. The SELECT command causes certain records in your table to be chosen, based on criteria that you define. Here is the basic syntax of SELECT:

```
SELECT [field names] FROM [table name]
WHERE [some expression]
ORDER BY [field names];
```

To select all the records in a table, use this:

```
SELECT * FROM [yourTableName];
```

To select just the entries in a given column of a table, use this:

```
SELECT [columnName] FROM [yourTableName];
```

To select all the records in a table and have them returned in a particular order, use an expression for ORDER BY. For example, if you have a date field for record entries and you want to see all the record entries ordered by newest to oldest, use this:

```
SELECT * FROM [yourTableName] ORDER BY [dateField] DESC;
```

DESC stands for "descending." To view from oldest to newest, use ASC for "ascending." ASC is the default order.

You can also perform mathematical and string functions within SQL statements, thereby using SELECT to do more than just echo existing data. Some examples follow.

A Few String Functions

This list contains only a few of the many string-related functions listed in the MySQL manual. Visit http://www.mysql.com/ and check out the entire manual for more information.

- You can concatenate values using the CONCAT() function. The syntax is

  ```
  SELECT CONCAT([field1],[field2],...) AS [newName] FROM
  [yourTableName];
  ```

- Convert your results to lowercase using the LOWER() function. The syntax is

  ```
  SELECT LOWER([field1],[field2],...) FROM [yourTableName];
  ```

- Convert your results to uppercase using the UPPER() function. The syntax is

  ```
  SELECT UPPER([field1],[field2],...) FROM [yourTableName];
  ```

A Few Date and Time Functions

This list contains only a few of the many date and time-related functions listed in the MySQL manual. Visit http://www.mysql.com/ and check out the entire manual for more information.

- Get the day of the week (1 = Sunday, 2 = Monday, ...) from a date field using the `DAYOFWEEK()` function. The syntax is

  `SELECT DAYOFWEEK([date]) FROM [yourTableName];`

- Get the weekday (0 = Monday, 1 = Tuesday, ...) from a date field using the `WEEKDAY()` function. The syntax is

  `SELECT WEEKDAY([date]) FROM [yourTableName];`

NOTE

The difference between the `DAYOFWEEK()` and `WEEKDAY()` functions is the starting point of the week. When getting the day of the week, the week starts at Day 1, which is Sunday. When getting the weekday (or "work week"), the week starts at Day 0, which is Monday.

- Get the day of the month (1 through 31) from a date field using the `DAYOFMONTH()` function. The syntax is

  `SELECT DAYOFMONTH([date]) FROM [yourTableName];`

- Get the day of the year (1 through 366) from a date field using the `DAYOFYEAR()` function. The syntax is

  `SELECT DAYOFYEAR([date]) FROM [yourTableName];`

- Get the month (1 through 12) from a date field using the `MONTH()` function. The syntax is

  `SELECT MONTH([date]) FROM [yourTableName];`

- Get the month name (January, February, ...) from a date field using the `MONTHNAME()` function. The syntax is

  `SELECT MONTHNAME([date]) FROM [yourTableName];`

- Get the day name (Monday, Tuesday, ...) from a date field using the `DAYNAME()` function. The syntax is

  `SELECT DAYNAME([date]) FROM [yourTableName];`

- Get the week (0 through 53) from a date field using the WEEK() function. Start the week with Sunday (0) or Monday (1). The syntax is

```
SELECT WEEK([date], [0 or 1]) FROM [yourTableName];
```

- Get the year (1000 through 9999) from a date field using the YEAR() function. The syntax is

```
SELECT YEAR([date]) FROM [yourTableName];
```

Using the SHOW Command

There are several types of SHOW commands, which will produce output to help you administer your MySQL database. The usual method for executing these commands is through the MySQL Monitor, the command-line interface to MySQL, which you used in Chapter 1, "Installing and Configuring MySQL."

The basic SHOW commands are SHOW DATABASES and SHOW TABLES, which simply display the names of the databases and tables on your server. If you use the SHOW CREATE TABLE command, it shows you the exact SQL statement used to create the specified table.

If you need to know the structure of the table but don't necessarily need the SQL command to create it, you can use the SHOW COLUMNS command:

```
SHOW COLUMNS FROM [testTable];
```

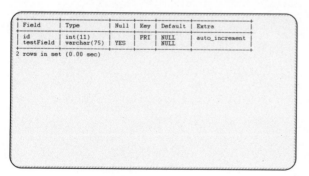

For administrative purposes, the SHOW STATUS and SHOW VARIABLES commands quickly provide important information about your database server. For more information on the numerous rows of output from these commands, please read the relevant sections of the MySQL manual, found at http://www.mysql.com/doc/.

E

Database Normalization

The database tables used in this book were designed for simplicity's sake to help you understand the basic interaction between PHP and MySQL. These are not "normalized" databases. "Normalization" is a word you'll hear a lot when you begin to create detailed database-driven applications, and it requires a different type of thought process—thinking in relational terms before seeing the relationships in front of you. In this appendix, you will learn the basics of database normalization.

Understanding Database Normalization

Database normalization is essentially a set of rules that allows you to organize your database in such a way that your tables are related where appropriate and flexible for future growth and relationships. The sets of rules used in normalization are called *normal forms*. If your database design follows the first set of rules, it's considered in the first normal form. If the first three sets of rules of normalization are followed, your database is said to be in the third normal form. We'll go through the normal forms using the concept of students and courses in a school, and eventually normalize the `my_contacts` table used previously in the book.

Applying the Normal Forms

Before explaining the first normal form, let's start with something that needs to be normalized. In the case of a database, it's the *flat table*. A flat table is like a spreadsheet with many columns for data. There are no relationships between multiple tables, as all the data you could possibly want is right there in that single flat table. This scenario is not the most efficient design and will consume more physical space on your hard drive than a set of normalized database tables.

Suppose you have a table that holds student and course information for a school. You might have the fields shown in Table E.1 in your flat table.

Table E.1   Students and Courses Table

Field Name	Description
StudentName	Name of the student
CourseID1	ID of the first course taken by the student
CourseDescription1	Description of the first course taken by the student
CourseIntructor1	Instructor of the first course taken by the student
CourseID2	ID of the second course taken by the student
CourseDescription2	Description of the second course taken by the student
CourseIntructor2	Instructor of the second course taken by the student

You might then repeat `CourseID`, `CourseDescription`, and `CourseInstructor` columns many more times to account for all the classes a student can take during their academic career. While redundant, this is the method used when creating a single flat table to store information. Eliminating this redundancy is the first step in normalization, so next you'll take this flat table to first normal form. If your table remained in its flat format, you could have a lot of unclaimed space and a lot of space being used unnecessarily—not an efficient table design!

Taking a Table to First Normal Form

The main rules for the first normal form are

- Eliminate repeating information
- Create separate tables for related data

Looking at the flat table design, with its many repeated sets of fields for students and courses, you can identify students and courses as its two distinct topics. Taking your student and courses flat table to the first normal form would mean that you create two tables: one for students (call it `students`) and one for students plus courses (call it `students_courses`). You can see the new table designs in Tables E.2 and E.3.

Table E.2   The students Table

Field Name	Description
StudentID	A unique ID for the student. This new field is now a primary key.
StudentName	Name of the student

Table E.3   The students_courses Table

Field Name	Description
StudentID	Unique ID of the student, matching an entry in the students table.
CourseID	ID of the course being taken by the student
CourseDescription	Description of the course taken by the student
CourseIntructor	Instructor of the course taken by the student

Your two tables now represent a one-to-many relationship of one student to many courses. Students can take as many courses as they wish and are not limited to the number of `CourseID`/`CourseDescription`/`CourseInstructor` groupings that existed in the flat table.

You still have some work to do, as the next step is to put the tables into second normal form.

Taking Tables to Second Normal Form

The basic rule for the second normal form is

- No non-key attributes depend on a portion of the primary key

In plain English, this means that if fields in your table are not entirely related to a primary key, you have more work to do. In the students and courses example we're using, it means breaking out the courses into their own table so that the original flat table is now just a table full of students.

`CourseID`, `CourseDesc`, and `CourseInstructor` can become a table called courses with a primary key of `CourseID`. The students_courses table should then just contain two fields: `StudentID` and `CourseID`. You can see the new table designs in Tables E.4 and E.5.

Table E.4 The courses Table

Field Name	Description
CourseID	Unique ID of a course
CourseDescription	Description of the course
CourseIntructor	Instructor of the course

Table E.5 The New students_courses Table

Field Name	Description
StudentID	Unique ID of the student, matching an entry in the students table.
CourseID	Unique ID of the course being taken, matching an entry in the courses table.

Believe it or not, you can go even further with this example to the third normal form.

Taking Tables to Third Normal Form

The rule for the third normal form is

- No attributes depend on other non-key attributes

This rule simply means that you need to look at your tables and see if more fields exist that can be broken down further and that aren't dependent on a key. Think about removing repeated data and you'll find your answer—instructors. Inevitably, an instructor will teach more than one class. However, the `CourseInstructor` field in the `courses` table is not a key of any sort. So if you break out this information and create a separate table purely for the sake of efficiency and maintenance, that's the third normal form. Take a look at the new `courses` table, and the `instructors` table, in Tables E.6 and E.7.

Table E.6   The courses Table

Field Name	Description
CourseID	Unique ID of a course
CourseDescription	Description of the course
CourseIntructorID	ID of the instructor, matching an entry in the instructors table

Table E.7   The instructors Table

Field Name	Description
InstructorID	Unique ID of an instructor
InstructorName	Name of the instructor
InstructorNotes	Any notes regarding the instructor

The third normal form is usually adequate for removing redundancy and allowing for flexibility and growth. Next, you'll normalize the `my_contacts` table, used previously in this book.

Normalizing the my_contacts Table

In the original my_contacts table, there's not a lot of repeating information, but there very easily could be if you expanded this to be an actual address book. In an address book, people usually have contact information for home and work, or multiple phone methods (land line, cell phone, etc.), and even multiple e-mail addresses. It would make much more sense to break all of those elements out into separate tables and attach the information to people through a primary key. Table E.8 shows the original my_contacts table as reference.

Table E.8   Original my_contacts Table

Field Name	Description
id	Creates a unique ID number for the entry
f_name	The person's first name
l_name	The person's last name
address1	First line of the address
address2	Second line of the address
address3	Third line of the address
postcode	Zip or postal code
country	Country in which the person resides
prim_tel	Primary telephone number
sec_tel	Secondary telephone number
email	E-mail address
birthday	The person's birthday

Now identify the different areas for which different tables will exist: address, phone, and e-mail are adequate for this example. Tables E.9, E.10, and E.11 show the fields for these new tables.

Table E.9 Fields for address Table

Field Name	Description
id	Creates a unique ID number for the address entry
contact_id	ID corresponding to a person in the master contact table
address1	First line of the address
address2	Second line of the address
address3	Third line of the address
postcode	Zip or postal code
address_type	Type of address, such as home, work, or other

Table E.10 Fields for phone Table

Field Name	Description
id	Creates a unique ID number for the phone entry
contact_id	ID corresponding to a person in the master contact table
phone_number	Phone number
phone_type	Type of phone number, such as home, work, cell, or fax

Table E.11 Fields for email Table

Field Name	Description
id	Creates a unique ID number for the email entry
contact_id	ID corresponding to a person in the master contact table
country	Country in which the person resides
email	E-mail address
email_type	Type of e-mail address, such as home or work

These new tables all contain the contact_id key, which corresponds to an entry in the new master contact table. The basic my_contacts table, used as the master contact table, should now look something like Table E.12.

Table E.12   New my_contacts Table

Field Name	Description
id	Creates a unique ID number for the entry
f_name	Person's first name
l_name	Person's last name
birthday	Person's birthday

With these new tables in place, you will have a much more flexible (and normalized!) set of tables for maintaining contact information.

F

Getting Help

One of the greatest aspects of the Open Source community is that people are eager to help you learn as much as you can so that you can become an advocate as well. However, you probably should attempt to find answers to your questions before posing them to the community at large. Doing so includes reading available manuals and FAQs, searching through mailing list archives, and visiting Web sites. Chances are good that someone else has had the same question you have.

The Web site for this book, and other books I have written, is http://www.premierpressbooks.com/downloads.asp. You will find book errata, downloadable code from the books, recommendations for books and other items, and anything else I think up in my spare time. I am also happy to answer questions if you're stumped about something you have read in my books.

PHP Resources

PHP-related Web sites, newsgroups, and mailing lists are popping up all over the place. The ones listed here are just a smattering of what's available.

Web Sites

The majority of these sites are maintained by normal people on their own time, so if you use any of their resources, try to give back to the community by helping others with their questions when you can, contributing code snippets to code repositories, and so forth.

www.php.net

The home of PHP is http://www.php.net. The annotated online manual is here, as well as the PHP FAQs, bug reports, links to ISPs that offer access to PHP, news articles, and much more!

www.zend.com

Zend Technologies, the folks behind the Zend engine of PHP, have created a portal site for PHP developers. This personalized site not only showcases how you can build a high-traffic, dynamic site using PHP, but it also provides pointers, resources, and lessons on how to maximize the potential of PHP in all your online applications.

Webmonkey (hotwired.lycos.com/webmonkey/)

The company that brings us *Wired* magazine also brings us HotWired, which spawned Webmonkey, a developer's resource site with a section devoted to PHP. Don't limit yourself to the PHP section of Webmonkey, for there's much information to be had in other sections as well. This is one of my favorites, not only because I have written articles for them, but because they're smart folks.

WeberDev (www.weberdev.com)

A longtime favorite of PHP developers, this site contains development tricks and tips for many programming languages (just to be fair) as well as a content management system for everyone to add their own code snippets, tutorials, and more! It has a great weekly newsletter and high traffic. Go contribute!

PHPBuilder (www.phpbuilder.com)

This is a very good tutorial site for intermediate and advanced PHP developers. It contains weekly How To columns for real-world applications, such as "Building Dynamic Pages With Search Engines in Mind," "Generating Pronounceable Passwords," and tons more. Recommended!

DevShed (www.devshed.com)

This site contains many user-submitted tutorials, news articles, interviews, and competitive analyses of server-side programming languages. Covers PHP as well as many other topics of interest to developers, such as servers and databases.

px.sklar.com

This is a bare-bones code repository, but who needs graphics when all you're looking for are code snippets? Borrowing from the "take a penny, leave a penny" mentality, you grab a code snippet to start with and then add your own when you feel confident in sharing.

PHP KnowledgeBase (php.faqts.com)

The PHP Knowledge Base contains questions and answers posed on PHP mailing lists. Anyone can answer questions at the Web site or ask new ones.

Mailing Lists

Several high-traffic mailing lists are available for PHP discussion in English as well as other languages. Please remember your netiquette when asking a question: be polite, offer as many examples as you can (if you're describing a problem), provide your system information (if looking for a solution), and did I mention to say please and thank you?

You can find mailing list subscription information in the Support section at http://www.php.net/. The English PHP mailing lists are archived and available for searching at http://marc.theaimsgroup.com/. Just look for the PHP-related lists under the WWW heading.

User Groups

Sometimes, knowing other developers in real life can prove helpful. You can find a list of PHP user groups at http://www.phpusergroups.org/.

MySQL Resources

Many of the PHP-related Web sites listed earlier also contain information on development with MySQL, but the MySQL Web site at http://www.mysql.com/ is the place to start for comprehensive MySQL information.

The online MySQL manual is immense, but it's so well-written and useful that its size should not scare you. You can find the manual at http://www.mysql.com/doc/. If you're looking for a quick introduction to MySQL, I have written a book called *Teach Yourself MySQL in 24 Hours*, available in bookstores worldwide.

As with PHP, several high-traffic mailing lists are available for MySQL discussion, in English as well as other languages. You can find mailing list subscription information at http://www.mysql.com/documentation/lists.html, and the MySQL mailing lists are archived and available for searching at http://marc.theaimsgroup.com/ as well.

Apache Resources

Start at the Apache Foundation Web site, http://www.apache.org/, for server documentation and a list of FAQs. Many of the developer-oriented Web sites offer Apache-specific tutorials—you just have to hunt them down.

Index

fast&easy web development